Intellectual Property Strategies for Start-ups

Elgar Practical Guides

Rich in practical advice, *Elgar Practical Guides* are handy, concise guides to a range of legal practice areas.

Combining practical insight and step-by-step guidance with the relevant substantive law and procedural rules, the books in this series focus on understanding and navigating the issues that are likely to be encountered in practice. This is facilitated by a range of structural tools including checklists, glossaries, sample documentation and recommended actions.

Elgar Practical Guides are indispensable resources for the busy practitioner and for the non-specialist who requires a first introduction or a reliable turn-to reference book.

Titles in the series include:

The UN Human Rights Council
A Practical Anatomy
Eric Tistounet

Start-up Law
Edited by Alexandra Andhov

Copyright in the Music Industry
A Practical Guide to Exploiting and Enforcing Rights
Hayleigh Bosher

The Law and Practice of Fine Art, Jewellery and Specie Insurance
David Scully

Financial Regulation and Technology
A Legal and Compliance Guide
Iain Sheridan

Intellectual Property Strategies for Start-ups
A Practical Guide
Edited by Stefan Golkowsky

Intellectual Property Strategies for Start-ups

A Practical Guide

Edited by

STEFAN GOLKOWSKY
PFENNING Patent Attorneys and Lawyers, Berlin, Germany

Elgar Practical Guides

Edward Elgar
PUBLISHING

Cheltenham, UK • Northampton, MA, USA

Original German language edition:
Stefan Golkowsky (Editor): IP-Strategien für Start-ups. Grundlagen, Aufbau und Umsetzung von Schutzrechten.
1. Auflage 2020. (ISBN: 978-3-7910-4729-4) originally published by Schaeffer-Poeschel Verlag für Wirtschaft, Steuern und Recht GmbH Stuttgart, Germany.

Published by
Edward Elgar Publishing Limited
The Lypiatts
15 Lansdown Road
Cheltenham
Glos GL50 2JA
UK

Edward Elgar Publishing, Inc.
William Pratt House
9 Dewey Court
Northampton
Massachusetts 01060
USA

A catalogue record for this book
is available from the British Library

Library of Congress Control Number: 2022931171

This book is available electronically in the **Elgar**online
Law subject collection
http://dx.doi.org/10.4337/9781802204025

Printed on elemental chlorine free (ECF)
recycled paper containing 30% Post-Consumer Waste

ISBN 978 1 80220 401 8 (cased)
ISBN 978 1 80220 403 2 (paperback)
ISBN 978 1 80220 402 5 (eBook)

Printed and bound in the USA

Contents

Contributors

Dr Daniel Brüggemann: Investment partner at Jindong Capital venture capital fund, Hong Kong; founding supervisory board member of DiaMonTech AG, Berlin, Germany.

Dr Rudolf Freytag: CEO of Siemens Technology Accelerator GmbH, Munich, Germany.

Dr Rainer Gith: Attorney at law; chairman of the supervisory board of DiaMonTech AG, Berlin, Germany; chairman of the supervisory board of gekartel AG, Dresden, Germany.

Dr Stefan Golkowsky: Partner at PFENNING Patent Attorneys and Lawyers, Berlin, Germany; founding supervisory board member of DiaMonTech AG, Berlin, Germany.

Dr Manuel F Juette: Patent engineer at PFENNING Patent Attorneys and Lawyers, Berlin, Germany.

Dr Ashkan Kalantary: Head of activities at KPMG Venture Services; partner, Deal Advisory at KPMG AG Wirtschaftsprüfungsgesellschaft, Berlin, Germany.

Peter Karge: German and European patent attorney; Former Head of Siemens AG IP Department in Berlin and Managing IP Counsel for Mobility Division, Germany.

Dr Christina Lubinski: Professor at Copenhagen Business School, Copenhagen, Denmark.

Thorsten Lubinski: CEO of DiaMonTech AG, Berlin, Germany.

Dr Werner Mäntele: Professor of Biophysics at Goethe University Frankfurt am Main, Germany; Chief Scientific Officer (CSO) at DiaMonTech AG, Berlin, Germany.

Uwe Schriek: German and European patent attorney; head of IP at Siemens AG, Berlin, Germany.

Christoph Viebig: PhD fellow at Copenhagen Business School, Copenhagen, Denmark.

Leif Zierz: Global Head of Deal Advisory, KPMG International.

Foreword

The Covid-19 pandemic caught the world by surprise with such force that it briefly fell into a state of shock. It quickly became apparent that we would only survive the global crisis through the active involvement of the entire population. While there is arguably never an ideal time for a global crisis, some would contend that today's innovative and digital companies are well placed to address the unique challenges we face. Never before have innovative start-ups joined forces with both investors and established companies to have such a dramatic impact on world affairs. Together, the advances they have achieved in medicine, technology and cybersecurity are charting a course out of the pandemic with extraordinary speed.

The recovery in the venture capital space has been particularly evident. Despite the significant uncertainty initially experienced in the market, transactional interest in highly innovative technology businesses quickly resumed across all sectors. The volume of invested capital in specialized funds is once again rising rapidly. Established companies are also increasing their investments in (disruptive) start-ups.

For individual start-ups in the process of raising capital, innovation has taken centre stage. However, other factors can attract investors and reduce the high risks that come with investing in a start-up. Protecting existing technology and intellectual property (IP) through copyrights, patents, licences and trademarks plays a prominent role in this regard. IP rights can help to make the value of a business more apparent to investors. They also create new tangible assets that can be independently valued by investors.

This book illustrates how IP protection – especially in the early stages of a business – helps to create both competitive advantages for start-ups and security for institutional investors and investment firms. The authors draw on many years of experience from their own start-up, consulting and supervisory board activities. They not only raise awareness of IP, but also give clear instructions on how to build an IP strategy. To this end, various categories of IP – in particular, the different types of IP rights (eg, patents, trademarks, designs) – are described. Later in the book, the hypothetical example of a medical technology start-up is used to demonstrate how young companies can implement IP strategies to protect them against loss of rights and loss of control and financial damage. Other examples – including the influence of employee inventions and a spin-off from a university – are shared to further explain the development of IP rights. Finally, recommendations are given on how start-ups can value and account for IP rights and position them as additional assets in negotiations with investors.

I wish all founders, investors, lawyers and interested readers much enjoyment in discovering how IP strategies can be successfully integrated into start-ups.

Leif Zierz

Global Head of Deal Advisory, KPMG International

Preface

The authors of this book come from different disciplines; but what we all have in common is that we all deal with the issue of intellectual property (IP). In writing this book, it was very interesting for us to learn about the different viewpoints of our co-authors; and in doing so, to rethink our own viewpoints. We hope that readers will also gain an insight into the various aspects of IP in this way. This will be particularly useful for start-up entrepreneurs and their advisers, and should help them to engage with discussion partners with different interests and use this new understanding to the advantage of their companies.

Particularly in the case of start-ups, IP is often given insufficient attention during the initial phase of the business. This can ultimately weaken the position of the founders. In this regard, IP and patents can be seen as a life insurance policy for founders and investors. The authors of this book have set out to raise awareness of IP as an instrument and to provide as clear instructions for action as possible. In this way, the book aims to impart practical knowledge so that you can credibly and confidently represent your IP position to various discussion partners.

The authors have already successfully developed many start-ups themselves and the book adopts an interdisciplinary approach, examining different aspects of IP from different perspectives. The authors are international (active in China, the US, the UK, Denmark and Germany). However, as the regimes in these countries diverge considerably, it was impossible to discuss every regulatory detail in each jurisdiction. Where special examples were needed, we primarily referred to the regulations in Europe – in particular, in Germany.

The book is divided into ten chapters written by different authors. The following rough outline can serve as a 'red thread' through the content.

Chapters 1 to 3 are written by patent attorneys and deal with the characteristics and strategic possibilities of IP rights, especially patents. Chapter 1 deals relatively comprehensively with the basics of patents, trademarks, designs, domains, copyright and trade secrets. Based on this, Chapter 2 goes on to describe the strategic structure of IP rights portfolios using examples as illustrations.

Chapter 3 discusses the very important issue of the law on employee inventions and its relevance and application to start-ups, with a focus on the German regime; it also provides a brief overview of the situation in selected other jurisdictions. In the authors' experience, in many due diligence procedures it is often unclear who holds the inventor rights to a particular patent and how the rights to the patent ultimately came to the patent holder entered in the register.

Chapters 4 and 5 are experience reports from start-up founders. Chapter 4 describes the experience with the university administration and the successful spin-off of DiaMonTech GmbH from the perspective of the chair holder for biophysics at the University of Frankfurt am Main. Chapter 5 complements this view from the perspective of a start-up series founder who now serves as CEO of DiaMonTech AG.

Chapters 6 to 10 throw light on the IP landscape from the perspective of different consultants. Chapter 6 deals with important aspects of contract drafting for start-ups, with a focus on IP rights. Particularly in the start-up phase, in case of a capital increase or exit (eg, a sale or initial public offering), the drafting of contracts and the allocation of IP to the company, as well as freedom to operate (FTO), are of central importance. The author of this chapter shares important insights from extensive experience and several very successful exits.

The author of Chapter 7 has helped to build many start-ups in his capacity as CEO of Siemens Technology Accelerator GmbH. He reports on the connection between business models and the IP that makes sense and is important to them.

In Chapter 8, the authors examine the requirements for IP throughout the lifecycle of a start-up from an economic perspective. Drawing on their teaching activities in the US and Europe, they also address differences between the US and Europe, especially Germany.

Chapter 9 explains how start-ups are assessed from the point of view of management consultancy and auditing firms. Exemplary valuation methods for IP rights are presented.

Finally, Chapter 10 approaches IP protection from the perspective of venture capital investors. Examples from the US and Chinese markets are also given.

Having read these chapters, I can draw some clear conclusions. During the preparatory work for this book, as well as the detailed discussions with my co-authors, many insights from my own practical work were confirmed. In addition, I learned about several new issues and have since viewed certain other matters through a different lens. In summary, I consider the following principles to be essential in connection with IP strategies for start-ups.

First, a start-up must have a clear focus, in terms of both content and region. This should – if at all possible – be cost-effectively protected by the appropriate IP rights, so that the business model cannot simply be copied by third parties. The IP rights thus represent a life insurance policy for founders and investors. In the case of IP rights, particular attention must be paid to compliance with the legal framework – for example, the law on employee inventions and the legal background for university inventions.

In addition to the acquisition of its own IP rights in line with its intended business model, it is also important that the start-up and/or its licensees can exercise the business model – in other words, that it has FTO. In this regard, it is important to recall that patents are only 'prohibition rights': the mere fact that a start-up holds a patent that can be used to prohibit a competitor does not mean that it can always be used by the start-up itself (eg, a competitor could hold an additional or earlier patent; see the tennis ball example discussed in Chapter 2, section 3.1).

Finally, it is important to clearly explain the start-up's IP rights situation to investors ('Do good and talk about it'). The specific interests and technical backgrounds of the relevant parties should be taken into account: M&A lawyers have a different focus from patent attorneys (albeit that both are essentially looking for legal pitfalls). Economists, on the other hand, pursue a somewhat different approach – although here too there are differences between venture capitalists and auditing firms; and there may also be different focuses depending on the region.

Having thus summarized the contents of the book, a few technical points should be noted to assist the reader.

First, to enhance readability, the use of gender-sensitive pronouns has generally been avoided; every passage should be understood in such a way that people of each gender are addressed.

Second, the literature cited in the ten chapters is collected in a complete bibliography at the end of the book, together with an index of relevant keywords. The actual text is preceded by a list of abbreviations. In addition, an attempt has been made to clarify the relationships between the individual chapters through cross-references between them; and to refer to definitions or quotations, for example, in order to avoid redundancies and duplication of content.

I would like to thank Luke Adams, head of law publishing at Edward Elgar Publishing, as well as the whole editorial team, in particular Fiona Todd, Barbara Pretty and Carolyn Boyle for their invaluable stylistic and conceptual advice and excellent organizational support for this project; and my colleagues David Weiß and Manuel F Juette for the initial proofread and corrections. Our special thanks also go to Silke Domann for her support in editing, as well as Andrea Rupp, Marita Mollenhauer and Jana Hartlaub of German publishing house Schäffer-Poeschel.

I hope that by presenting the issue of IP from different perspectives, the reader will gain comprehensive insight on this subject. The aim is to avoid fundamental mistakes when setting up a start-up; in this way, the inevitable IP due diligence in the event of an exit will be significantly expedited and potential problems avoided.

Stefan Golkowsky
November 2021

Abbreviations

AI	Artificial intelligence
ArbnErfG	German Employee Inventions Act
BGB	German Civil Code
BGH	German Federal Court of Justice
BVK	German Private Equity and Venture Capital Association
DPMA	German Patent and Trademark Office
EBIT	Earnings before interest and taxes
EPC	European Patent Convention
EPO	European Patent Office
EUIPO	European Union Intellectual Property Office
FRAND	Fair, reasonable and non-discriminatory
FTO	Freedom to operate
IAS	International Accounting Standards
IFRS	International Financial Reporting Standards
IGE	[Swiss] Federal Institute of Intellectual Property
IP	Intellectual property
IPO	Initial public offering
M&A	Mergers and acquisitions
medtech	Medical technology
NDA	Non-disclosure agreement
OIN	Open Invention Network
OSS	Open source software
PCT	Patent Cooperation Treaty

PPH	Patent Prosecution Highway
R&D	Research and development
ROI	Return on investment
SEO	Search engine optimization
TRL	Technology readiness level
USPTO	United States Patent and Trademark Office
VC	Venture capital(ist)
VR	Virtual reality
WIPO	World Intellectual Property Organization

1 Basics of Intellectual Property rights with a focus on start-ups

Uwe Schriek, Manuel F Juette and Stefan Golkowsky

1. Introduction: can't we do it without patents?

Why should a start-up concern itself with intellectual property (IP)?

Here's what we know: not all start-ups depend on IP protection; but many start-ups can fail if IP protection is not handled properly.

The importance of IP to a start-up depends on a number of factors, which are discussed in more detail in this chapter. One thing is certain, however: investors will want to know whether IP is a priority for a start-up in which they are considering investing. They will want to know whether everything has been done to ensure the economic value of the start-up and to minimize the risk to their investment through good and sustainable IP work.

Otherwise, a start-up may find itself in a difficult situation, as the following examples illustrate:

- The technology that is used is protected by a third-party patent.
- The start-up has acquired a licence to a third-party patent on which it depends, but the negotiated terms are unfavourable or the licence is endangered by the possible insolvency of the patent holder.
- The start-up develops a new technology, but fails to protect it. Financially strong competitors then copy the new technology and enter the market without the start-up's involvement.
- The start-up's chosen name or product name is already protected by

a third-party trademark.
- A service offered by the start-up depends on data which may not be readily used (eg, due to copyright or data protection laws).

You can avoid such problems by acting early enough and identifying which IP-related measures are absolutely necessary for your company – and which would at least be beneficial.

2. Types of IP

The following overview outlines the types of IP rights that exist, what each of them protects and which aspects require particular attention. We will then explore the details of:

- how to protect your own IP; and
- how to avoid infringing the IP rights of others.

This book is intended for persons with little prior knowledge of IP rights. For this reason, the following section attempts to explain the basics in a way that will be easily understandable to laypersons. The text aims to increase awareness of the protection of IP and to encourage vigilance. If you get the impression that action is required at your company regarding the protection of IP, it may be advisable to consult a patent attorney. Patent attorneys combine technical understanding (in many jurisdictions, qualification as a patent attorney requires the completion of a technical degree) with knowledge of the legal requirements and options. To provide comprehensive advice, your patent attorney should also understand how your business model works.

2.1 The main categories of IP rights

This book deals with the subset of IP that is relevant to commercial enterprises – also referred to as 'industrial property'. Typical relevant IP rights include patents, utility models, industrial designs and trademarks. Copyright is not usually regarded as an industrial property right; but for the purposes of this book, it may be treated as such, as only certain aspects of copyright of particular importance to start-ups are discussed.

Table 1.1 *Most important types of IP rights*

Patent	Utility model	Design	Trademark	Copyright
Protects technical inventions	Protects technical inventions	Protects external appearances	Protects names, graphics and the like	Protects works of art, including software
Protection obtained by filing with an IP office	Protection obtained by filing with an IP office	Protection obtained by filing with an IP office	Protection obtained by filing with an IP office	Protection obtained by law – no filing required
Formal and substantive examination	Formal examination only	Formal inspection only	Formal and substantive examination	
Term of up to 20 years	Term of up to ten years	Term of up to 25 years	Renewable indefinitely	Expires 70 years after the death of the last co-author
European Patent Office (EPO), national patent offices	Certain national patent offices	European Union Intellectual Property Office (EUIPO), national patent offices	EUIPO, national patent offices	

Table 1.1 outlines the most important types of IP rights. The various IP rights are explained below using the example of international and national IP rights in Europe (with Germany serving as an illustration). An introduction to the extension of protection to other countries (within or outside Europe), and to the development of a region-specific protection strategy, is set out in Chapter 3, section 7.

2.2 Patents

The European Patent Convention states as follows:

Article 52

(1) European patents shall be granted for inventions, in all fields of technology, provided that they are new, involve an inventive step and are susceptible of industrial application …

Article 54

(1) An invention shall be considered to be new if it does not form part of the state of the art.
(2) The state of the art shall be held to comprise everything made available to the public by means of a written or oral description, by use, or in any other way, before the date of filing of the European patent application …

Article 56

(1) An invention shall be considered as involving an inventive step if, having regard to the state of the art, it is not obvious to a person skilled in the art …

Section 1(1) of the German Patent Act and many other national patent acts of EU states mirror this language almost verbatim. Patents protect new technical inventions – for example, new products or improvements to products, as well as new processes. What is protected is specified in the patent claims by a definition in text form.

To obtain a patent, a patent application must first be filed with, and examined by, a patent office. During examination, the invention is compared with the prior art in the form of patents, technical articles and other information known to the public. A patent application may be filed with any national patent office in order to obtain protection for that country. Alternatively, in member states of the EPC, it is possible to submit a European patent application to the European Patent Office (EPO). Member states of the EPC include all member states of the European Union and certain other countries, including the United Kingdom, Switzerland, Norway and Turkey. A European patent filed with the EPO is not (necessarily) a unitary international protection right. A European patent application should be understood as a unified path to obtaining a set of national patents subject to the respective national regulations. However, a unitary EU patent conferring the same rights in all EU states has been a longstanding goal, and the legal basis for such a right may enter into force in the near future (although some hurdles remain to be cleared).

The minimum official fees for an online application, examination and grant of a patent amount to €390 in Germany and €4745 at the EPO.[1] Once the patent has been granted, renewal fees are payable annually, which in Germany start at €70 per year for the third patent year and increase annually to €350 for the 10th patent year and €1940 for the 20th year, with a maximum possible lifetime of 20 years. In the case of a European patent, renewal fees after grant are due for each country in which protection is maintained and are payable to the respective national patent offices.

2.3 Utility models

In some countries (eg, Spain, Italy, Austria, China, Japan and Germany), utility models are in a certain sense 'small patents' (the application fee for electronic filing is just €30), which also protect technical inventions. German utility model protection is available for all fields of technology for which patent protection is also possible, with the exception of processes (ie, protection is available only for embodied objects). To obtain a utility model, an application must also be filed with the patent office; but this is examined only for formal requirements, and not for content. Unlike in the case of a patent, the inventor need not be named. A utility model is usually registered without further substantive examination, affording immediate protection. A utility model is cheaper to obtain and maintain than a patent; but it can only be kept alive for a maximum of ten years by paying annuities (€210 after three years, €350 after six years and €530 after eight years). Furthermore, the protectability of a utility model in terms of its subject matter is examined (by either the patent office or a court) only if the utility model is cited in legal proceedings against a competitor or tested in cancellation proceedings. In the meantime, the owner (and the competition) face a certain degree of uncertainty as to the validity of the IP right.

---

[1] All fees referenced in this chapter were effective as of 31 October 2021.

2.4 Design rights

The Community Design Regulation of the European Union states as follows:

Article 3

For the purposes of this Regulation

(a) "design" means the appearance of a whole or a part of a product resulting from the features of, in particular, the lines, contours, colours, shape, texture and/or materials of the product itself or its ornamentation ...

Article 4

1. A design shall be protected by a Community design to the extent that is new and has individual character ...

Article 6

1. A design shall be considered to have individual character if the overall impression it produces on the informed user differs from the overall impression produced on such a user by any design which has been made available to the public …
2. When assessing individual character, the degree of freedom of the designer in developing the design shall be taken into account.

A design right, such as the EU Community design and comparable national rights, protects a performance that manifests itself in the external appearance of an object. Unlike the European patent in its current form, the Community design is a unitary right – that is, it confers the same protection in all EU member states (please note that design protection in the United Kingdom can no longer be obtained by registering a Community design). To obtain a registered design, an application must include formally correct illustrations. These are only formally examined by the office. As with the utility model, the protectability of the design is examined only in the event of a dispute. The protection is comparatively inexpensive: the official electronic application fees for a single German design amount to €60; while registration and publication of a Community design with the European Union Intellectual Property Office (EUIPO) cost €350. In both cases, the renewal fees due every five years from the sixth year of protection increase from €90 to €180.

2.5 Trademarks

The EU Trademark Regulation states as follows:

Article 4

> An EU trade mark may consist of any signs, in particular words, including personal names, or designs, letters, numerals, colours, the shape of goods or of the packaging of goods, or sounds, provided that such signs are capable of:
>
> (a) distinguishing the goods or services of one undertaking from those of other undertakings; and
> (b) being represented on the Register of European Union trade marks ('the Register'), in a manner which enables the competent authorities and the public to determine the clear and precise subject matter of the protection afforded to its proprietor.

A trademark protects a sign which identifies to the relevant class of persons that the marked goods or services originated from a particular undertaking/enterprise. Trademarks can in most cases be represented graphically; but protection can also extend to names without limitation to a specific graphic representation. In addition, trademark protection is possible for sound signs, the shape of goods or their packaging and other perceptible forms. A trademark is registered by filing a trademark application with the EUIPO or a national patent office, such as the German Patent and Trademark Office (DPMA) (please note that trademark protection in the United Kingdom can no longer be obtained by filing a Community trademark). Before doing so, however, it is first examined whether the trademark is fundamentally eligible for registration – that is, whether it is suitable for the public to understand it as an indication of origin. The protection is comparatively inexpensive: the official costs of an EU trademark application (in digital format) amount to €850 and the renewal fee due every ten years is €850 (compared with a €290 application fee and €750 renewal fee for German trademarks).

2.6 Copyright

EU Directive 2009/24/EC requires all member states to protect computer programs under national copyright law. For instance, the German Copyright Act states as follows:

Section 69a(3)

1. Computer programs are protected if they constitute individual works in the sense that they are the result of the author's own intellectual creation.
2. No other criteria, in particular no qualitative or aesthetic criteria, shall be applied to determine their protectability.

In principle, copyright law protects artistic achievements, but protectability also extends to software to the extent that it is represented by a program code (source code). In order to obtain protection, it is not necessary to apply for copyright registration or deposit the code. However, in the event of a dispute, it must be proven that the rights holder created the code itself or holds rights of use; and that in the case of a copy, this first legally substantiated code served directly as a model. The ideas and principles that underlie a computer program (cf Section 69a(2) of the German Copyright Act) are not protected by copyright. However, their application can in many cases be protected by patents.

3. Ways to protect your IP

It's a nightmare for any start-up: a product has just been successfully launched on the market after intensive development work, when it turns out that a competitor is offering a very similar product. Or perhaps a foreign company that you have never heard of quickly adopts the solutions you have developed and offers copies of your product.

These scenarios will reveal whether your start-up is in good shape IP-wise. If protection measures were considered in good time, in many cases it will be easy to take action against copies with the help of protective rights. At the very least, you will be prepared for these scenarios and know your options.

The following sections outline good practices aimed at securing the best possible protection for your innovative solutions.

3.1 Inventory: what is already there?

The resources of a start-up are naturally scarce. Therefore, before thinking about what can be protected, it is worth taking stock of your existing legal assets. Many may already exist and may thus be available at no extra cost.

Start-ups usually have a history. Often, the founders will already have been professionally active in the relevant field and will have collected ideas along the way. In many cases, a start-up emerges from activities at a university or research institute; in this event, it is possible that patent applications may already have been filed for the technical developments on which the start-up is based. The founders must clarify whether they are allowed to take the resulting patents with them, or at least to use them. Many universities greatly appreciate it when their research activities give rise to business opportunities that lead to spin-offs. Therefore, in many cases, the founders can hope for some support from the university. On the other hand, the university may want a stake in the business or to benefit from its financial success. It is therefore to be expected that either paid licences will have to be acquired for the patents or the patents will have to be bought from the university. This subject is discussed in detail in Chapter 4.

It is highly recommended that the start-up acquire the IP rights, if possible, in order to be able to use them freely. It is also desirable that any payments (eg, royalties) or profit-sharing due to the university in the event of economic success either be avoided altogether or at least be made manageable for investors.

Care should be taken where the founders develop their ideas while still working for a company as employees, even if no patent applications have been filed. In such cases, if the ideas developed contain technical inventions, it should be examined whether they legally belong to the former employer (see Chapter 3). If so, it is essential to find a legal solution with the former employer before the start-up takes off.

In some cases, software may have been programmed on an experimental basis before the start-up was founded. If so, the copyright may already be owned by the founders and should be entered on the credit side of the balance sheet. It is not absolutely necessary, but conceivable as a cost-effective option, to deposit the software with a notary as proof of the existence of the software and when it was created.

In many cases, open source software (OSS) may make economic sense, as it significantly reduces development time and powerful software libraries are available. On the other hand, the resulting programs will be very difficult to protect. It is in the interests of open source projects to make the resulting software available to the public. However, there are ways to keep the results of one's own programming efforts proprietary, and avoid the so-called 'copyleft' effect of open source licences, if the proprietary software can be sufficiently separated from the OSS in one's own product or if OSS is not used at all.

Perhaps a domain name has already been registered. This can be done with minimal financial effort and, in addition to direct ownership of the domain, can serve as a good starting point for the later registration of a trademark. For example, the future name of the company or a product can be protected in this way.

The founders may already be in possession of trade secrets on which they wish to build their business. Trade secrets are protected by national law in accordance with Directive (EU) 2016/943, provided that appropriate safeguards have been put in place (see also section 3.5.4). This protection is helpful, for example, if the trade secrets are unlawfully disclosed to a third party which uses them commercially. However, a trade secret provides no control over a situation where a third party independently develops and uses the relevant information.

An initial stocktake of your own IP helps to identify existing assets and weaknesses and forms the starting point for an IP strategy.

3.2 What does your business model look like?

The founders of start-ups no doubt appreciate that a mere idea or even a technical solution does not yet constitute a business model. By definition, a business model describes the logical functioning of a company and, in particular, the specific way in which it generates profit (see Morris et al 2012). 'Fundamentally, the description of business models should help to understand, analyse and communicate the key factors of a company's success or failure' (see Business Model nd).

In particular, the key factors of business success should be examined to see whether they can be reserved or monopolized for the start-up. It is not unusual for the business model to change during the development phase, or for another model to be chosen or added. Therefore, it should be clarified at the outset which alternative business models may potentially be viable, in order to consider them for possible protection. After all, competitors operating under different conditions may also try to compete with the start-up with a modified business model.

In some cases, it may even be worthwhile to adapt the business model to what is protectable for the start-up: if a claim can be staked using an IP right, it can later be used to 'dig for gold' – that is, to implement your business model in a protected manner. In some cases, this can be more promising than digging in another area alongside many competitors.

One key factor of success, which is sought after by many investors, is the scalability of the business model – in particular, the ability of the business to expand and grow its revenue with good operational cost efficiency. Scalability can and should be supported by a well-thought-out IP strategy.

Let us assume that you want to set up an online ordering and delivery service for food. This is not a completely new idea and you will probably struggle to find an aspect for which your start-up could obtain IP protection in this context. But you might consider asking users who place orders about the size of their households and the age of household members; on the basis of an order, you can thus calculate and indicate the 'lifespan' of the delivery – that is, how many calories the order contains and for how many days, if any, these will be sufficient. You can also take into account the shelf life of the food and give an estimate of whether it will be reasonably consumed before the expiry date. These calculations could give you a unique selling point, which you could try to protect with a patent (ie, the way in which the data is determined) or a design (eg, if results are displayed using a special traffic light design, with red indicating that too much has been purchased).

Finally, you should also consider whether the same business model will be adopted in all regions or countries in which your start-up wishes to operate. The protection that you can generate through IP rights is in most cases country-specific – that is, a separate IP right must be generated and paid for in each country. On the one hand, it can make sense – in the interest of scalability – to structure the business model in such a way that it is as homogeneous as possible and functions in the same way in many countries. On the other hand, this can be difficult due to legal and social conditions, so regional adjustments may be necessary. Careful consideration should be given to selecting the countries in which it makes sense to acquire protection and to whether it is necessary to tailor protection specifically to individual countries. This is discussed in more detail in section 3.7.

The influence of different business models on available protection options is explained in more detail in Chapter 2, using further examples.

3.3 What can be protected?

3.3.1 Patentable inventions

Below is a list of items that may be patentable or may indicate patentable inventions. The list is neither comprehensive nor free from overlap; it is merely intended to give you a general idea of the types of subject matter that may potentially be patentable:

- Embodied objects:
  - mechanical constructions;
  - electrical and electronic circuits;
  - new arrangements of known components;
  - measuring circuits;
  - control circuits;
  - devices for data collection;
  - devices for image generation and speech processing;
  - data storage devices;
  - devices for data transport and communication;
  - materials, alloys; and
  - active ingredients, pharmaceuticals and molecules.
- Processes/methods:
  - methods with a new sequence of known steps;
  - manufacturing processes;
  - new operating procedures for known or new devices;
  - measurement procedures;
  - control methods;
  - methods for collecting, determining, analysing or processing data (under certain conditions); and
  - methods for the storage, output, representation or transport/communication of data (under certain conditions).

The conditions under which patents are actually granted are very complicated, fill entire patent law commentaries and cannot be explained exhaustively here. For a more reliable assessment or to elaborate on an invention, it is thus advisable to discuss the matter with a patent attorney in each individual case.

In some cases, where the items listed above are not protectable themselves, it is often possible to identify a protectable invention in connection with other components. This is especially true for inventions that are reflected in software. Although under the EPC and national patent acts, computer programs are not protectable *per se*, applications or computer-implementable processes containing a technical aspect may be protectable (cf Articles 52(2)(c) and (3) of the EPC).

Below are two examples of new application software that has been created as the basis for a business model, in an attempt to sound out useful protection options.

Example 1

Software/computer-implementable method

In a procedure performed by a computer, various icons arranged on the graphical user interface are rearranged on the screen according to a selectable prioritisation. For this purpose, the computer records or determines for a certain period the amount of processor capacity that the individual programs have used. The icons are then arranged, for example, according to the order of used capacity, with distance increasing from the start or home button.

This process may be patentable in principle if formulated correctly. In a further step, the patent office will still examine whether an identical or similar process is already known from the literature (ie, examination as to novelty and inventive step).

Example 2

Artificial Intelligence

In examining patentability, it is important to determine whether a so-called 'technical contribution' within the meaning of the Patent Act can be identified. In many cases, this is also the case when using artificial intelligence (AI). The European Patent Office's 2019 examination guidelines on AI provide as follows (EPO 2019):

> Artificial intelligence and machine learning find applications in various fields of technology. For example, the use of a neural network in a heart-monitoring apparatus for the purpose of identifying irregular heartbeats makes a technical contribution. The classification of digital images, videos, audio or speech signals based on low-level features (eg edges or pixel attributes for images) are further typical technical applications of classification algorithms ... Where a classification method serves a technical purpose, the steps of generating the training set and training the classifier may also contribute to the technical character of the invention if they support achieving that technical purpose.

Applications for patents on AI are increasing, particularly in jurisdictions such as China.

3.3.2 *Identification of protection options*

Particularly in the case of innovative business models and start-ups with highly flexible work processes, the identification of new and protectable units can be difficult.

In the classic so-called 'waterfall' process of product development, which is applied in established companies, innovation runs in regulated – but also strictly limited – paths. In each case, a product is analysed in its current state; possible customer needs are then identified; and finally technical problems are solved or additional functions added by means of targeted development. Potentially patentable improvements can often be identified relatively easily. It is often a good idea simply to compare the existing product with the new product and go through the technical changes in search of inventions.

However, this procedure is not possible for completely new products and services, as is often the case with start-ups. That said, this allows for innovations to be designed or tailored at one's own discretion and according to the protection requirements. This requires significant experience in dealing with innovations and protection options.

The following questions can be helpful in identifying protectable ideas:

- Who is the customer/purchaser/user of the product?
- Are several potential customer groups relevant?
- What benefits/advantages does the customer/various customer groups derive from the product?
- Through which (especially technical) measures is the benefit/advantage achieved?
- Is the benefit achieved through a single measure or through several interacting measures?
- Can a partial benefit already be achieved through a subset of the measures?
- Is a known problem solved in a new way?
- Is a technical or non-technical problem solved that did not previously occur or that was previously unknown?
- Are one or more of the measures to solve the problem of a technical nature?
- Can blocking one or more of the measures prevent the product from being used effectively by the customer?
- Are there other conceivable solutions or modifications of individual measures to solve the problem?

Examples of business ideas and the development of protection strategies are presented in Chapter 2.

3.4 Against whom and against which actions should protection be directed?

To answer this question, one should consider the scenario of a functioning business model and identify who the start-up would compete or cooperate with in this situation and who would be potential users of the product offered.

In most cases, IP rights entitle the owner to prohibit third parties from using them or to offer a licence in return for compensation.

According to Section 9 of the German Patent Act, a patent gives the holder the right to prohibit any third party from:

- manufacturing, offering, putting in circulation or using a product which is the subject matter of the patent, or either importing or possessing it for such purposes;
- using a process which is the subject matter of the patent or, if the third party knows or it is obvious under the circumstances that the use of the method is prohibited without the consent of the patent holder, offering it for use within the scope of the law; or
- offering, putting in circulation or using a product directly produced by a method which is the subject matter of the patent, or either importing or possessing it for such purposes.

However, the devil is often in the detail. A possible trap for patent protection – for example, for Internet or cloud-based services – is that only certain procedural steps of a patent claim are carried out by the end user; while other steps are carried out by a provider, platform operator or database operator. Only clever formulation of a patent can succeed in identifying a single person or company to which all steps of the patented process can be attributed.

Another potential problem is that not all method steps may be carried out within the territorial scope of the patent. If such cases are anticipated in good time, problems can often be avoided through the appropriate selection and formulation of the features to be protected.

The following rules are important when assessing the content of patent protection:

- The substantive protection is determined by the (granted) patent claims.
- The fewer features that the claims contain (ie, the fewer 'limitations' there are), the wider the scope of protection.
- Also of interest are several 'independent claims' of the same or different categories (eg, device, method).
- Similar protection options exist worldwide for most areas of technology.

There are, however, country-specific restrictions on protection, especially in the case of computer-implementable inventions and medical procedures. In this context, it should also be determined as early as possible in which countries it is intended to enable litigation based on patents. The territorial effect of patents is limited to the country for which they were granted. More detailed considerations are set out in section 3.7.

3.5 Resources and consultants

3.5.1 Budget

It makes sense for a start-up to establish a budget for IP rights and IP protection as early as possible. It is very difficult to make general statements about a reasonable amount that should be invested in IP. Large companies in innovative industries often have IP budgets that are linked, as a percentage, to total R&D spending. The IP budget of a start-up can vary considerably depending on the technology, size of product range, product maturity and environment.

Funds must be spent not only on applications for new patents (ie, official fees and patent attorney fees), but also on 'prosecution' – that is, the ongoing examination procedures at the patent offices. In these procedures, the prior art identified by the patent offices is analysed in the form of documents and compared with the relevant invention. Differences are discussed and reasons for and against a lack of novelty or lack of inventiveness of the claimed invention are exchanged.

It may be useful to file as few patent applications as possible, with each containing a plurality of ideas. Admittedly, this is not what the patent offices are looking for – which is why they will often object to such applications for lack of 'unity'. However, a good patent attorney can still take advantage of this by dividing the application into several 'divisional applications' at a later date, if necessary, which can be pursued separately. For this purpose, separate fees must be paid to the patent office at the time of division; but this can be deferred into the future. This may fit into the financial planning of a start-up – for example, if a financing round or an exit is anticipated (see also section 3.6). A strong investor may still be able to develop a comprehensive patent portfolio from this.

3.5.2 Patent attorney

Patent filings and representation in the examination procedure before the EPO, the United States Patent and Trademark Office (USPTO), the United Kingdom Intellectual Property Office or the DPMA can be formally handled by the inventor or an authorised in-house person. However, it is usually helpful to hire a patent attorney who can draw on his experience in order to avoid any gaps in protection and achieve the broadest possible scope of protection by correctly formulating the patent claims. Since the protection depends as much on the wording of the patent claim as on the invention itself, much can be gained from a professional formulation. Even an ingenious invention must be perfectly defined in words; it cannot defend itself!

But remember: the patent attorney will usually be a stranger to the company. He will know only what he is told about the invention, the potential opportunities and risks, and the successes and challenges of the company. It takes time to keep the patent attorney updated and informed. However, if you involve him throughout the process on an ongoing basis, he can achieve the best possible protection for your company, adapted to your respective situation.

3.5.3 Patent workshops

Boring afternoons with no meaningful tasks are a rarity at start-ups! Employees seldom have the time (or the priority) to check for new developments at the company to see which might be suitable subject matter for a patent application. Moreover, it is not always easy to identify the most valuable ideas.

Therefore, it is both helpful and efficient to schedule half an afternoon (or longer) for a patent workshop from time to time. This is a well-known method of identifying the good ideas that have recently been developed and/or outlining initial ideas for solving tasks that lie ahead. When several ideas are considered together, it is also easier to compare them in terms of quality and to prioritize which should be selected for patent applications.

As part of this process, it is helpful to consult an independent person who can also lead the workshop. That person could be, for example, an innovation manager of the company, an external consultant or an experienced patent attorney.

Various methods can be adopted for the workshop, in terms of how best to search for and evaluate new ideas. Group work is generally recommended, in order to generate momentum in the discussion. As the focus of the workshop is not the resolution of technical problems, but rather a search for protectable subject matter, the usual workshop methods should be modified accordingly. In doing so, the focus should be directed both to solutions that have already been realized and to challenges lying ahead. This is because not only concrete solutions, but also solution concepts at the drafting stage may be protectable.

A good starting point is often to analyse the characteristics of the planned product or service which will ultimately be appreciated by the end customer or which represent value. Another suitable starting point is to analyse a few exemplary patents of competitors in the same field of the business (eg, what do they do differently? Why? What can be protected?).

3.5.3.1 SAILS method

The SAILS method examines recognizable innovations to see whether they fall within the following categories:

- Standards: Are new standards set or existing standards met?
- Architecture of the system: Is it about an overall structure?
- Integration of components: Will existing elements be integrated into other elements in the course of the new development?
- Linkages of components: Are elements connected/coupled in a new way?
- Substitutions: Are elements replaced?

By discussing the above questions, protectable aspects can easily be identified in the workshop.

3.5.3.2 Diamond structure

In another possible workshop format, the diamond structure set out in Figure 1.1 is used systematically.

3.5.3.3 Layer model

In many other cases, the analysis and search for protectable objects in start-ups can be based on the following layer model (from bottom to top):

- Digital services;
- Data analysis;
- Connectivity;

- Sensors/actuators; and
- Product.

The treatment of inventions is often simplest at the lowest level, in the case of a technical product (hardware) which physically exists. The second level – the provision of sensors or actuators – can also still be treated through classical means; as can the third level, connectivity, which deals with data preparation and data transport or communication. Here, for example, communication protocols, transmission and reception processes and data transport paths play a role.

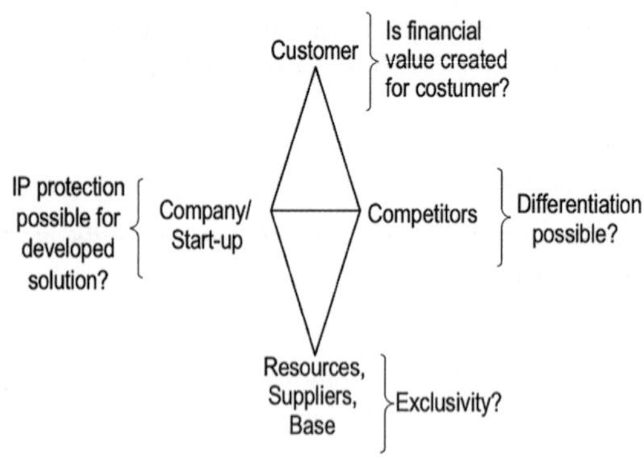

Figure 1.1 *Diamond structure*

For the two upper layers – data analysis and digital services – the task of identifying patentable technical inventions is the most difficult. Various sub-processes or aspects can be extracted from the overall process, suitably delimited and defined; but this process requires keen insight into the approach of patent examiners to examination. Even if you feel that you can identify a patentable idea, a patent attorney will still try to identify alternatives, generalize concrete steps and find out a lot of information that should be disclosed in a patent application, should the solution to be protected need to be further narrowed down during the examination procedure.

In data analysis, methods of AI or methods for structuring and providing data suitable for analysis may be eligible for protection.

One potential problem with digital services is that intensive interaction with the customer may be required to provide the digital service. This means that the entire process is realized through cooperation between the provider and the customer. Therefore, in many cases, it may be useful to check the process steps undertaken by the provider and those undertaken by the customer separately for possible protectability.

3.5.3.4 'Scrum process' in agile development

In traditional development processes utilized at well-established companies, process milestones are usually based on certain things that must be worked through; and the issue of protectable ideas can be linked to this.

However, start-ups do not normally have such processes in place. For example, many work with 'agile' processes, rely on self-organization of teams and structure development work in 'sprints'. Employees are under immense time pressure and everything that does not directly serve the achievement of the development goal is pushed aside.

It is then the responsibility of management to create room to discuss protectable inventions. Ideally, this should happen at the end of a sprint, when the achievement of objectives is discussed. It may also be useful to put an 'IP hat' on an employee during the sprint, so that he stays on the lookout for possible inventions.

3.5.4 Trade secrets

In certain cases, instead of filing a patent application, it may make sense to keep developed technology secret if it is not immediately recognizable from the product or service. To this end, the first step is to determine what the valuable 'secret' is; while the second is to ensure its actual secrecy – that is, to actively prevent the technology from being made accessible to outsiders. These are the basic criteria that must be met to qualify as a trade secret.

It also makes sense to make the technology a trade secret in a formal sense. To this end, it is necessary to take relevant concrete measures to ensure its secrecy in accordance with Directive (EU) 2016/943 of the European Parliament and of the Council of 8 June 2016 on the protection of confidential know-how and confidential business information (trade secrets) against unlawful acquisition, use and disclosure, and its implementation into national law. These measures should be well documented should it subsequently become necessary to invoke the trade secret. To do so, it is recommended to use a company-owned IT network; train your employees on the subject of confidentiality; and draw up proper documentation. This is the only way to ensure that an unlawfully 'leaked' trade secret can be traced and a third party can be prohibited from using it. This also applies, for example, where cooperation partners or the start-up's own employees take secrets with them when they move to a new employer

3.6 Timescales, financing rounds and exit

The timescales for the examination of patent applications are often frightening for start-ups, as it can take several years before a patent is granted.

However, this can also have its advantages. Once the initial costs of a patent application have been paid, peace and quiet is restored for a while. During this time, all rights are reserved as a result of the filing, on the one hand; and almost no further costs arise, on the other.

It is important for the start-up to synchronize the 'patent track' with its broader schedule. Essentially, most start-ups are keen to defer costs into the future, wherever possible. At the same time, however, rights must be reserved as early as possible. There are a number of options to achieve this – for example, a centralized international application procedure under the Patent Cooperation Treaty (PCT) (see current version WIPO 2019a). This procedure involves the issue of a preliminary opinion on protectability by a single central office once an application has been filed; for a few thousand euros, a period of at least 30 months can then be bought before attorneys must be retained and documents filed in all countries in which patent protection will potentially be sought.

Where only a German patent is sought, the patent application can be filed with the DPMA and the request for examination of patentability can be postponed for up to seven years. During this period, only annual fees are payable – and then only after the examination procedure has commenced. The disadvantage of this lengthy postponement is that during this period, it is not clear whether a patent will in fact be granted and to what extent it will offer protection.

Another advantage of delaying the examination procedure for as long as possible is that it affords some considerable time in which to shape the wording of the patent claims (within the boundaries set by the original disclosure). If the actual solution changes, one should examine whether it is reasonable to adapt the patent claims accordingly within the scope of what was initially disclosed.

It could be even more exciting to keep an eye on competitors' products while your own patent application is under examination at the patent office and then, at the appropriate time, 'tailor' your own patent claims as far as possible to those competing products (again, within the scope of what was originally disclosed in the patent application).

One particularly suitable way to pursue this approach is through the filing of divisional applications. In most countries, a pending patent application can be divided during the examination procedure (against payment of an additional fee). Of the resulting two patent applications, one (the parent application) can quickly lead to the grant of a patent; while the other (the divisional application) goes through the patent office examination process again. This saves time; and the options for shaping the divisional application largely correspond to those of the parent application, with the only condition being that the two granted patents must be different in the end.

Through this procedure a divisional application can be kept alive for quite a while – for example, until the exit of the start-up – with all options kept open, so that an investor/buyer can then still fully exploit the desired protection possibilities.

It may also be extremely useful for an upcoming financing round if the start-up can show that it has been granted a patent. At the EPO and the DPMA, for example, a free-of-charge request for acceleration is possible. Close cooperation between the patent attorney and the patent office is often helpful in this regard – for example, by requesting telephone or personal interviews with the patent examiner instead of relying on correspondence.

In some cases, the patent office proceedings can be accelerated even faster if desired. For example, the USPTO offers a 'Track One' procedure, through which a US patent can be granted within about a year (albeit at additional cost) (see also USPTO 2019).

The Patent Prosecution Highway (PPH) offers further possibilities for acceleration, especially if the examination is being conducted in parallel in several countries (eg, if an invention is to be protected in the US, Europe and China). Under the PPH, in order to reduce their overall workload, certain patent offices will at least partially adopt the results of another patent office. This should lead to faster grant and more uniform patents.

Several PPH agreements have been established for different groups of countries; a good overview can be found on the homepage of the World Intellectual Property Organization (WIPO) (see WIPO 2019b). The best known is the IP5 PPH, which includes the EPO, the Japanese Patent Office, the Korean Intellectual Property Office, the State Intellectual Property Office of the People's Republic of China and the USPTO.

3.7 Region-specific protection strategy

An IP right such as a patent offers protection only in the countries for which it has been granted. Patents are usually granted for individual countries/states; but there are also international agreements that allow for regional validity, such as the planned unitary patent of the EU (as noted above, the current EPC aims to secure the country-by-country validity of patents and merely centralizes the examination and grant process independently of EU member state membership).

The first filing of a patent application with a single patent office (eg, the DPMA) will suffice to establish the date that will be regarded as the date of filing worldwide, provided that the relevant documents are subsequently filed with other patent offices in the following 12 months. The decision on the countries in which protection will be sought must therefore be made just a few months after the first filing (in extreme cases, shortly before the 12-month period expires).

For the subsequent enforcement of patents, it is also important that the patent law allows the patent holder to prohibit the unauthorized activities of third parties. For example, Section 9 of the German Patent Law provides as follows:

> The effect of the patent is that only the patentee is entitled to use the patented invention within the limits of the applicable law. Any third party shall be prohibited, without his consent
>
> > to manufacture, offer, put in circulation or use a product which is the subject-matter of the patent, or to import or possess it for those purposes
> > to use a process which is the subject-matter of the patent or, if the third party knows or it is obvious in the circumstances that the use of the process is prohibited without the consent of the patent proprietor, to offer it for use within the scope of this Act;
> > offering, putting in circulation or using a product directly obtained by a process which is the subject-matter of the patent, or either importing or stocking it for these purposes.

Thus, the holder of a German patent can prohibit not only the use of an infringing product in Germany, but also the import of infringing products from abroad. The holder can also prohibit the manufacture in Germany of products that are intended for export.

The question of in which countries protection should be sought will depend on the budget, the markets in which the start-up wishes to be active and the countries in which possible competitors are based and/or competing products sold.

However, this does not necessarily mean that all eligible countries must be covered by national IP rights. If it is possible to protect some important markets, a competitor will be left with only the remaining markets and thus correspondingly reduced potential sales; so a good competitive position can be secured in the case of economies of scale.

The following issues are important in considering a region-specific patent protection strategy:

- Worldwide protection is seldom useful. Depending on the company and its products, individual geographic coverage ('footprint') will usually make more sense. This should be considered before each patent application.
- A patent prohibits both the unauthorized manufacture and the unauthorized sale of a product. Therefore, it is often sufficient to have a patent either in potential 'manufacturing countries' or in target 'consumer countries'.

- In the case of technically complex products, registration in only a few countries (eg, Germany, the US and China) will often suffice to block the world market for competitors.
- The costs of granting and maintaining a patent vary from country to country (eg, in the US, obtaining a patent is expensive; but maintaining a granted patent is comparatively cheap year on year).
- The costs of enforcing rights in case of patent infringement should also be considered (these are comparatively low in Germany, but usually high in the UK).
- Consideration of the formal requirements is very important, but is often overlooked:
    - Many countries require that an invention which is made in the home country also be registered in that country first (eg, the US, China, India, Italy, Spain). A good overview is provided by the World Intellectual Property Organization (see also WIPO 2019c).
    - The laws of some countries impose a general 'obligation to file' (eg, Chapter 3 of the Law on Employee Inventions in Germany; and Russian law).
    - Transnational joint developments in groups of companies may prove problematic. In this case, an application for a foreign filing licence is often the only available option. But remember: non-compliance with the regulations will also be apparent to third parties!

What is stated above in relation to patents also applies analogously to other types of IP rights, although the costs for these are typically much lower than for patents. The DPMA provides a good overview with useful further links (for trademarks, see DPMA 2019a; for designs, see DPMA 2019b).

As previously mentioned, international protection for an invention may be obtained by initially filing an application for a patent or utility model in one country (or with the EPO) and subsequently, within a 'priority interval' of 12 months, extending the territorial scope of protection by filing subsequent applications for the same invention in one or more additional countries. This priority right also exists for designs and trademark rights filed either nationally or with the EUIPO (with a shorter priority interval of generally six months).

This procedure may be quite costly and cumbersome if protection in many countries is desired. An alternative mechanism – which is often simpler and more cost effective – is available in the form of 'bundled' international filings which are submitted to a central authority and allow respective national protection to be obtained in multiple member states. For patents, this mechanism – known as an 'international patent application' – is made possible by the PCT (which was previously mentioned above in connection with timing considerations). For designs and trademarks, international registration under the Hague System (for designs) and the Madrid System (for trademarks) serves a similar purpose.

3.8 Employees, freelancers and cooperation partners

A start-up usually has scarce resources, little time and often limited experience. To keep costs low, the number of permanent employees is kept to a minimum. It is therefore often helpful to be able to rely on freelancers, development cooperations and 'business angels' (see Business Angels Netzwerk Deutschland eV (2020)) for certain tasks.

However, in case of such arrangements two important considerations with regard to the IP protection should be borne in mind:

- The start-up must keep track of protectable work results and encourage external partners to communicate protectable results; and
- The start-up must ensure that it is entitled to both rights to use all work results and rights to all emerging IP.

This applies to research and development cooperations; development contracts and supply contracts for the development or adaptation of products; and cooperations with freelancers.

Example

A start-up produces temperature sensors for heating systems that will be connected via radio. For the radio connection, a cooperation partner is commissioned to design and manufacture an application-specific integrated circuit (ASIC) with a transmitting and receiving device. A written contract is not concluded. In this case, the cooperation partner supplies the work results and ASICs, but can also freely dispose of the results and utilize the developed component in cooperation with other sensor manufacturers. As the development is paid for once, the device can even be sold to the start-up's competitors at a lower price.

A contractual arrangement under which the start-up would secure all or part of the IP rights to the development would enable it to obtain this component exclusively, at least for a period of time.

A similar problem can arise when freelancers are employed. Unless otherwise agreed, all inventive ideas that freelancers may have will remain their property, and patent or utility model applications may be filed in respect of those ideas. Such persons usually have an insight into the technical problems at hand and thus have a good starting position from which to file for patents and grant licences. It is not difficult to regulate cooperations with freelancers by means of a contract which includes provisions on the assignment of rights to inventions; you just have to think about this in time!

If external persons are invited to cooperate – for example, by participating in a workshop to discuss solutions to problems and perhaps also inventions that could lead to a patent application – there is a twofold danger:

- Formally, every idea discussed becomes known to a person outside the company who is part of the public. Thus the idea becomes formally public and cannot be the basis of a patent application; and
- Contributions to solutions made by external persons are legally owned not by the start-up, but rather by their respective providers. Only those external persons can apply for the corresponding IP rights to those ideas – or transfer them to the start-up (eg, in return for monetary compensation).

Both problems can be solved through relatively simple contractual arrangements: in the first case above, a non-disclosure agreement; and in the second, a cooperation agreement. The two can also be combined.

By contrast, in the case of permanent employees of the start-up, the rights to their ideas are normally assigned to the employer. Here, the relevant legal conditions and the automatic consequences thereof should be kept in mind. In Germany, the right of employee inventors to inventor's remuneration is particularly worth mentioning. This should be settled contractually by the start-up with its employee inventors for each invention as early as possible – not least so that the inventors' claims are transparent for investors. These issues are explored in more detail in Chapter 3.

4. How to avoid infringing third-party IP rights

In 2017, more than three million patents were registered worldwide (see WIPO 2019d). These must be observed by third parties which are commercially active in the respective countries. Fortunately, both granted patents and published patent applications are easily accessible online (on various platforms provided by IP offices and third parties), organized by technical fields according to a very granular patent classification system.

Of course, it is a lot to ask to be aware of all granted patents in one's field of work; but ignorance is not a valid excuse. All companies have a legal obligation to monitor patents in their respective field of activity with 'due care'.

To this end, you can either conduct your own regular research or have a service provider do this for you. Either way, a well-informed employee of the start-up should examine all IP rights that the research turns up. The analysis of whether a third-party IP right may affect your own product is simple in many cases: if the patented solutions are obviously completely different from your own, they will present no problems.

In other cases, however, the analysis may be more difficult, and only a patent attorney can interpret the patent claims and identify with a degree of certainty which solutions fall within and which fall outside the scope of protection.

Such analyses should be carried out in detail only once a route to a marketable product has been determined. At that point, investment decisions will be taken that require legal certainty regarding technical feasibility and freedom from third-party rights.

The following procedure is a pragmatic way of dealing with third-party IP rights at moderate cost.

First, monitor your own field of activity by signing up for internet alerts (see EPO 2019b). These provide regular news about technical innovations in your field of activity and, depending on your search profile, about published patent applications and patents.

NOTE

At least in principle, submitted patent applications are not published by patent offices worldwide until 18 months after the first filing. Before that date, applications are not visible to third parties. This gives the patent applicant a lead time for implementation or further development. Often, the applicant will not inform the public of its invention, even in technical articles, until the corresponding patent applications have been disclosed.

Patent searches should also be commissioned at certain development milestones (eg, several times in the course of product development), in order to obtain an overview of the evolving IP rights situation. Depending on the complexity of the product, you will then be provided with several or even several dozen patent documents to deal with.

A search service offered by the Swiss Federal Institute of Intellectual Property (IGE) has proved to be a practical and (comparatively) inexpensive option in this regard. ip-search is a company affiliated with the IGE (see IGE 2019). The scope of the search, the depth of the analysis and the extent of the preparation can all be specified by the client. The price is based on the amount of work that can be determined in advance. The search yields results of a standardized and recognized quality to facilitate risk management at a comprehensible level, which can also be easily explained to investors.

In principle, the search for third-party IP rights in the field of software development is particularly challenging. It is often difficult to determine whether one's own process steps fall under one of the multitude of existing patents – especially since these are often formulated in a relatively abstract way.

Complete certainty is thus an unrealistic aspiration. However, a strategic approach may be useful: it should be gauged which stages of software development are on the one hand costly and on the other hand solve problems which in all probability must also be solved or may have been solved by competitors in the same or a neighbouring area. At this point, it is worth taking a closer look at whether relevant patents already exist. If such solutions also concern interfaces for the transfer of data or communications, the risk of patent infringement increases, as for such purposes certain boundary conditions or standards must be observed, which will probably make it more difficult to modify the software at a later point in order to avoid patent infringement.

NOTE

Where an important third-party patent has been identified, the start-up has the option of taking a licence if possible or seeking to modify its own product to circumvent the patent. To make this more difficult for competitors, patent attorneys usually try to find terms for all features that are as comprehensive as possible, in order to ensure that the scope of protection is as broad as possible. On the other hand, during the patent examination, patent offices will take care to ensure that the protection is not unduly extended. In any case, when it comes to developing around the scope of protection of a patent, a patent attorney should be consulted to help with the interpretation of the patent and with finding ideas for design-around.

Even the use of OSS cannot ultimately protect against patent problems. Where OSS is described as 'free', this is true only to a limited extent, since the users involved license their copyrights on a reciprocal basis. Where a software solution falls under the patent of a third party, that third party is not obliged to license it.

For this reason, initiatives have been established by OSS users – such as the Open Invention Network, established by Google, IBM and Microsoft, among others – through which their own patents are collected and made available for joint use in order to provide a counterweight against possible future patent lawsuits (see OIN 2019).

5. Use of third-party patents as a source of information

Patent applications and patents are published, in part, to make them available to society as a source of information on innovation. As patent publications are generally available free of charge online, they can and should be used as a source of information. For example, they can provide information on:

- what solutions have been found for specific problems (these solutions may be freely available);
- which players are utilizing those solutions (these could be approached as cooperation partners or avoided as potential competitors); and
- which inventors have been involved in achieving those solutions (these could be poached).

6. Conclusion

IP rights exist to fulfil a social function: monopoly rights are granted to individual innovators to reward investment in technology development. This is intended to promote innovation. However, protection can be obtained only against payment and only for a limited time. After that, the new development becomes free for all to use. As a rule, information on protected new developments is publicly accessible at the latest 18 months after submission of the patent application.

IP rights also ensure that an inventor is rewarded and (if he so wishes) is identified as such to the public. This is part of the inventor's right of personality.

Irrespective of the social functions of IP protection, IP rights must be used as strategic instruments in competition. An understanding of the possibilities for such use helps those companies that innovate most.

2 Basics and development of an IP strategy for start-ups

Uwe Schriek

1. Introduction

This chapter demonstrates how the instruments and tactics presented in Chapter 1 can be correctly applied in practice and aligned with a long-term strategy. Section 2 outlines the fundamental strategic issues; while section 3 concretizes them in more detail by examining important individual questions. Section 4 discusses protection options and possible business models for a hypothetical company. In section 5, the development of an overall strategy is then outlined, based on the example of hypothetical medtech company SugarLight. In the start-up phase, the leverage of IP rights and IP in general for the planned company must first be determined and the initial stock of IP must be recorded. This includes the ideas of the founders, as well as purchased or in-licensed IP rights. It is important that as many rights as possible are held by the start-up itself. Maintaining the consistent confidentiality of know-how (especially aspects that are not visible in a product that will subsequently be marketed) is also an option. In addition, freedom-to-operate (FTO) analysis should be carried out to ensure that products can be marketed with the greatest possible certainty, with no risk of infringing third-party rights.

2. Fundamental strategic issues

2.1 What must a start-up consider with regard to IP?

Among other things, IP rights are intended to enable innovative companies to monopolize their innovations for a certain period of time by protecting the results of their work through patents, trademarks or designs, enabling them to recover their investment in the development of the innovation through market exclusivity. As start-ups rely on their innovations for success, they should not hesitate to exploit this opportunity. They often have few other factors on their side (eg, an extensive distribution network, customer loyalty or strong capital cover). Thus, start-ups would be well advised to secure IP protection for their innovations, enabling them to monopolize those innovations to strengthen their competitive position.

Like all companies, start-ups must take care not to infringe the patents of third parties. To complicate things, a patent may be inadvertently infringed where, for example, a start-up implements its own idea, but this has already been independently developed and patented by a third party. The earlier patent will prohibit the realization of this idea by the start-up, even if the start-up developed its idea independently. Care should thus be taken to ensure that newly developed products and processes – or at least the core ideas – are not protected by third-party property rights; or in other words, that the start-up has FTO.

2.2 Which strategic IP goals can be pursued?

A start-up may have various IP goals. For example, the sole aim could be to obtain patents quickly and cheaply. This is particularly pertinent for research institutions that have no production facilities themselves and are not commercially active. A granted patent conveys the message that the institution has conceived or developed something really new and unique; and the institution will enjoy the status of an inventor as a result.

However, a variety of IP goals may exist beyond the mere accumulation of granted patents. These should be aligned with the corporate strategy: the start-up should determine which of the IP goals discussed below are most important for it.

One legitimate IP goal is to build a reputation. Granted patents are regarded as proof of innovative strength. For example, patent offices regularly publish 'record lists' of the companies that have filed the highest number of patent applications or been granted the highest number of patents over the past year.

Product or service exclusivity further means that third parties can be prevented both from copying those products or services (direct copies) and from adopting the concept of the solution by prohibition rights. The yardstick for determining which activities third parties are prohibited from pursuing is the final patent claims of the granted patent. This is why, in patent applications, the patent attorney usually expresses the invention as broadly – that is, as generally – as possible. As a rule of thumb, concepts are protected primarily and concrete solutions only secondarily. Exclusivity can often be achieved through strong IP rights; but in some situations it can also be achieved through effective secrecy, provided that it may be anticipated that the secret would not be recognizable by third parties from the product or service – including through reverse engineering.

A start-up can also secure bargaining power by obtaining IP rights that are of interest to third parties, including competitors. The start-up may not only assert these rights as prohibition rights, but also use them as 'technology currency' to exchange rights with third parties, enabling it to use their technology where this is deemed useful.

FTO can be established through good patent clearing, whereby foreign IP rights that could prove to be obstacles are identified early on and are circumvented systematically and with reasonable effort. However, complete certainty cannot be achieved, because the IP rights of third parties are not published until 18 months after submission and only then become visible to competitors. FTO can also be achieved, for example, by having a patent position that is so strong that other companies do not dare to attack for fear of retaliation or are prepared to negotiate licence exchanges.

Through licensing income or other consideration for the grant of licensing rights, a start-up can generate a regular income stream, which will be beneficial to its financial situation. Other consideration can also be negotiated in return for the grant of IP rights, such as favourable supply conditions or prices from a supplier. When granting licences, preference should be given to licences for use in markets which the start-up itself does not serve ('off-core' licences). For example, a manufacturer of light switches could license a new, burn-off resistant contact material for switching contacts to a manufacturer of welding electrodes and thus would not damage its own business.

Another interesting strategic objective is the possibility of using IP rights as collateral for bank loans or investors. While it is difficult to objectively evaluate IP rights for this purpose, recognized methods of valuation have been developed, for example, to ensure that the trade in IP rights within a group of companies is fair and transparent from a tax point of view, and occurs at reasonable prices (for tax reasons, such transactions must be able to withstand what is known as a 'third-party comparison' – that is, the conditions under which they are carried out must be the same as those which would have applied in a corresponding transaction with an unrelated third company).

An overriding strategic IP objective is an accurate assessment of the start-up's IP position at the point of exit – for example, when selling the company or going public. The start-up's value should be as high as possible at the point of exit. One aspect of a good company valuation is a strong IP position, which must be transparent and verifiable for potential investors. This includes the following aspects, among others:

- patents and patent applications which protect the start-up's products from being copied and ensure that it can utilize the competitive advantages monopolized by the property rights in its business;
- in-depth FTO analyses which provide a certain degree of certainty that no foreign property rights are being infringed, and that market entry cannot be delayed or prevented by patent disputes;
- good contracts with cooperation partners, in which IP is clearly assigned (if possible to the start-up); and
- certainty that the IP rights really belong to the start-up, and not to the private founders or a research institute from which the start-up emerged as a spin-off; to cooperation partners; or to individual inventors (eg, who are also employees of the start-up) who still hold shares in the rights to the invention.

NOTE

It is possible to assess IP in several different ways, depending on the relevant perspective. In the context of this book, this is discussed several times throughout this book – for example, in:

Chapter 3 – IP from the perspective of the law on employee inventions;

Chapter 9 – IP from the perspective of consultancies/auditing firms;
Chapter 10 – IP from the perspective of venture capital investors.

2.3 Which aspects are important to safeguard your own work results?

The scope of protection of patents should be optimized – that is, the 'smallest marketable unit' should be monopolized; and in addition, possible circumvention solutions should be addressed. Finally, the scope of protection should remain flexible for as long as possible (eg, through divisional applications), in order to be able to react more easily to possible problems and changing circumstances.

When formulating patent claims, different categories (eg, device or process) can be claimed, even cumulatively. It is important to understand that, for example, the manufacturer or importer of a measuring device can be attacked on the basis of a device claim, but possibly not directly on the basis of a process claim, as the measuring method is used only by the customer. Caution is also required when deciding whether the protection should be directed at a navigation device for a motor vehicle or at a motor vehicle with a (built-in) navigation device. In the latter case, it is more difficult to attack the manufacturer of the navigation device than in the former case, since the navigation device manufacturer neither manufactures the vehicle with the navigation device nor puts it into circulation (however, there are also possibilities for prosecution in the latter case in the context of so-called 'contributory patent infringement').

The rights to the invention should be clearly documented (which could be problematic if external consultants or similar have been involved in producing the invention). To this end, it is important to clarify and reach agreement on the concomitant circumstances of each invention in a timely manner.

The aim should be to achieve the greatest possible global protection – at least in the main markets (eg, the US, the EU and China; only in rare cases will protection in Germany alone suffice), as well as in the countries of manufacture, where appropriate. In many cases, it is not necessary to cover all markets as long as a certain world market share is covered. In such case competitors could only supply the 'remaining markets' with rival products, which often makes no economic sense.

As far as possible, costs should be managed or spread out over time. The best institutionalized way to do this is to file a worldwide Patent Cooperation Treaty (PCT) patent application, for which a prior art search and an examination are carried out centrally once only, and which can be validated 30 months later in (almost) all countries of the world at the applicant's behest. The filing fee is just a few thousand euros; and it is not until 30 months later that fees must be paid for the selected countries in which protection is then sought. In principle, it is also possible to file a very inexpensive patent application with the German Patent and Trademark Office (DPMA) and then, according to the Paris Convention for the Protection of Intellectual Property (WIPO 2019e), file subsequent applications in selected individual countries up to 12 months later, claiming the initial filing date ('priority'). However, in this way all international fees become due after 12 months (see also the timescales set out in Figure 2.1 for details).

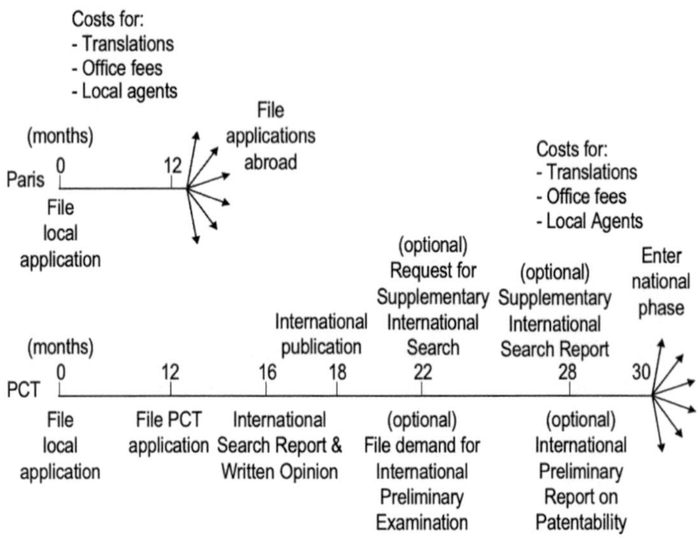

Figure 2.1 *Timescales for international patent applications for basic filing routes and PCT*

In addition to these routes regulated by international treaties, certain tactical behaviours can accelerate or delay patent office procedures. These are explained in more detail in, for example, Chapter 1, section 3.6.

2.4 How can you ensure freedom to operate?

By taking the following steps, you can gain a degree of certainty that your products or services do not infringe the rights of third parties.

First, the core features of your own product/service should be identified and then FTO research should be carried out. In order to achieve good-quality FTO at optimal cost, it is important to be clear about the basis (possibly patent-free) on which you are starting your development, and about which core features have been added that are important for the functioning or marketability of your product/service or business model. At least these core features should be thoroughly researched by an expert who specializes in patent searches. This may also reveal clues about related solutions or previously unknown competitors.

Next, the results should be analysed together with a patent attorney and further expert opinions should be commissioned if necessary. An assessment of the legal situation should then be conducted by a patent attorney after thorough analysis and discussion with the experts of the start-up. On the one hand, analysing the scope of protection of a patent is technically and legally challenging; and on the other, there are often additional aspects that must be considered, such as prior use rights or defects in the analysed patents, which may not be legally valid or to which the registered owner may not in fact be entitled. In addition, in the event of a potential infringement, it should always be considered whether a problematic patent can be circumvented – perhaps through minor product modifications ('design-around').

Finally, trademarks that are similar to the start-up's company name or product name should be researched in order to avoid infringement. There are often third-party trademarks which, depending on the classes of goods and services to which they apply, may legally conflict with the start-up's company name or product name. However, the trademark owner may or may not use or need them in the start-up's field of activity. These problems can often be solved with little effort by entering into a so-called 'delimitation agreement' with the trademark owner. The alternative is to rename the company or product as soon as possible, in order to establish valid designations on the market as early as possible. Trademarks should then be registered for these as soon as possible.

2.5 In a nutshell: the most important IP issues for founders

The **founders** should conduct IP due diligence with exit in mind from the very beginning. The following should be ensured as an absolute minimum:

- The start-up's own IP protects at least its own products;
- Inventor rights/ownership rights to the IP have been clarified; and
- FTO has been established, at least to some extent.

3. What can you do wrong with IP in general?

3.1 Can a patented product be marketed without further ado?

A patent merely prohibits third parties from using the invention of the patent holder; it does not automatically entitle the patent holder to use the invention himself. Every patent may thus depend, for example, on other, older patents.

EXAMPLE

Company C obtained a patent in 2015 for tennis balls made of a certain particularly durable material. Company L obtains a patent in 2021 for tennis balls with a fluorescent coating that allows play to continue in twilight. Company C can thus prevent Company L (and anyone else) from manufacturing or marketing tennis balls made of the protected material; while Company L can prevent Company C (and anyone else) from manufacturing or marketing tennis balls with a fluorescent coating.

In principle, therefore, Company L cannot use its own patented invention (fluorescent coating) if it also makes use of the older patented invention of a third party.

3.2 The main pitfalls of IP protection - especially in the medical field

Business models *per se* are excluded from patent protection – at least in Germany and generally in Europe. A certain degree of technical content is required for patentability. However, at least some technical aspects are necessary for many business models. These can be either in products or services themselves or in data processing – for example, in combination with an app or even in a payment system for which a new communication channel or encryption is invented.

An additional problem for start-ups in the medical technology sector – especially in Germany and Europe – is that many medical procedures are excluded from patentability. According to Article 53(c) of the European Patent Convention, 'methods for treatment of the human or animal body by surgery or therapy and diagnostic methods practiced on the human or animal body' are excluded from patentability. However, surgical and diagnostic tools or materials, including those for use in the aforementioned processes, are eligible for protection.

3.3 Identification of weak points through IP due diligence

IP due diligence aims to clarify the IP situation of a company in a secure, comprehensible and legally watertight manner. This includes the following aspects:

- The company's IP – for example:
  - trademarks;
  - designs; and
  - patents.
- Formal aspects of the IP – for example:
  - Are protective rights in force?
  - Have they been granted or are they still under examination or the subject of opposition proceedings?
  - Is the company aware of legal defects, such as conflicting prior art, which the patent offices have not found?
  - Who is entitled to the rights and how were they acquired?
- Essential content characteristics of the IP – for example:
  - Does it protect the company's own or planned products?
  - Is it used by third parties which have a licence or a right of prior use; or which are simply infringing the patent?

- FTO – for example:
  - Have problematic third-party property rights been identified?
  - Was FTO analysis carried out? What were the results?
- Licensing – for example:
  - Are there licence agreements in place?
  - Are licence fees payable?

These points should be considered from the very foundation of a start-up, so that in case of exit, IP due diligence will yield the best possible results.

4. Case study of the 'SceneMark' platform

Let us consider as an example a company called SceneMark – which owns a hypothetical software information platform for films.

SceneMark has developed a program, which can be bought by end users and installed on computers or other devices. The program enables these devices to capture users' data as they watch films. At the beginning of the film, the user enters the film title and the program determines the length of the film by accessing a database. The user makes an entry on the program at the start of the film, as well as every time he stops the film. The user presses an 'enter' key at any point in the film that he finds particularly interesting or important. In addition, or alternatively, the user may be asked to press the 'enter' key at particularly cruel or offensive parts of the film. The various locations are linked to the film as time positions and stored in a database. This data is then made available for future users, who can pay to access this data either with money or by undertaking their own 'marking' of films.

A first possible business model may allow information on important or offensive scenes to be sold to future users for a few cents. A user could then see, for example, whether he had missed anything important if he had to stop watching for a few minutes due to an interruption. Parents could also see, for example, whether there are any scenes that are not suitable for their children and at what point in the film they occur.

A second possible business model could give film producers access to the corresponding markings – in particular, markings made by many users.

The producers could then use these markers, for example, for the automatic generation of trailers.

4.1 Analysis of protection possibilities

The code of the program that runs on the mobile device enjoys copyright protection against unauthorized use by a third party without any further measures being necessary – at least as long as no open source components have been used. (If OSS components have been used, special OSS licence regulations will apply.) However, this copyright protection protects only against direct copies of the code, and not against reprogramming, which is often possible with limited effort. In principle, patent protection is also possible for the storage structure of the generated data; and the database containing the marked films may also be protectable.

4.2 Other technical aspects

It may be more useful to identify and mark the interesting scenes in the film by measuring the viewer's physiological data. For example, a data connection could be established to the viewer's fitness tracker; or his pulse or skin moisture could be measured by using a finger ring. This would save the user the trouble of entering the data manually; the data collection would be objectivized and automated with minimal effort; and some features would have good prospects of patentability. The collection of measured values through technical sensors and the evaluation, classification and storage of data with a time stamp in connection with a predetermined total running time would be a good candidate for a process patent. In a patent application, the possibilities of manually entering the data and data acquisition by sensors could also be summarized or abstracted. These could then be examined in case of a dispute with the patent office during the examination procedure, to determine how far protection could be extended. The way in which users are credited for marked films and the way in which films marked by third parties are made accessible could also be protected by process patents; as could the mechanisms for encrypting data to prevent unauthorized access. The combination of a mobile device with a connected sensor, a time base and a database could also be protected as a system.

4.3 First additional business model

Now let's consider the modifications that could result from a change in the business model. If the focus is not (only) on use by viewers, but also on use by film producers to create trailers, then a statistical evaluation of the data (eg, how many viewers found certain scenes interesting; which scenes were marked as interesting by the highest number of viewers) could be more useful than the simple markings of the scenes themselves. Therefore, film producers could be offered corresponding statistically evaluated data. In this case, a patent application for a process patent could be slightly modified to include the process for linking the marking data of different viewers.

4.4 Second additional business model

The markings made by one viewer could also be linked to the markings of other viewers and correlations could then be evaluated. On this basis, further films (or other products) could then be suggested to the viewer. This business model could be targeted at providers of film streaming services or online shops. The entire process – including the recording of markers and the delivery of film proposals – could thus be protected through a process patent.

4.5 Other types of IP protection

It may be useful to purchase or reserve an impressive or catchy domain name. A website could be made available for uploading the data collected.

Consideration could also be given to the registration of a trademark for the service – for example, the product name ('SceneMark', if not already registered) as a word mark; or a graphic design that emphasizes the SceneMark name as a word or picture mark.

Several aspects may also be considered for design protection. For example, the design of the outer shape and colour of sensors on a device that are used to record data could be protected; as could the 'look and feel' of a display on the device on which the program is running, or individual icons displayed on the screen.

However, design protection, copyright protection, protection through a figurative mark, protection through a 3D mark and supplementary protection under competition law are all relatively closely related to the actual design of the shape applied for; and recognisable variations may already fall outside the scope of protection.

5. Development of an IP protection strategy for medical technology start-up SugarLight

5.1 Inventory and technological levers

Hypothetical start-up SugarLight is a company that emerged from the activities of the biophysics faculty of a university. The company aims to produce a device for non-invasive blood glucose measurement, which would replace the current method of taking blood samples and then chemically testing them using test strips. If it worked with the requisite accuracy and reliability, such a device would have an immense market and would make the lives of many diabetics much easier. As a result, numerous attempts have previously been made to develop various alternatives to the current method, including spectroscopic methods for non-invasive blood glucose measurement. However, many of these approaches have failed for technical reasons. It may therefore be assumed that the right technology, once found and mastered, will be the key to success. There is therefore a strong technological lever; and a company which can develop and monopolize a functioning technical solution will enjoy a major advantage over its competitors.

In the case discussed here, the basic functioning of the technique (thermo-optical spectroscopy in the mid-infrared range) was demonstrated in the laboratory setup at the university and the university had already applied for a basic patent. SugarLight – which was founded on the basis of the activities of the biophysics faculty – initially had a licence agreement with the university granting it exclusive use of the university's basic patent. The patent had been granted as a national German patent by the DPMA. A subsequent international application (PCT) designating all contracting states had also been filed in the name of the university. The university had the idea of dividing the PCT application and offering SugarLight a patent application limited to the measurement of blood glucose levels in patients' blood for transfer; while the international patent for other applications would remain with the university.

However, the university was subsequently convinced that this division of the PCT application would be unhelpful, as it would have to be reflected in different claims and the divisional applications (possible in a later phase) probably would not have the same scope of protection as the comprehensive basic patent. Moreover, the university quickly realized that the large number of countries in which SugarLight wished to file patent applications was not at all practical for it.

It was therefore agreed that all of the IP rights would be transferred to SugarLight in return for consideration. The basic IP rights were thus in SugarLight's possession. Some of these rights had already been granted in Germany; while others could be formulated in the wording during the patent examination and grant procedure.

5.2 Basic strategic orientation

SugarLight sought to exert the leverage of its protective rights – especially patents – to the greatest possible extent, in order to secure the exclusivity of its products. To this end, it set itself several sub-goals, as follows.

The first sub-goal was to strengthen its own IP by testing various possible implementations and applications of the technology and safeguarding against potential circumvention possibilities. The focus here was, for example, on the analysis of bodily fluids in general and the possibility of measuring depth profiles of substance concentrations in the skin with the technology. This could also be useful, for example, in dermatological tests for the cosmetics industry.

The second sub-goal was to further develop the technology to facilitate the exploration and protection of parallel technical solutions. This included, for example, further development of the requisite quantum cascade lasers in cooperation with laser manufacturers and the possible consequences for the measurement method; and the development of other sensor solutions for the measurement of spectra. As far as possible, the results should belong to SugarLight, or at least be usable for it. With regard to the further development of lasers in cooperation with laser manufacturers, it is only natural that the manufacturers themselves would want to become the owners of the IP rights and could potentially demand this as a condition of cooperation. In that case, however, it may be possible to negotiate a licence for SugarLight which would allow it to purchase lasers according to the invention from other manufacturers or would allow for the establishment of a 'second source'. It is also conceivable, for example, that SugarLight could help to design a laser array consisting of several lasers, each with a fixed wavelength, and invent the optimum selection of wavelengths required for spectrum evaluation. A patent application could be filed for this selection and the start-up could be entitled to a patent for the laser array.

The third sub-goal was to protect related uses of the technology (eg, for the detection of other substances) as business opportunities. This might include checking the quality of blood during dialysis; measuring the usual laboratory values in blood; measuring the contents of foodstuffs and so on.

5.3 Regional distribution of patent applications, filing routes and general tactics in examination procedures

It was also important for SugarLight to select the right countries in which to seek protection in order to strengthen its IP position. To this end, the focus was mainly on countries in which a large number of end customers would use the measuring instrument or a large number of suppliers would sell it. Jurisdictions with sufficiently high gross domestic product and a large number of diabetics – such as the US, Canada, Mexico, Brazil, China and Europe – proved to be promising candidates. With a view to the available financial resources, those countries with well-functioning patent offices and courts were then selected.

In the next step, before publication of the subsequent application which the university had filed, two further international (PCT) patent applications were filed in which all modifications of the basic invention that still seemed plausible were recorded. These were formulated in a way that combined the basic idea with each individual modification, so that a multitude of parallel possibilities for improvement of the technical solution emerged – all of which could potentially lead to the grant of a patent. The next step was to obtain patents for the most attractive variants, initially in Europe and the US. Once this was achieved, divisional applications were filed with the aim of obtaining further patents on other variants already mentioned in the text or the sub-claims. As it was unclear at the outset which variants were most promising, it was important for the divisional applications to exhaust all time limits in the patent office examination procedure in order to gain as much time as possible to work out the most successful solutions, on which protection should then be focused.

For a quick first patent grant at the European Patent Office, among other things, an examiner interview was requested in an attempt to determine the extent to which the examiner would be prepared to grant a patent.

In the US, one of the patent applications was processed under the 'Track One' procedure, under which the US Patent and Trademark Office offers a particularly fast examination procedure for divisional applications upon request and upon payment of a fee, under certain conditions. The US patent was thus granted less than one year from filing of the application.

The non-accelerated US parent application with the same content continued in parallel through the normal examination procedure, in order to obtain a parallel patent with a supplementary scope of protection with a time delay.

One potential tactic with regard to the content of a patent application is to describe and include possibilities which have not yet been implemented, but whose implementability would be plausible to the skilled person or could at least be presented plausibly to the patent examiner. It is not necessary to prove that all possibilities have already been tested in practice.

For example, the measurement method used by SugarLight involved the measurement of continuous spectra recorded by a relatively expensive tunable quantum cascade laser. However, it would be conceivable to measure only several discrete wavelengths that are selected to cover the interesting parts of the spectrum. These could also be measured with a tunable quantum cascade laser; but a more cost-effective solution could involve the use of a certain number of individual, inexpensive fixed-wavelength lasers. These could be combined into a so-called 'array' and produced at low cost. The measurement of spectra with a laser array was claimed in the patent applications as a parallel possibility to the use of a quantum cascade laser. If measurement with a laser array proved to be economically advantageous, the patent application could be reformulated in this direction during the examination procedure – albeit only within the scope of the content initially laid down in the patent application. Thus, even if a patent were actually granted for it, the path of measurement using laser arrays could be blocked for competitors, even if the start-up itself preferred to use another device (ie, a tunable quantum cascade laser).

5.4 Attractive protectable objects

In determining the target direction of the patent protection to be obtained, SugarLight determined, based on the criteria outlined above, that the following areas of development should be regularly checked for new patentable ideas:

- Mechanics: device frame, optical crystal, fixing of the excitation laser;
- Optics: optical integration, alignment, laser setup, temperature control;
- Biophysics and extraction of physiological data from the spectra;
- Software, data processing, data preparation, cloud use, data transport;
- Human-machine interface; and
- Handling, housing.

It should be kept in mind that it is not always the most technically complex solutions that lead to the most powerful patents. For example, it was clear from the outset that the blood glucose meter should be reduced in size and should ultimately be wearable on the wrist. This resulted in a need for small housing (it was simply assumed that the meter would fit into this at some point), which was already formulated in the initial patent that the university applied for. If a patent were eventually obtained for this, the housing design would be protected even independently of the measuring method. In this specific case, for example, it was considered that the measuring surface of the wearable device should face outwards – that is, away from the patient's body – as unlike with existing pulse monitors, the measurement would not take place on the wrist itself, facing inwards; rather, one finger of the other hand would be placed on the measuring surface.

The applications also described the opportunities that the measuring device could present for end customers and users, such as direct control of an insulin pump based on the measured values; or the identification and indication of recipes and foods to be consumed. The connection of the measuring device to a cloud – with all of the attendant medical, administrative and data protection consequences – was also addressed.

5.5 Types of IP rights

In principle, SugarLight considered protecting its device through patents, utility models, designs, trademarks and know-how/trade secrets. Right at the outset, a trademark (strictly speaking, a word mark and a word/picture mark) was applied for in SugarLight's name, in order to prevent other companies from using that name and from registering their own identical or similar trademarks. SugarLight refrained from applying for designs until it had created its own product ready for serial production.

In order to protect business and trade secrets, it was proposed that access to development and test results be granted to employees on a 'need to know' basis only; barriers to access by third parties be established; and appropriate training be provided for the start-up's employees. The protection of know-how and trade secrets should also be reflected in cooperation agreements.

Staggering the procedure for building an IP portfolio also required strategic decisions to be made. As the IP budget was limited, the costs of filed applications were at least partially deferred 30 months into the future by using the PCT filing route. Only after this 30-month period had elapsed were the costs of national prosecution of IP rights incurred in each case. At the same time, the numbers of first applications were limited, in order to keep costs low. In return, the individual applications were made very substantial, in order to be able to separate divisional patent applications at a later date if necessary and pursue them with retroactive payment of fees. This ensured that the start-up could react flexibly to its evolving financial situation.

However, some basic IP rights were secured quickly in order to demonstrate to investors that the technology was protectable in Europe and the US.

5.6 Negotiation of contracts in the interests of the company

SugarLight decided that all product-related IP should be assigned to it. This decision was initially reflected in its negotiations with the university on the ownership of the basic IP rights. SugarLight was prepared to take on considerable financial burdens in order to own the basic patents. In cooperation with consultants and cooperation partners, care was also taken to ensure that any IP that potentially emerged would be assigned to

SugarLight. In some cases, cooperation partners were even selected based on whether they were prepared to accept this arrangement (eg, when awarding the contract for prototype development and the contract for the development of a new sensor).

In order to achieve this goal, it was ensured from the very beginning that the boundary conditions of the German Law on Employee Inventions (see Chapter 3) were observed. In order to make clear to investors whether any compensation would be due to employees in the event of success, the aim was to settle all compensation claims as far as possible.

Care was also taken to ensure that shareholders' contributions to technical problem solutions were allocated to SugarLight in the shareholders' agreement. As shareholders will often understand the technical problems at hand in detail, their contributions should not be excluded and may be helpful. However, these contributions must be usable by the start-up without reservation and should be protected if they are attractive.

As shareholders are often associated with or may work for other companies, it must also be ensured that they can freely dispose of the rights to their ideas and that these rights will be transferred to the start-up, if possible without any reward.

As in the present case the shareholders included several physicists, engineers and computer scientists, it did not seem out of the question that the shareholders – and especially the founders – would contribute to the solution.

5.7 Principles of patent work

SugarLight's initial situation was favourable, in that no competing product based on the same technology existed; only a few used similar measuring principles; and the details of relevant players in the scientific community were already partly known. An initial overview of the state of development of potential competitors could be gained from a review of scientific articles. In addition, it was possible to search the Internet for patent applications filed by known participants.

The next step was to subscribe to various search engine alerts that reported new mentions of the technology or similar technologies. The relevant sites were followed up in each case. These search results also included patents and patent applications.

A higher level of certainty was achieved by commissioning a search using 'ip-search', a service provided by the Swiss Federal Institute of Intellectual Property (see IGE 2019). The service provider was shown drawings of the current design of the measuring device and the concept was explained to it. A patent search was then conducted and the few hits it yielded were delivered to SugarLight. Based on this, it was possible to clarify whether the current design of the device might infringe a patent that was in force and had been granted.

This research and analysis should be repeated at the different stages of product development. However, it should be kept in mind that a search cannot identify with 100 percent certainty all patents of third parties; and that patent applications are published by default only 18 months after the application date.

5.8 Principles of IP management

SugarLight attached great importance to a strong IP portfolio, as this is helpful in attracting investors. For some investors, pending or granted patents may be a decisive factor for investment. For similar reasons, it was also important for SugarLight to own the IP rights itself and provide for this in development contracts. The technical contributions of shareholders were also attributed to SugarLight wherever possible. It was also agreed that the entire development process would be continually monitored in order to identify ideas worthy of protection at the earliest possible stage and, if necessary, take the necessary steps to obtain protection. Of course, a start-up must also consider a possible exit; and SugarLight factored this into its planning from day one.

3 Basic principles of the law on inventions and their relevance for start-ups

Peter Karge

1. Introduction

The law on the allocation of the work results of employees – and in particular, the law on employee inventions – is regulated differently from country to country and is also very complex in certain jurisdictions. Remarkably, there have been no efforts to harmonize this within the European Union.

In particular, the German law in this field has certain pitfalls. Some exemplary templates are presented in the appendix to this chapter. These aim to raise awareness of this issue – in particular, for investors based outside of Germany. The chapter's overall objective is to give start-ups an initial overview of the system and structure of the German regime; the associated risks and problems it presents; but also the potential opportunities and creative freedom it affords. In addition, a high-level summary of the legal situation in some other countries is presented. The law on employee inventions – which is very important to consider when drafting contracts for start-ups – is also addressed in Chapter 6, section 2.7.

This chapter does not claim to be exhaustive, as very case-specific consideration may be required, depending on the circumstances. It is strongly advised in individual cases to seek advice from an expert in the relevant law in the respective country.

2. Employee Inventions Act

2.1 Introduction

The German Employee Inventions Act (ArbnErfG) came into force on 25 July 1957 and sets out detailed regulations on inventions made by employees, which in some cases can result in very heavy administrative burdens for the employer.

The basic system of the law has remained unchanged for more than 60 years. No major changes have been introduced, apart from a fundamental reform of the regulations for inventions of university personnel in 2001; the amendment of the procedure for transferring rights in employee inventions to the employer (so-called 'claiming of invention rights'); and revisions to reflect modern methods of communication (eg, email, fax) in 2009.

The Act aims to resolve the contradiction between the general provisions of labour law – according to which all work results belong to the employer – and the special provisions of patent law, according to which the right to an invention and the right to a patent (initially) lie with the inventor. The legal solution is that, in principle, the employer can transfer the rights to a so-called 'service invention' to itself. The employer is completely free to decide whether to transfer the rights and the employee has no say in this. However, especially in small companies and start-ups, it can be very beneficial for the corporate culture to involve the employee inventor in the decision-making process.

If the employer decides to transfer the rights to the invention to itself, this will result in considerable obligations and the employee will have corresponding claims against the employer. One principle is that the employee should participate in the economic advantages which his employer will enjoy as a result of his invention. The ArbnErfG is thus designed to resolve the conflict between the principles of labour law and the rights provided under patent law, and aims to protect both parties to the employment contract – but particularly the employee. Accordingly, the ArbnErfG contains a number of mandatory provisions from which it is not possible to deviate – or at least, not in advance and in a general manner. In particular, the ArbnErfG prohibits the imposition of advance regulations for service inventions that have not yet been reported. For example, provisions in the employment contract which deviate from those of the ArbnErfG to the disadvantage of the employee – even if this is in return for an additional substantial payment or other benefit by the employer – are invalid.

Only a few countries, such as Austria and Turkey, have similarly detailed – and pro-inventor – legal regulations. China has also developed more complex regulations on employee inventions, which also – unusually – extend to design rights. By contrast, in other countries, such as Korea, employee invention rights are only rudimentarily regulated; and in Canada and the US, there are no specific regulations on employee inventions. In these countries, the allocation of invention rights is often regulated within the framework of individual employment agreements; and recognition of inventions in the form of bonuses or similar is also common.

In principle, the law of the country that applies to the employment relationship in question will also apply to employee inventions. The applicable law is not freely negotiable, but is subject to the provisions of the Rome I Regulation, according to which the choice of law must not result in, for example, a German employee being deprived of protection which would be available under the relevant law (ie, in this case, the ArbnErfG) in the absence of a choice of law (see Bartenbach/Volz, KommArbnErfG, 6th Ed. Section 1 Marg. 32).

2.2 Scope

Inventions (and technical improvement proposals) made by employees in the private sector are subject to the ArbnErfG (Section 1 of the ArbnErfG).

2.2.1 Material scope

The ArbnErfG applies only to technical inventions which, by their nature, must be patentable or eligible for utility model protection (Section 1 of the ArbnErfG). Technical improvement proposals, which are also mentioned in the ArbnErfG, are generally subject to the same regulations and, where applicable, to the bonus regulations under the company proposal scheme. Only so-called 'qualified technical improvement proposals', which grant the employer a similar preferential competitive position to an IP right, are subject to remuneration under Section 20 of the ArbnErfG. In practice, however, proposals for improvements that qualify under this provision are extremely rare.

Any doubts or disputes between the employer and employee concerning the eligibility of the invention to be protected by a patent or utility model will not lead to the inapplicability of the ArbnErfG. The ArbnErfG has automatic application if the invention is by nature a protectable invention –that is, not something which is not considered an invention under Section 1, paragraph 3 of the Patent Act, for example.

Note

Doubts as to whether an invention is eligible for protection by patent or utility model will not release the employer from its obligations under the ArbnErfG.

This means that, in principle, the employer must fulfil its obligations under the ArbnErfG despite any doubts as to whether an invention is eligible for protection by a patent or utility model; otherwise, this could lead to claims for damages by the employee.

2.2.2 Personal scope

The ArbnErfG regulates only the relationship between the parties to an employment contract – that is, the employer and the employee. Section 1, paragraph 1 of the law covers employees in the private and public sectors, civil servants and soldiers. Hereinafter, this chapter focuses exclusively on employees in the private sector. The ArbnErfG applies only if the employment relationship is subject to German law. The formal existence of an employment relationship is crucial; and interruptions in work performance (eg, due to illness or vacation) are irrelevant. The ArbnErfG ties in with the concept of an 'employee' as defined under German labour law. The main criterion is that the employee is obliged to perform instruction-bound work in personal dependence on another person based on an employment contract under private law (see Section 611a, paragraph 1 of the Civil Code (BGB) 18/9232 of 20 July 2017 – 'Legal definition of the employment contract'). Accordingly, under the law on inventions, an 'employee' is also deemed to be, for example, a student who takes a job in a dependent position. This cannot be determined differently in the employment contract, so it will depend on the actual work situation.

Although an employment contract should in principle be in writing, a *de facto* employment relationship can also exist if a person performs instruction-bound, externally determined work with the knowledge and will of the employer, and is in a personal dependency relationship (eg, due to corresponding payment of wages). Provisions in the employment contract which change the rights and obligations under the ArbnErfG to the employee's disadvantage are generally invalid (Section 22 of the ArbnErfG).

> **Note**
>
> The distinction between freelance work and an employment relationship can often cause difficulties (eg, in the case of trainees or PhD students). Thus, in all cases it is recommended to establish a clear definition of – and, where there is no employment relationship, clear regulations on – the rights to inventions.

2.2.2.1 Temporary personnel

Special regulations apply to the supply of temporary personnel subject to approval under the Temporary Employment Act (AÜG). Section 11, paragraph 7 of the AÜG sets out special provisions on employee inventions which exceptionally deviate from the principle that the ArbnErfG regulates the legal relationship between employee and employer. The company that provides the temporary employee remains his employer; but Section 11, paragraph 7 of the AÜG provides that the hirer (ie, the company at which the temporary worker is temporarily employed) is deemed to be the employer within the meaning of the ArbnErfG. Therefore, the mutual rights and obligations which are explained in further detail below arise between the temporary employee and the company for which he is temporarily working.

2.2.2.2 Managing directors and executive body members

The ArbnErfG does not apply to members of executive bodies (eg, the managing directors of a company with limited liability; the members of the management board of a stock company) or shareholders, as these do not have employee status (OLG Düsseldorf, Mitt 2014, 337 – *Rapssaatenschälung*; OLG Frankfurt, GRUR-RR 2017, 294 – *Transportfahrzeuge*). For these persons, as for freelancers and freelance service providers, the treatment of any inventions that may arise can be regulated in advance and completely differently from the ArbnErfG.

Note

In the case of personnel who do not fall within the personal scope of application of the ArbnErfG (managing directors, freelancers, free inventors), clear and comprehensive provisions on inventions should be included in advance in the relevant contracts (eg, employment contracts for managing directors and contract agreements for freelancers).

From the start-up's point of view, it is not advisable to agree on the applicability of the ArbnErfG for such persons, because this would also imply all obligations under the ArbnErfG – some of which may be subject to dispute and/or involve a high administrative burden for the employer.

2.3 Service inventions and free inventions

The ArbnErfG distinguishes between two categories of inventions: so-called 'bound inventions' (service inventions) and free inventions (Section 4(1), paragraph 2 of the ArbnErfG).

Service inventions are inventions which are made during the formal duration of employment and which meet one of the following criteria:

- The invention has arisen from the employee's duties in the company (so-called 'obligation inventions'; Section 4, paragraph 2, No 1 of the ArbnErfG); or
- The invention is largely based on the experience or work of the company (so-called 'experience inventions'; Section 4, paragraph 2, No 2 of the ArbnErfG).

All other inventions of employees are free inventions. The ArbnErfG also imposes obligations and restrictions on free inventions (Sections 18 and 19 of the ArbnErfG). For example, an employee who makes a free invention during the course of the employment relationship must immediately notify the employer in 'text form', providing sufficient information about the invention and – if necessary – its creation to enable the employer to assess whether the invention is free or not.

Note

The old version of the ArbnErfG (ArbnErfG ov) applies to inventions that were reported or notified before 1 October 2009, according to which the report pursuant to Section 5, paragraph 1 of the ArbnErfG or the notification pursuant to Sections 18 and 19 of the ArbnErfG had to be submitted in written form. To fulfil this requirement, the document had to be signed with the original signature of the signatory (Section 126 of the BGB).

Upon receipt of the notification, the employer has three months to dispute in text form (according to ArbnErfG ov, in written form) the claim that the invention notified to it is free if the employer is of the opinion that it is not a free invention, but rather a service invention. If it misses this deadline, it can no longer claim the invention as a service invention.

The obligation to notify the employer of free inventions does not apply if the invention is obviously not usable in the employer's field of business. This assessment may be relatively easy for an employee inventor in a small company or a focused start-up; however, in more complex company structures, the company's field of business will not always be completely clear to the individual employee. In case of doubt, it is advisable that the employee notify his employer of an invention which is presumed to be 'free'.

Before the employee exploits a free invention during the course of his employment, he must first offer his employer at least a non-exclusive right to use the free invention on reasonable terms if, at the time of the offer, the invention falls within the employer's existing or projected field of business. The employee can make the offer at the same time as notification of the free invention, according to Section 18 of the ArbnErfG. Here, too, the employer must respond within three months; if it does not accept within three months of receipt of the offer, its preferential right expires.

The question of whether an employee invention is a service invention is also of particular importance for the employer because it determines the extent to which it can claim (transfer) all rights to the invention to itself.

The decisive criterion is that the invention was made 'during the course of employment'. In purely formal terms, this means the period from legal commencement to legal termination of the employment relationship. What matters is the point at which the invention was completed in the sense of patent law – that is, when it became reworkable by a person skilled in the art. It is irrelevant whether the invention was completed during the employee's working hours or time off. It is therefore irrelevant whether the inventor completed the invention on a holiday, in his spare time or while on vacation.

If the employment relationship is terminated before the invention has been completed, an invention which is completed thereafter will not constitute a service invention *vis-à-vis* the former employer. Questions of proof in this regard – in particular, whether the invention was completed before the employee left the company – are extremely difficult to resolve in practice. It is therefore recommended that employers – especially those whose assets are primarily IP rights – ensure that development activities are documented through laboratory books, report books and so on.

Note

Section 4 of the ArbnErfG is based on the (formally) existing employment relationship, and not on working hours.

Recommendation

Especially in companies whose main value lies in IP, it is advisable to regularly document the work results of employees and check whether they could potentially contain inventions.

An obligation invention exists if the employee has been assigned certain R&D tasks explicitly or implicitly through the employment contract, or through instructions from his employer or on its behalf (eg, by the employee's superior), and the invention results from this activity. The employee's activity is determined by his actual position in the company and the specific work and duties assigned to him. In this context, it is generally assumed that the higher up in the company hierarchy the employee's scope of work and duties, the wider the scope of work and duties.

In order to classify an invention as an experience invention, the invention must be substantially based on the experience or work of the company. In other words, the experience and work of the company (also referred to as 'internal prior art') must be causal for the invention and must have contributed substantially to the invention.

In the case of start-ups in particular, it is therefore very important to determine what technical knowledge was available and whether it was accessible to the inventor. The mere provision of supporting aids or operating equipment is not sufficient for an experience invention.

2.3.1 Service invention – reporting obligation

If an employee has made a service invention, he must report it to his employer without delay through a so-called 'invention disclosure' or 'invention report'. The ArbnErfG has relatively onerous requirements on the form and content of the invention disclosure, because receipt of an invention disclosure by the employer triggers significant legal consequences. For this reason, the invention disclosure must make clear to the employer that an invention made under the conditions of Section 4, paragraph 2 (service invention) is being disclosed to him. The circumstances and the persons involved in the invention must be described and disclosed in a way that allows the employer to assess the invention and make a well-founded decision on whether to claim or release it (see section 2.3.2). The invention disclosure therefore also serves an informational and warning function for the employer. For this purpose, the law stipulates that the invention disclosure must be submitted separately, and must be clearly marked in a way that ensures the employer will understand that it is an invention disclosure. The employer should appreciate that it is not being informed of a general work result, but rather of a work result which is associated with special legal consequences and deadlines, and which may be eligible for IP protection.

The employee must report the service invention to his employer. The notification to another employer – for example, of another co-inventor, within a framework for cooperation between several companies in which various co-inventors from different companies are involved – will not suffice in this respect. Several co-inventors of the same employer can jointly report the invention to their employer. The employer must immediately confirm receipt of the notification to the inventor and each co-inventor, respectively.

According to the ArbnErfG nv, which applies to invention reports received by the employer from 1 October 2009, text form will suffice for such invention disclosures. 'Text form' requires that the invention disclosure be submitted in a document or another manner that is suitable for permanent reproduction (eg, fax or email); that the person (ie, the inventor) is named; and that the conclusion of the declaration (ie, the invention disclosure) is recognizable as such. Thus, the electronic transmission of an invention disclosure is now legally effective. The employer cannot impose any requirements on the form of the invention disclosure which are stricter than text form. For invention disclosures received prior to 1 October 2009, however, the so-called 'written form' requirement (ArbnErfG ov) still applies, which requires a handwritten signature.

In the invention disclosure, the employee must describe the technical task addressed; the solution; and the process through which the service invention was created. He should also enclose records to the extent that these are necessary to understand the invention. The inventor should specify any instructions or guidelines given to him in the course of his work, and the cooperation or participation of the company; and emphasize what the reporting employee considers to be his contributing share to the invention. The employer is entitled to all of this information. Subsequent improvements, further developments and additions to a reported service invention may also be subject to an independent reporting obligation.

To be able to enforce its information rights in case of an incomplete invention disclosure, the employer can state, within two months of receipt of the invention disclosure, that the invention disclosure requires supplementation and the respect in which this is necessary (Section 5, paragraph 3 of the ArbnErfG). The employer must support the employee in supplementing the invention disclosure to the extent necessary. If the employer misses this two-month deadline, the invention disclosure is deemed to be proper.

Recommendation

The invention disclosure and its content are of significant legal importance. Particularly in the case of a company sale or initial public offering, when it is important to prove all IP rights, all relevant documents must often be submitted in the course of due diligence. It is therefore highly recommended – even if this may seem very bureaucratic for small companies – to provide inventors with suitable templates or forms for their invention disclosures; and to ensure that invention disclosures are handled with care (see section 4).

2.3.2 Essential legal effects of receipt of an invention disclosure

In principle, the employer must immediately – that is, without culpable delay (Section 121, paragraph 1 of the BGB (German Civil Code)) – register or file the reported service invention for protection in Germany (Section 13, paragraph 1 of the ArbnErfG). In general, the employer must apply for a patent for an invention which is patentable, unless utility model protection appears more appropriate after a reasonable assessment of the exploitability of the invention. In this case, the employer must bear all costs associated with the application for a patent or utility model. The purpose of this provision is to ensure the earliest possible priority date, irrespective of whether the employer actually claims (transfers) the invention to itself at a later point in time. However, as this may involve considerable cost, the employer must be granted a reasonable period of time for examination and decision making, which also includes conducting a search for existing prior art. However, the employer bears the risk if the patentability of the invention is jeopardized by a late application – for example, due to publications in the meantime – and the employee suffers damage as a result.

The employer is released from the obligation to file an application for an IP right in Germany only if it releases the service invention or if the employee agrees with the decision not to file (Section 13, paragraph 2 of the ArbnErfG).

Alternatively, the employer has the option (although this is seldom exercised in practice) to declare a service invention a trade secret and not to file an application for an IP right if its legitimate interests require that the service invention not be disclosed – which would happen once an application for an IP right was published. In doing so, the employer must acknowledge the protectability of the service invention to the employee or have it assessed by the Arbitration Board for Employee Inventions at the German Patent and Trademark Office (DPMA). An essential risk in this context is that the employer must, as a matter of principle, pay for the use of an invention declared a trade secret as if an IP right has been granted for the service invention. This also applies if the invention or trade secret was actually prior art, or if the trade secret will subsequently become public knowledge.

Note

Considerable risk is associated with the declaration of a service invention as a trade secret – with regard to both any remuneration for use of the service invention and the permanence of the protection. This option should thus be carefully considered.

Further significant legal effects of receipt of the invention disclosure include the start of the claiming or release period and the possibility of entering into agreements that deviate from the ArbnErfG with respect to the reported service invention (Section 22 of the ArbnErfG). In addition, notification of the invention gives rise to mutual confidentiality obligations (Section 24, paragraphs 1 and 2 of the ArbnErfG). The employer must keep the invention reported to it secret for as long as the legitimate interests of the employee require this. Accordingly, the employee must keep his service invention secret as long as it has not become free (Section 8 of the ArbnErfG).

2.3.3 Claim or release of a service invention

According to the ArbnErfG nv, the regulations and systematics discussed below apply to employee inventions reported as of 1 October 2009. For service inventions reported prior to this date, the ArbnErfG ov will apply; among other things, this imposed stricter formal requirements and set out a procedure for the transfer of rights to a service invention (so-called 'claiming') which was dangerous and error-prone, and thus also often subject to dispute.

Pursuant to Section 6 of the ArbnErfG nv, the employer can claim the invention and thereby effect the transfer of all rights to the service invention to itself. Only the personal rights of the inventor remain with the employee (Sections 6 and 7 of the ArbnErfG nv).

The ArbnErfG stipulates that a statutory fiction of claiming – that is, the transfer of rights to the reported service invention – occurs, unless the employer expressly declares to the employee in text form that the service invention has been released by the end of the claiming period (Section 6, paragraph 2 of the ArbnErfG nv). The claiming period – or, more precisely, the period for the release of the reported service invention – is four months after receipt of the proper invention disclosure.

In other words, if the employer takes no action after receipt of the invention disclosure, the invention rights are automatically transferred to it. However, this also creates corresponding obligations for the employer as set out in the ArbnErfG. If the employer wishes to avoid these obligations and therefore to release the invention, it must act and release the reported service invention to the inventor in text form in due time. This could also be relevant in the context of a company valuation and the assessment of the company's possible existing liabilities and obligations, and should therefore be well documented.

According to the law, the employee or inventor has no say in the employer's decision on the claim or release of his service invention. Nevertheless, it may be expedient to involve the inventor in the decision-making process and to explain the decision to him – this is helpful in supporting an innovation-friendly company culture.

2.3.3.1 Release and its consequences

The declaration of release form provided for under Section 6, paragraph 2 of the ArbnErfG must be issued in text form to each co-inventor, where several co-inventors are involved. In the case of an informal form – for example, an oral release declaration – the fictitious effect according to Section 6, paragraph 2 applies; in other words, the invention will not be released, but the invention rights will be transferred to the employer.

The release of a service invention (Section 8 of the ArbnErfG) has an *ex tunc* effect – that is, the rights to the invention remain with the original rights holder (ie, the inventor), with effect from the beginning. The employee can dispose of a released service invention without the restrictions of Section 18 (obligation to notify a free invention) or Section 19 (obligation to offer) of the ArbnErfG.

This is the entrepreneurial risk associated with releasing a service invention, because the employee can license or transfer the service invention to a third party, for example. However, as long as the employment relationship exists, the employee himself may not enter into direct competition with his employer by using the invention, due to his duty of loyalty under the employment contract.

2.3.3.2 Claiming of the invention rights and its consequences

Upon claiming the invention rights, the employer is generally obliged to pay remuneration as compensation for the transfer of the invention rights to it (Section 9, paragraph 1 of the ArbnErfG).

The amount of remuneration is determined by whether and how the employer exploits the invention – for example, by using it in its own products. This is a free entrepreneurial decision of the employer. In principle, the employee has no right to exploit the invention and no right to have the invention released to him if the employer does not exploit the invention itself.

By claiming the invention, the employer is entitled – but not obliged – to file applications for IP rights for the service invention in foreign countries (Section 14, paragraph 1 of the ArbnErfG). For foreign countries in which the employer does not wish to acquire IP rights, it must release the service invention to the employee in due time and of its own accord. If the employee then wishes to acquire foreign IP rights in those released countries himself, he can use the priority rights from the first application. At the same time as this so-called 'foreign release', the employer may reserve a non-exclusive right to use the service invention ('proviso') in the respective foreign states against reasonable remuneration. This right of use is tied to the employer's business and cannot be licensed to third parties, for example. In practice, such a proviso – which in itself incurs no costs or remuneration obligations – is highly recommended. Reasonable remuneration is due only when the right of use is actually exercised.

Note

Simultaneously with the release for foreign countries, the employer should, as a precautionary measure, reserve a non-exclusive right to use the service invention ('proviso') in the respective foreign countries in return for reasonable remuneration.

In practice, however, Section 14 of the ArbnErfG creates a very high administrative burden for many companies and the aim of this provision – namely, to enable the employee to exploit the invention abroad himself – is seldom realized. If the employer may potentially be deterred by the effort and cost involved in filing subsequent applications abroad, the employee will usually be even less able to file or exploit the invention abroad. A residual risk remains that the employee could transfer the invention released for foreign countries to a third party.

It has become widespread practice in industry to waive the rights provided by Section 14 of the ArbnErfG once the invention has been reported in exchange for payment of a sum of money or other compensation.

A similar protection provision for the employee concerns the abandonment of pending IP rights or granted IP rights (patent or utility model applications or granted patents or registered utility models, respectively) by the employer. If the employer is no longer interested in an IP right – both in Germany and, where applicable, in other countries in which it initially filed applications – it must notify the inventor (or, in the case of several inventors, each co-inventor) of the intended abandonment of the respective IP right. The employer also must, at the inventor's request and expense, transfer the IP right to him (Section 16, paragraph 1 of the ArbnErfG).

If an employer executes this right, the employee need not reimburse the costs incurred by the employer until the transfer. The employee will bear only the costs incurred by the transfer itself and all costs incurred thereafter (eg, the costs of the filing proceedings, maintenance and, if applicable, patent attorney fees).

Here too, the employer can reserve a non-exclusive right to use the service invention ('proviso') for reasonable remuneration at the same time as the aforementioned notification. This proviso of use is also bound to the employer's business. In practice, such a reservation of use – which *per se* incurs no costs or obligation to pay compensation – is highly recommended. Reasonable remuneration is due only when the right of use is exercised.

Note

Simultaneously with notification of the intended abandonment of an IP right, the employer should reserve a non-exclusive right to use the service invention against reasonable compensation, as a precautionary measure.

Section 16, paragraph 2 of the ArbnErfG is problematic for the employer – particularly with regard to the time limits set out in multinational cooperation agreements such as the European Patent Convention and the Patent Cooperation Treaty – because in principle, the employee has a period of three months for consideration after receipt of notification of the intended abandonment of the IP right. It is therefore advisable for the employer to inform employee inventors as early as possible about the intended abandonment of an IP right.

Similar to Section 14 of the ArbnErfG, many companies have started to offer waiver or purchase arrangements to employee inventors under Section 16 of the ArbnErfG after receipt of a service invention report, which releases the employer from its obligation to offer the invention under Section 16.

Pursuant to Section 8 of the ArbnErfG nv, it is generally provided that a service invention becomes free if the employer releases it by declaration in text form. As Section 8 is not related to the invention disclosure and the claim-or-release period, the Arbitration Board for Employee Inventions and parts of the commentary opinion (Bartenbach/Volz, KommArbnErfG, 6th Ed., Sect. 8 n.v., marginal no. 7) assume that this is an independent provision for a release even after the expiry of the four-month period under Section 6 of the ArbnErfG nv, and before any application for an IP right. However, this interpretation is not uncontroversial and has not yet been confirmed by the courts.

If an IP right application has already been filed, unilateral release is no longer possible. In this case, the employer must apply the procedure described above in accordance with Section 16 of the ArbnErfG.

2.4 Remuneration for claimed service inventions

According to Section 9 of the ArbnErfG, the main consequence of claiming a service invention is the inventor's claim to reasonable remuneration, which arises on the merits. 'On the merits' means that the claim exists, but the amount and due date are determined by the concrete situation of use or exploitation of the service invention by the employer. If several persons (co-inventors) have contributed to the invention, each co-inventor has an independent claim to reasonable remuneration. According to the wording of Section 9 of the ArbnErfG, for the remuneration claim there is no requirement that an IP right has already been applied for or granted.

The claim for remuneration is a claim of its own kind, and in this respect is not compensation for work; although the tax and social security regulations for salary payments apply accordingly in the case of inventor remuneration payments.

The right to remuneration follows the so-called 'monopoly principle'. This means that the employee is entitled to a share in all economic advantages which the employer causally gains from the invention due to the preferential or monopoly position it creates. These advantages must therefore be causally related to the invention. This is also known as the 'principle of causality'.

In Germany, unlike in many other countries, the remuneration thus does not represent compensation for the transfer of the invention rights – which, according to the inventor principle, are initially held by the employee inventor – to the employer, which can then exploit them at its discretion and in accordance with its own free entrepreneurial decisions.

If the employer generates revenues using the invention, but makes no profits or even makes a loss, it is still basically liable to pay remuneration. This is oriented towards the licensing market for free inventions, where the licensor usually also tries to be as independent as possible from the profit or loss situation of the licensee. Possible loss situations or low margins are usually taken into account in licence agreements through a correspondingly lower licence rate.

The appropriate amount of inventor's remuneration depends on the kind and scope of use or exploitation which the employer undertakes. Common types of use or exploitation include:

- the production of its own products using the invention;
- the internal use of the invention (eg, in manufacturing processes or testing methods);
- the use of the invention as a blocking right (this is very rare in practice);
- the out-licensing to third parties of IP rights or the invention on which it is based; or
- the sale of IP rights or the invention on which they are based.

Several types of use – in particular, in-house production and licensing to third parties – may exist in parallel; in which case the inventor must be remunerated for all kinds of use. The remuneration (in terms of amount) can only be determined and falls due for payment when the employer actually receives economic advantages from the use of the service invention. This could be, for example, the turnover generated through the sale of products incorporating the invention; or the receipt of a licence payment once the corresponding licence has been granted.

In the case of own sales, the inventor's remuneration is usually determined on a post-calculation basis – that is, after the end of the employer's fiscal year. According to the common practice of the Arbitration Board for Employee Inventions and practice in industry, agreement on and payment of the inventor's remuneration should be made within three to six months of the end of the respective remuneration period (fiscal year).

The claim for remuneration is due regardless of whether the IP right granting procedure (or, in the case of a utility model, the registration procedure) has been successfully completed.

As repayment of remuneration already paid cannot be demanded (Section 12, paragraph 6 of the ArbnErfG), the risk will lie solely with the employer to pay remuneration for a service invention which ultimately does not lead to a registered utility model or granted patent, or to a patent that is revoked after a subsequent opposition procedure. On the other hand, the case law of the Federal Court of Justice (BGH: GRUR 1963, 135 – *Cromegal*; BGH: GRUR 1971, 475 – *Gleichrichter*) has confirmed (BGH: GRUR 2002, 609 – *Drahtinjektionseinrichtung*) that the employer must pay provisional remuneration for acts of exploitation which occur in the period from commencement of use until final rejection of the IP right. This is of significant practical importance, as the grant rate for all patent applications at the DPMA ranges from just 50 to 60 per cent. The case law of the Federal Court of Justice is based on the fact that under Section 2 of the ArbnErfG, the rights and obligations (in this case, the employer's obligation to pay remuneration) are generally linked to protectability – that is, the objective possibility of obtaining an IP right; and that an employer with an existing IP rights application has a competitive advantage over its competitors, even if actual grant may appear doubtful.

The amount of provisional remuneration may differ significantly from the remuneration that would be granted for a granted IP right if the risk of rejection of the application is high. For this reason, according to the common practice of the Arbitration Board for Employee Inventions and practice in industry, the remuneration which the inventor would receive if the IP right were granted is first calculated, and then a deduction is made depending on the likelihood of grant. The amount after the deduction represents the provisional remuneration and is to be paid by the employer accordingly. Once the IP right has been granted, the inventor is entitled to the full remuneration and the retained deduction must be paid. If no IP right is granted or if the IP right is revoked with final and binding effect, the provisional remuneration is final (ie, the deduction is not paid) and, according to Section 12, paragraph 6, need not be paid back. The claim for remuneration expires only from the point at which the IP right is denied with legal effect.

The deduction is based on the prospect of grant in the individual case. In practice, a standard deduction of about 50 per cent has been established for the usual risk of patent grant. However, if substantial doubts as to patentability are raised in an examination opinion or search report, or if the patent application has been rejected at first instance, the provisional remuneration may be reduced to between 10 and 30 per cent (for further examples see Bartenbach/Volz, KommArbnErfG, 6th Ed.)

2.4.1 *Factors influencing inventors' remuneration*

The inventor's remuneration is calculated taking the following factors into account:

- the invention value;
- the co-inventor's share (which is 100 per cent if there is only one inventor and which otherwise depends on the individual contributions of the co-inventors to the invention; see section 2.3.1); and
- the 'share factor'.

In 1959, the Federal Ministry of Labour issued Guidelines for the compensation of employee inventions in the private sector to determine the reasonable remuneration (available on the DPMA's website at www.dpma.de/docs/dpma/richtlinienfuerdieverguetungvonarbeitnehmererfindungen.pdf). The Guidelines are not binding; but if applied correctly, there is a (rebuttable) presumption that the remuneration is reasonable.

In principle, the remuneration is determined according to the following formula:

$$V = E \times M \times A \text{ (Guideline 39)} \quad (3.1)$$

where:

- V is the remuneration amount (Euro);
- E is the invention value (Euro);
- M is the co-inventor share (percentage); and
- A is the share factor (percentage).

A deduction (risk deduction R) is to be made from the determined amount to (initially) reflect the risk that the IP right may ultimately be denied if the IP right has not yet been granted, and to ensure that this risk is not borne unilaterally by the employer.

2.4.1.1 *Invention value*

The invention value (E) is the price which the employer would have to pay to an independent free inventor for the transfer or use of the same rights to the invention had the invention not been created in its own company (BGH: GRUR 2010, 223 – *Türinnenverstärkung).*

The determination of the invention value depends on the respective concrete use of the invention and is only briefly explained below. For inventions which are used by implementation in sold products, the so-called 'licence analogy' (Guidelines 6 et seq) is to be applied (BGH: GRUR 2010, 223 – *Türinnenverstärkung*; BGH: Mitt 2012, 285 – *Antimykotischer Nagellack*). Here, the invention value is the (fictitious) licence fee which the employer would have to pay to an independent freelance inventor if it concluded an exclusive licence agreement with the latter for the same invention, granting it the same rights of use as for the service invention. In its case law, the Federal Court of Justice is guided by what reasonable licence agreement the parties would have entered into.

However, in applying the licence analogy, it is difficult to determine a reasonable royalty rate and the so-called 'reference value' to which the royalty rate refers. Usually, the terms of licence agreements are secret, so there is little public guidance available in this regard. Although Guideline 10 provides guidance on royalty rates for various industrial sectors, these vary widely and do not seem feasible from today's perspective. Moreover, the respective reference value is not apparent.

When determining the invention value, the first step is to determine the technical-economic reference value according to Guideline 8, which roughly defines the problem or field of application to which the invention relates in the case of a complex product consisting of several components or problem areas (see BGH: GRUR 2010, 223 – *Türinnenverstärkung*). The reference value to be determined in this way must at least comprise all parts or elements/limitations necessary to carry out the invention. In addition, it may include components which are significantly influenced or characterized by the invention.

Subsequently, according to Guideline 7, an economic value – usually the net turnover achieved from the invention after the deduction of taxes, duties and levies – must be assigned to the previously determined technical-economic reference value. As the determination of these sales relating to special reference values is often costly or even impossible in practice, in such cases the production cost or the purchase price for the employer of the corresponding reference value is assumed in practice. This price is then multiplied by an extrapolation factor (approximately 1.2 to 1.6, depending on the sector) to determine the fictitious sales with the reference value.

Recommendation

The user-friendly compilation of the longstanding practice of the Arbitration Board for Employee Inventions in Hellebrand/Rabe 6th ed. 2021, which is structured by International Patent Classification classes, is a good aid for determining appropriate standard licence rates.

Moreover, in the licence analogy, increasingly high sales are often based on competitive advantages which are not in the sphere of the invention, but rather in the sphere of the employer (eg, a large worldwide distribution network; a good reputation), and are thus no longer causally related to the service invention alone. According to the abovementioned principle of causality, the inventor should receive only a reasonable share of the economic advantages of the employer which are causally related to the invention. For this reason, Guideline 11 provides for a staggered reduction (so-called 'gradation') of the licence factor for cases that involve a so-called 'causality shift', insofar as this is common in the industry taking into account the individual case.

For the other common cases of invention exploitation – that is, the sale of IP rights or the invention on which they are based, or the licensing of the invention – Guidelines 14 and 15 (licensing income) and 16 (sale of the invention or the IP rights on which they are based) provide for an invention value determination which is based on the net licensing income or the net purchase price after the deduction of specific deductible costs and (if applicable) the know-how. The net income is by no means equal to the invention value; rather, an arithmetic conversion factor must be applied.

In practice, however, it must be ensured that – especially in the case of licence or purchase price income, as well as for own use and any risk deductions made in the payment of remuneration – appropriate accruals are made for the inventor's remuneration, which must be calculated and paid after the end of the fiscal year. In addition, other asset benefits and income earned by the employer (eg, damages or compensation payments by patent infringers) must also be valued as income that is subject to remuneration.

The inventor has a fundamental right to information and to accounting, in order to be able to check the appropriateness of the remuneration statement and the remuneration paid to him. This claim is derived from the case law on Section 242 of the BGB. The scope of this fundamentally justified claim has been extended by the courts – in some cases very far – which can present an extraordinarily high administrative and economic burden for the employer.

Note

Satisfying the claim to information and accounting for an exploited service invention can not only generate high costs – especially in the case of employees who have left the company – but also involve risks with regard to the protection of business data. It is therefore advisable to agree with the inventor on the compensation at an early stage, through final arrangements which are as transparent and as comprehensive as possible.

Recommendation

In business practice, therefore, to mitigate the administrative burden, the right to information is contractually specified in advance by agreements with the inventor and limited to certain information which must provide the inventor with sufficient possibilities of verification.

2.4.1.2 Share factor

As explained above, the system of inventors' remuneration is based on a comparison with a (fictitious) identical invention made by an independent inventor. However, as a service invention is not a free invention, but is created within the framework of an employment relationship and with the support of the employer, the employee inventor will receive only a fraction of the invention value. This fraction is determined by the so-called 'share factor' (A).

Section 9, paragraph 2 of the ArbnErfG lists as decisive criteria for this purpose the tasks and position of the employee in the company; and the company's share in the creation of the service invention. Thus, the share factor compares the situation of the employee inventor with that of an independent inventor (see Ministry of Labour Guidelines 30 et seq), and takes into account that the employed inventor need not invest upfront or bear economic risks, like an independent inventor. Rather, the employee inventor is supported by his employer in the development of the invention through suggestions, orders, personnel and material and technical means.

In order to determine the share factor, the Ministry of Labour Guidelines provide for three value numbers – (a), (b) and (c) – which reflect different aspects in the history of the invention. Value number (a) takes into account the share and initiative of the employee in identifying the objective (task) of the invention and its solution. Value number (b) reflects the extent to which the employer has supported the inventor in solving the task. Value number (c) depends on the actual (not the nominal) hierarchical position of the inventor in the company. Relevant to these value numbers are the prevailing conditions at the time of completion of the invention. To calculate the share factor (A) from the abovementioned value numbers, a table in Guideline 37 provides for a range of between 2 and about 90 per cent. Usual share factors lie somewhere between 8 and 15 per cent; or up to about 20 per cent in special cases.

2.5 Possibilities and limits of contractual freedom

As is already clear from this superficial presentation of the ArbnErfG, the statutory regulations are relatively complex and administratively burdensome. For many employers, it would thus be favourable to avoid their obligations under the ArbnErfG in advance altogether – even if this necessitated additional compensation payments.

However, as the ArbnErfG is a protective law, especially for employees, the possibilities for regulation and, in particular, for waivers have been severely restricted by the legislature.

The provisions of the ArbnErfG cannot be waived to the employee's detriment (Section 22 of the ArbnErfG). A 'detriment' in the sense of Section 22 already exists if an agreement could theoretically be to the employee's disadvantage. For example, even if the employer were to pay a substantial premium for waiving obligations under the ArbnErfG, this would in principle be an impermissible agreement. Section 22 aims to prevent provisions on inventions from being included in employment contracts in advance to the detriment of the employee, because the employee would be under pressure in this situation – for example, he might feel obliged to waive rights in order to secure employment. However, the legislature has left it to the contractual autonomy of the parties to the employment contract to reach individual agreements on a reported invention that is thus in concrete existence. Therefore, agreements on employee inventions that have been reported are permissible (Section 22 of the ArbnErfG).

Agreements permitted under Section 22 of the ArbnErfG are also subject to the so-called 'equity test' under Section 23, paragraph 1 of the ArbnErfG, according to which agreements on service inventions permitted under the ArbnErfG are invalid if they are substantially unjust. As a rough guideline, inequity is generally assumed if the inventor's remuneration owed differs from the remuneration paid or agreed by more than 100 per cent upwards or 50 per cent downwards (this would be unjust to the disadvantage of the employer). Decisive to the assessment of inequity is the point at which the agreement was concluded. This means that any changes that occur subsequently and that were not foreseeable or known at the time the agreement was concluded will not constitute inequity.

2.6 Particularities of inventions made at universities

Following the amendment of the ArbnErfG in 2001, the ArbnErfG now also applies in principle to universities and universities of applied sciences and their personnel. However, special regulations are set out (Section 42 of the ArbnErfG) that do not apply to non-university research institutions (eg, Fraunhofer-Gesellschaft). In principle, a university, as an employer, also has the right to claim a service invention (ie, an obligation invention or experience invention) under Section 6 of the ArbnErfG made by an employee during the employment term (Section 4 of the ArbnErfG). A particularity, however, is that the university-employed inventor is entitled to refrain from disclosure of his invention (and thus avoid the submission and subsequent publication of an application for an IP right) if he enjoys freedom of teaching and research guaranteed by constitutional law. In such circumstances, contrary to Section 5, paragraph 1, an inventor is thus not obliged to report a service invention to his employer (the university) (Section 42, No 2 of the ArbnErfG).

In addition, the inventor is entitled to disclose the service invention in the course of his teaching and research activities if he has notified the employer in due time – usually two months in advance. This is a significant simplification of the otherwise generally applicable secrecy requirements under Section 24, paragraph 2 of the ArbnErfG.

Another particularity for university-employed inventors is that they enjoy a special remuneration scheme. If the university exploits the invention, the amount of remuneration paid to the inventor is 30 per cent of the income generated by the exploitation, without deductions and without consideration of an individual share factor. In this respect, inventors employed at a university are significantly better off than other employee inventors.

Note

When awarding contracts to or cooperating with universities, the special privileges enjoyed by university employees must be taken into account – especially with regard to possible negative freedom of publication (ie, the freedom not to publish) and access to any inventions arising in the course of (industry-financed) projects.

2.7 Arbitration

Especially in the case of ongoing employment relationships, the ArbnErfG offers the parties to an employment contract the possibility to resolve any disputes arising from the ArbnErfG amicably out of court with the help of the Arbitration Board for Employee Inventions established at the DPMA. Each party to the employment contract may appeal to the Arbitration Board by submitting a written request stating the facts of the case and indicating the names and addresses of the other parties involved. The request is then sent to the other parties, which are invited to comment on the request within a certain timeframe. The arbitration is voluntary; no party is forced to participate in the proceedings. The Arbitration Board has extensive experience and expertise gained over decades.

In the arbitration proceedings, the parties involved can present the dispute from their own perspectives and can also represent themselves. Proceedings before the Arbitration Board are free of charge. At the end of the proceedings, the Arbitration Board will render a so-called 'settlement proposal' to the parties, which is reasoned in detail. The settlement proposal is deemed to be accepted if neither party objects to it in writing within one month of receipt of the proposal. In the event of unsuccessful arbitration proceedings, claims under the ArbnErfG may be asserted by way of an action before the Patent Litigation Chambers of the regional courts. In the case of an ongoing employment relationship, such an action is subject to prior proceedings before the Arbitration Board, even if unsuccessful.

Recommendation

Referral to the Arbitration Board for Employee Inventions is an option which both parties to the employment contract should consider in the event of disputes arising from the ArbnErfG.

3. Legal situation with respect to employee inventions in other countries

3.1 Overview

If a start-up operates across borders – either initially or while geographically scaling up its business – the laws regarding employee inventions (as well as all other laws pertaining to inventions and ensuing rights) of all relevant countries must be taken into account. As these provisions can vary substantially, complex situations may arise and care must be taken to reconcile the different requirements – with respect to both the rights in an invention and the development of an appropriate international IP filing strategy.

For instance, some countries require the filing of a domestic patent application for an invention made in the respective country (or even by a citizen or resident of that country) before any foreign applications may be filed. Such provisions apply, for instance, in the United States, China, India, Italy, Spain, France and Russia. These requirements may conflict or compete with one another, as well as with specific national provisions on employee inventions – for instance, the ArbnErfG requires an employer to file a domestic IP application when claiming a service invention.

In this situation, often the only way to resolve the contradictions between the different requirements is to apply to the respective competent patent authority for a foreign filing licence.

In this section, the legal situation regarding employee inventions in a few selected countries is outlined to highlight the divergences between such regimes, which range from rigid material and procedural frameworks to an almost complete absence of specific regulations pertaining to employee inventions (and, correspondingly, marked flexibility in contract drafting). As noted above, a comprehensive treatment cannot be provided and individual legal advice should be sought in cross-border situations.

3.2 United States

Federal law in the US does not regulate employee inventions. The laws of the individual states therefore apply. Accordingly, the regulations and case law vary from state to state. By default, an invention and any derived patents belong to the inventor.

However, it is common to contractually assign an inventor's rights in an invention to the employer (eg, as part of the employment contract). Such agreements are also subject to state law. In some states, such an assignment by employment contract requires case-by-case consideration and notice to the employee – in particular, where inventions do not fall within the usual tasks of the employee ('hired to invent'). In some states, in the absence of an explicit contractual assignment, the employer may be entitled to a royalty-free non-exclusive implied licence ('shop right') – for instance, if its resources were used in developing the invention.

There is currently no federal or state law that generally requires remuneration of an inventor for an invention or patent. However, many businesses and universities have remuneration policies in place.

3.3 United Kingdom

In the UK, employee inventions are governed by Sections 39–43 of the Patents Act 1977. Accordingly, an invention belongs to the employer in either of two scenarios:

- It was made in the course of the employee's normal or specifically assigned duties and the circumstances were such that an invention

'might reasonably be expected to result from the carrying out' of those duties; or
- It was made in the course of the duties of the employee where, because of the nature of those duties, the employee had a special obligation to further the employer's interests.

Any invention that does not fall within the scope of these definitions belongs to the employee inventor; and this provision cannot be excluded by contract.

The Patents Act provides for mandatory compensation for certain inventions (unless a relevant collective agreement applies, in which case that agreement takes precedence) – in particular, for inventions belonging to the employer from which the employer has derived an outstanding benefit. In the case of an invention belonging to the employee which has been assigned to the employer (or for which the employer has been granted an exclusive right of use), the employee may be awarded compensation if the proceeds obtained by the employee from a transfer agreement (or licence agreement) concluded with the employer are unreasonable in comparison with the employer's proceeds from the patent.

3.4 France

In France, the National Patent Act (Article L611-7 of the Intellectual Property Code) contains provisions on employee inventions. Accordingly, inventions made by an employee will belong to the employer if they are made in the performance of an employment contract comprising an inventive mission, or while carrying out studies and research work expressly assigned to the employee. The employer must inform the employee of any patent application (or grant) in respect of such an invention. The employee may also benefit from additional remuneration under applicable collective agreements, company agreements or individual employment contracts.

All other inventions belong to the employee; although in cases where the employee has made an invention in the performance of his or her duties, in the scope of the employer's work, or on the basis of knowledge or information specific to the employer, the employer may have ownership or use of the rights arising from the patent either in whole or in part. For the transfer of such rights, the employee is entitled to appropriate remuneration which, in the absence of agreement between the parties, is determined by an arbitration commission or the court of first instance.

3.5 China

According to Article 6 of the Chinese Patents Act, inventions made by a person in the performance of duties assigned by the employer or with the predominant use of the employer's resources (service inventions) belong to the employer. Therefore, the employer has the right to apply for a patent for a service invention. This also applies to the service inventions of former employees for up to a year after the employee inventor left the company if the invention is a solution to a task that arose from the previous employment relationship. For any invention which is not a service invention, the inventor has the right to file a patent application.

The inventor is entitled to compensation for a service invention. If the employer uses the patented invention, the compensation will be based on the extent of distribution and application, as well as the economic benefits obtained. The implementing provisions of the Patents Act stipulate the nature and amount of the compensation, but individual contractual agreements can be concluded in this regard and will take precedence over such provisions.

3.6 India

Indian law has no dedicated regulations on employee inventions, which are therefore regulated under general contract law and case law. According to widespread opinion, an employer is in most cases entitled to an employee's invention made during the employment relationship; although recent case law of the higher courts recognizes exceptions if the employee was not hired to conduct inventive activities. Separate compensation for employee inventions is generally not required, but an increasing number of employers have agreements in place which provide for such compensation.

3.7 Japan

According to the Japanese Patent Act, an 'employee invention' is an invention which, by its nature, belongs to the employer's field of business and arises from activities which form part of the present or past official duties of the employee.

The assignment of the rights arising from such inventions by the employee to the employer may be regulated in advance by contract or on the basis of company regulations or other agreements. In the absence of such an agreement, the employee will generally retain the rights to his invention. However, the employer is always entitled to a non-exclusive licence and no remuneration is required in this case.

In case of the transfer of an employee invention to, or the grant of a right for exclusive use by, the employer, the employee will be entitled to remuneration in the form of a 'reasonable amount of money or other economic benefits', according to a 2017 revision to the Patent Act. This remuneration is limited to any additional value over the non-exclusive licence to which the employer is entitled – that is, it concerns only the 'monopoly profit' arising from the exclusive right of use.

Inventions which are not employee inventions are not subject to a non-exclusive licensing obligation and cannot be contractually transferred from the employee to the employer in advance.

3.8 South Korea

In South Korea, employee inventions are regulated by the Invention Promotion Act. An 'employee invention' within the meaning of this Act is an invention made by an employee in connection with his duties, provided that it falls within the scope of the employer's business and that the activities which led to the invention fall within the employee's present or former duties.

The employee must immediately notify the employer in writing of any such invention. The employer must notify the employee within a certain timeframe as to whether it claims rights to the invention.

Regarding the nature of these rights, a distinction must be drawn between small and medium-sized enterprises (SMEs) and other businesses. In the case of SMEs, the employer is entitled to a non-exclusive licence to a patent based on an employee invention. In all other cases, the employer is entitled to such a licence only if a corresponding agreement exists (eg, an employment contract or company regulation). The assignment of the rights to the patent or an exclusive licence may also be agreed in this way.

If an employee invention is transferred to the employer or an exclusive right of use is granted, the employee is entitled to appropriate compensation. The employer must ensure that appropriate provisions as to the amount of compensation are in place.

Appendix

3A.1 Exemplary communication templates and forms (according to the provisions of ArbnErfG)

3A.1.1 Invention Disclosure Form

To the management/chief technology officer (CTO)/personnel officer[1] *... by fax/email/letter*[2]

Invention Disclosure

*** Confidential ***

I / we, Inventor #1[personal details]; Inventor #2 [personal details]; ……….….. etc.

hereby report the following service invention with the title/short name: ……….…..

1. Description of the technical task of the invention: What is the technical problem underlying the invention or which is solved by it?

   [Please provide detailed information]
   ….

2. Which known state of the art/prior art (eg, known solutions, predecessor model ...) is the invention based on? What disadvantages of the prior art should be overcome by the invention?

   [Please provide detailed information]

---

1 It is recommended to clearly state to whom or to which department invention disclosures should be sent within the scope of the employer's right of direction. Due to the rights and obligations associated with receipt of an invention disclosure and the deadlines to be observed, it is not advisable to allow invention disclosures to be submitted to individual (email) addresses. It is advisable to enter a special postal address, company mailbox or email address for the subject of inventions as sender.

2 The written form (ie, an original document with the inventor's handwritten signature) can be requested, but not demanded by the employer; transmission by email, for example, will suffice according to the legal regulations (ArbnErfG nv).

…

3. Describe the solution according to your invention:

How does your invention solve the technical problem described under no. 1?

What measures and technical means does your invention use for this purpose?

Describe – depending on the nature of the invention – the specific design, the necessary procedural steps, the material components, etc.

What advantages or positive effects does your invention achieve?

[Please provide detailed information]

…

4. Describe the genesis and history of the invention:

Have you received instructions, advice, suggestions for solutions etc.? Have you been given the technical task by the company? Did you use existing preliminary work, experience or knowledge for the technical solution in the company?

Which technical aids were used?

…

Who were the persons involved in the creation of the invention? Are these people co-inventors? [Please specify]

5. What do you consider to be your individual contribution to or share in the invention?

[Please specify]

…

6. Please attach documents, documentation, drawings and the like which contribute to a better understanding of the invention.

…

Declaration of the co-inventors (if applicable) in their individual shares (contributions) to the invention.

...

Inventor's signature(s)/name(s)/date

3A.1.2 Acknowledgement of Receipt

From management/CTO/personnel officer[3] ...by fax/email/letter

To: Inventor #1 .... [if applicable: individually to each co-inventor]

Acknowledgement of Receipt of your Invention Disclosure from XX.YY. ZZ, received on [Date]

[File number/Title/Short description]

*** Confidential ***

Dear Ms/Mr [inventor],[4]

Your invention disclosure identified above was received by us on [Date].

We have assigned the internal name/title given in the subject.

Your responsible contact person is [...]

Please inform us immediately if you make any improvements and further developments to your invention. Please also inform us immediately of any other changes – including to your address or availability.

We will immediately check the conditions of protectability.

---

3 The department/contact person responsible for invention disclosures. It is advisable to enter a special postal address/company mailbox/email address for the subject of inventions as sender.

4 Note for co-inventors: according to Section 5(1) of the ArbnErfG, the receipt of the invention disclosure must be confirmed to each co-inventor.

If we believe the invention disclosure is in need of supplementation, we will inform you immediately (Section 5, paragraph 3 of the Employee Invention Act (ArbnErfG)).[5]

As a precautionary measure, we would like to draw your attention to your obligation to maintain secrecy.

We thank you for your innovative commitment.

With kind regards

Company signature or name/date

3A.1.3 Release of a Service Invention (Section 6, paragraph 2; Section 8 of the ArbnErfG)

From management/CTO/personnel officer[6] ...by fax/email/letter

To: Inventor #1 [...]

Release of Your Invention

[File number/Title/Short description]

*** Confidential ***

Dear Ms/Mr [inventor][7]

We do not claim the abovementioned service invention reported by you on [Date]. Instead, we hereby release this service invention to you (Section 6, paragraph 2 in conjunction with the Employee Inventions Act (ArbnErfG n. v.).

---

5 Note in case of co-inventors: if the co-inventors did not file their invention disclosures together but separately, the periods triggered by this – in this case, the period for objection according to Section 5(3) of the ArbnErfG – will correspondingly expire at different times.

6 The department/contact person responsible for invention disclosures. It is advisable to enter a special postal address/company mailbox/email address for the subject of inventions as sender.

7 Note in case of co-inventors: the release of the service invention must be declared to each co-inventor. If the co-inventors did not submit their invention disclosures together but separately, the periods triggered by this – in this case, the release period – will correspondingly expire at different times.

You are thus entitled to apply for an industrial right for the invention yourself (Section 13, paragraph 4 of the ArbnErfG).

In addition, we would like to point out that you can dispose of the released service invention without the restrictions of Section 18 and Section 19 of the ArbnErfG (Section 8 of the ArbnErfG).

However, as a precautionary measure, we would like to point out that you are not entitled to disclose or exploit other company knowledge, experience or trade secrets to third parties.

We ask you to confirm receipt of this release declaration for our files by returning the signed duplicate attached or by email to [...] by [Date].

With kind regards

Company signature or name/date

3A.1.4 Release for Foreign Countries with Reservation of Right of Use (Section 14, paragraphs 2 and 3 of the ArbnErfG)

From management/CTO/personnel officer[8] *...by fax/email/letter*

To: Inventor #1 [...]

Release for Foreign States Subject to a Right of Use

[File number/Title/Short description]

*** Confidential ***

Dear Ms/Mr [inventor][9]

We will register/file your abovementioned service invention for protection in the following foreign countries:

---

[8] The department/contact person responsible for invention disclosures. It is advisable to enter a special postal address/company mailbox/email address for the subject of inventions as sender.

[9] Note in case of co-inventors: the release for foreign countries and the reservation of use must be declared to each co-inventor.

[List of the states in which the employer has filed or will file own applications for protective rights].

We do not wish to acquire any industrial property rights in the remaining foreign countries. For these foreign countries, we herewith release the service invention to you.

We will be pleased to fulfil our legal obligation to support you in the acquisition of foreign protective rights on request. The costs of any property right filing or granting proceedings in these foreign states are to be borne by you.

As a precautionary measure, we would like to point out that the priority period for subsequent foreign applications expires on [Date].

At the same time, we reserve a non-exclusive right to use the service invention in accordance with Section 14, paragraph 3 of the German Employee Invention Act (ArbnErfG).

If applicable: We request you to take into account our company's obligations under the currently existing contracts for the service invention when exploiting the released invention in the foreign countries listed below [...].

These are in detail the following contracts/obligations [...].

We ask you to confirm the receipt of this declaration of release and the reservation of use for our files by returning the signed duplicate attached or by email to [...] by [Date].

With kind regards

Signature or name/date

3A.1.5 Notification of the Intention to Abandon with Reservation of the Right of Use (Section 16, paragraphs 1 and 3 of the ArbnErfG)

From management/CTO/personnel officer[10] *...by fax/email/letter*

[10] The department/contact person responsible for invention disclosures. It is advisable to enter a special postal address/company mailbox/email address for the subject of inventions as sender.

To: Inventor #1 […]

Notification of the Intended Abandonment of the Property Right Application Subject to a Right of Use

[File number/Title /Short description]

*** Confidential ***

Ms/Mr [inventor],[11]

We do not wish to pursue or maintain the above-identified property right(s) based on your service invention.

We ask you to inform us as soon as possible (at the latest within three months after receipt of this letter) whether we shall transfer this/these property right(s) to you at your expense and hand over the related necessary documents.

The next (annual) maintenance fee is due on [Date].

If you do not wish the transfer of this property right or these property rights within the above-mentioned period of three months, we are entitled to abandon the property right(s).

At the same time, we hereby reserve a non-exclusive right to use the service invention pursuant to Section 16, paragraph 3 of the German Employee Invention Act (ArbnErfG).

We ask you to confirm the receipt of this notification and the reservation of use for our files by returning the signed duplicate attached or by email to […] by [Date[.

With kind regards

Company signature or name/date

[11] Note in case of co-inventors: the notification and the reservation of use must be made or declared to each co-inventor.

4 Patenting and spin-offs at universities

Werner Mäntele[1]

1. Preliminary remarks

This chapter outlines the author's experiences in R&D projects at Goethe University, Frankfurt am Main, Germany, from 1997 to 2018, and as a co-founder of a start-up from 2015 to 2020. It describes the processes that led to the establishment of IP at Goethe University and to the foundation of the start-up, based on application-oriented research in the field of medical technology. In particular, the chapter considers how universities deal with applied research, the involvement of industrial partners and the foundation of start-ups by university employees. It also describes the role played by student participation and the theses they produce (eg, bachelor's theses, master's theses and PhD theses). Even habilitations are concerned. The attitudes towards these issues can vary significantly from university to university and from country to country. The experiences described in this chapter can thus be understood only as examples.

[1] The author would like to thank Dr Otmar Schöller (managing director of Innovectis GmbH until 2017) and his successor, Dr Martin Raditsch – as well as the entire Innovectis team – for their helpful cooperation in patenting and in R&D projects with industrial partners; and for their support in the initial phase of our start-up, DiaMonTech. Thanks also go to the many employees at the Institute of Biophysics for over 20 years of joint, innovative and productive R&D work.

2. Development of a patent portfolio at universities

2.1 Initial situation

Many universities have a technology transfer department which advises scientists on how to establish IP rights. However, this task is conducted through very different structures and with varying degrees of commitment – often neglected and somewhat listless; seldom professional and efficient. Some universities have delegated this task to regional transfer companies, which often 'serve' several universities and are rarely visible to individual scientists. However, it is not only local structures that determine the quality of patenting and patent exploitation, but also the universities' commitment to patenting and transfer, and the human and financial resources that they devote to this (after all, patenting costs money at all stages of the process, which must be provided from universities' already tight budgets).

Back in the 1980s, the Goethe University was already advising scientists on technology transfer (although the term was not yet in use at the time) and the development of IP. However, the numbers of patents filed and industrial collaborations established were very manageable.

The Employee Inventions Act of 1957 introduced the so-called '*Hochschullehrerprivileg*' ('university teacher privilege'), under which the inventions of professors were considered free inventions and the inventors could freely dispose of them. In the author's opinion, this version of the law reflected the constitutionally guaranteed freedom of teaching and research.

However, the university teacher privilege was practically abolished by a 2001 amendment to the Employee Invention Act (*Gesetz über Arbeitnehmererfindungen*) (ArbnErfG). While the regulations otherwise applicable under the ArbnErfG essentially remained force, universities – like other employers – were given the option of releasing the privilege under Sections 6 and 8 of the ArbnErfG. If the release option was not exercised, the university became the owner of the property right. As a result of this amendment, university scientists thus became mere 'service inventors'. In case of the exploitation of a patent – for example, through licensing or sale – the amended law obliges universities to pay the inventors a total of 30% of the (gross) income generated by the exploitation (see Section 42, No 4 of the ArbnErfG). Further details on university inventions are set out in Chapter 3, section 2.6.

2.2 Foundation of Innovectis GmbH

In 2000, even before this change in the law, subsidiary enterprise Innovectis GmbH was founded at Goethe University to manage patenting and technology transfer. From today's perspective, this was a very far-sighted decision by the then president of the university. The role of Innovectis was to advise scientists; identify and patent inventions that were worthy of protection; systematically build up a portfolio of patents and patent families; take care of the maintenance and marketing of these patents; and, in cooperation with university scientists, initiate and coordinate industry cooperations based on the patents.

However, university scientists are very differently knit when it comes to the commercial exploitation of their ideas. Some researchers are so addicted to noble basic research that they would never even consider patenting their ideas and reject this on principle, preferring to disseminate their ideas exclusively through scientific publications. That said, such scientists are clearly in the decline, so we will not pay them any further heed here. Of those scientists who are basically 'willing to patent', there are some who tend not to consider their ideas innovative ('We have always done so; this is nothing new'). Others tend to overestimate the significance of their inventions and would like to patent everything they achieve in their research. The wide range of assessments of innovations by university scientists is mainly due to the fact that very few scientists in the relevant field of research consider patent specifications in addition to publications in scientific journals. If you are looking for scientific publications in specialist journals, check the literature list for cited patents – you will rarely find any.

Here it is important to enhance awareness among university scientists of inventive step, together with knowledge of the stages through which one can progress from an invention to a patent – and above all, what can go wrong in this process. In order to sensitize the next generation of scientists to these issues, we have included lectures and seminars on patent law, IP development and the foundation of companies in some natural science subjects at Goethe University at as early as bachelor's level.

2.3 Implementation: from invention report to patent

At Goethe University, subsidiary Innovectis has implemented a procedure that charts the path from invention to patent and – in accordance with the Employee Invention Act – enables IP to be established in a way that is fair (for the scientists) and affordable for the university. For this purpose, a committee for the evaluation of inventions) was established, comprised of equal numbers of university professors and representatives from industry in the Greater Frankfurt area. The committee meets approximately every two months to review incoming invention reports. In this way, the deadlines set by the Employee Invention Act for the acceptance or release of inventions can be met. The author of this chapter was a member of this committee until 2018.

Innovectis is active in the run-up to the committee meeting. Scientists who have made (or at least, who believe they have made) a patent-relevant invention are encouraged to contact Innovectis as early as possible. Innovectis employees then advise on the design of the invention disclosure and, together with the inventors, explore the environment of the invention to be disclosed. The timeframe set by the Employee Invention Act begins to run from receipt of the invention disclosure. With the help of external patent attorneys, Innovectis conducts a minimal and thus cost-effective patent search and – possibly after the conclusion of a confidentiality agreement – conducts initial discussions regarding exploitation with possible interested parties from industry ('pre-patent exploitation'). Based on the searches conducted by Innovectis and an initial assessment by the patent attorneys, the evaluation committee makes recommendations on the decision to claim or release the invention. The decision criteria are patentability and the chances of exploiting the invention. This procedure – in which only about one in four invention disclosures leads to a patent application, according to the experience of recent years – has proven itself effective over many years. It reduces the number of 'patent corpses' and focuses the university's scarce resources on the patents and patent families with the best chances of exploitation. Notably, almost no inventors whose inventions have been recommended for release by this committee have subsequently applied for a patent with their own funds.

3. Patenting and publishing at universities: a contradiction?

3.1 'Publication urge' at universities

'Publish or perish' – this is an overarching principle at our universities. Without the right number and quality of publications, a scientist will receive no research funding; no job; no higher qualifying degree such as a doctorate. Numerical parameters – such as the Hirsch Index, which provides details of the publication activity of a scientist; or the Impact Factor, which indicates how often the articles of a particular journal are cited – are used as seemingly objective parameters to assess the quality of a scientist's work.

But how does patenting fit in with publishing; the confidentiality agreement with public speaking; the withholding of information with free access to research results?

3.2 Patenting versus publishing

Many colleagues at universities are of the opinion that patenting and publishing are completely incompatible, and have therefore opted for the latter. However, our own experience is that patenting and publishing are compatible if certain rules are observed. This starts with sensitizing laboratory staff to confidentiality: research results and details of procedures and devices are confidential information that must remain within a working group and have no place in social media or chat groups. In delicate projects with patentable results, we have also concluded internal confidentiality agreements within the research group – including with bachelor's and master's students, and even more so with doctoral students – or have passed on confidentiality agreements with industrial partners internally.

Scientists publish by writing articles for scientific journals and by presenting posters or lectures at conferences. Articles for scientific journals are submitted as manuscripts to the publisher or editor, and usually undergo a review process with several reviewers, which is considered confidential. If their vote is positive, the article is accepted and nowadays appears promptly as a publication in the electronic version of the journal and later in the printed form, if it (still) exists. Alternatively, the reviewers can request corrections; in which case the manuscript is returned and later submitted again as a revised manuscript. This process typically takes several weeks, and in many cases months. In principle, all parties involved should be obliged to maintain confidentiality throughout the process from submission to publication. One could therefore use the time from submission of a manuscript to publication to formulate and file a request for a patent.

However, we know from our own experience that submitted manuscripts are often passed on by the publisher, the editor or reviewers to third or fourth parties, often in good faith, to obtain a further opinion for a correct and fair assessment.

RECOMMENDATION

We therefore believe it is safer to submit manuscripts for professional journals and patent applications at the same time, in order to have provisional protection for the IP during the review phase of the manuscript for the professional journal. In practice, this means that work on the manuscript and on the draft patent application must be carried out simultaneously. However, this can be advantageous and helps, for example, to ensure that both texts are formulated precisely.

4. Theses of students and dissertations

In a working group at a university, professors, research assistants, doctoral candidates and students work closely together. This results in drafting of theses such as bachelor's or master's theses, doctoral theses and postdoctoral dissertations. The respective staff members have the right to present their research results in the thesis and these theses are basically open to the public. This applies all the more so to dissertations written by doctoral students, both for detailed work and for so-called 'cumulative work', where several publications together with a short summary constitute the doctoral thesis. In addition, theses and dissertations must be evaluated by at least two reviewers – creating a risk of 'leaks' that could potentially be patent damaging.

RECOMMENDATION

Internal and especially external reviewers of papers to be approved should sign confidentiality agreements.

In order to solve this dilemma to a certain extent, we have adopted a procedure – in consultation with the examination offices and doctoral commissions – whereby theses and dissertations are examined under the seal of confidentiality and can be kept under lock and key for a certain period of time (possibly several years) after completion of the course of study or after the doctoral examination. In practice, this means that internal and external reviewers receive a written indication of the confidentiality of the process along with the paper and must countersign it. Although this has repeatedly caused surprise and even displeasure among colleagues, it has always been accepted. At some universities, the doctoral regulations also provide for so-called 'circulation', where copies of the dissertation together with the reports are presented in turn to all professors in a department. These professors can give their consent, add comments or, in the worst case, raise objections. This process, which can take weeks, also presents considerable risk of leaks, which could potentially be damaging to the patent. This can be solved by making the dissertations available together with the expert opinions in the dean's office, where they can only be viewed and signed off by staff who have signed the confidentiality agreement. This also applies analogously to the habilitation process at universities and the review of habilitation theses.

All of these procedures may appear shaky auxiliary constructions to prevent the patent-damaging dissemination of information. Indeed, it would be desirable if study regulations, examination regulations and rules for doctorates and habilitations contained passages from the outset which clearly regulated the protection of IP for the university (and thus also for the inventors). This is a clear mandate for universities to take appropriate steps to facilitate efficient technology transfer. However, we are still a long way off from this: too much university business is still characterized by the attitude of 'free knowledge for all'.

5. Lectures and posters at conferences

Another common method of disseminating knowledge at universities is the presentation of research results in the form of posters and lectures at conferences. These are easier to control. We first check each draft poster or lecture that a member of the working group wishes to present, externally or internally, for possible harmfulness for patenting and release it only when we are sure that no confidential information will be disclosed. Such procedures are taken for granted in industry – why not at a university? Here, the help of a transfer office is important – in our case, university subsidiary Innovectis.

An example from our research group illustrates this further. Together with an industrial partner, we developed a measuring device for the quantitative determination of the ingredients of beer ('beer sensor') – a project that not only was scientifically highly interesting, but also provided us with numerous samples of all possible types of beer, thus creating true beer sommeliers. Our industrial partner invited us to present the prototype of the sensor at their booth at a trade fair, which we gladly accepted. By chance, a patent attorney working with Innovectis learned about this project just three days before the trade fair. He convinced us that no patent protection could be obtained at the latest once the prototype was unpacked and presented at the trade fair to the public and journalists. As a result, the patent draft was completed in barely three days. At the same time as confirmation of receipt of the patent application arrived from the German Patent and Trademark Office in Munich, the prototype was unpacked at the trade fair.

RECOMMENDATION

A regulated approval process is particularly recommended for posters and conference presentations.

6. 'Roof' patents instead of 'wall' patents

Patents at universities are almost always made with the intention of obtaining protection for a very specific process or device, which will be implemented or used as a novelty or as a significant improvement (for a detailed description, see Schilling 2014). They should therefore look fundamentally different from those in industry, where patents are often grouped like a wall or barrier around a (patented) process and aim to prevent similar or related processes. A helpful distinction is between 'roof' patents (in universities) and 'wall' patents (in industry). This is very much in line with universities' limited financial resources for patenting. A 'typical' roof patent at a university could therefore resemble the structure illustrated in Figure 4.1.

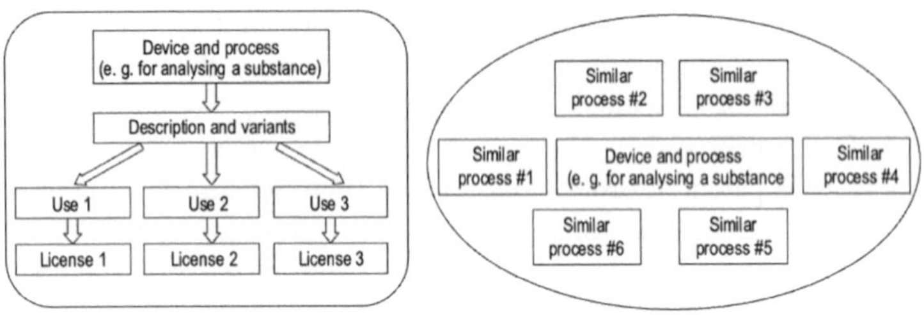

Figure 4.1 *Different structures of patents at universities (left) and in industry (right)*

From the perspective of a university, this structure has the advantage (at least in theory) that with only one patent, a whole series of marketing of devices and processes – for example, with different partners – is possible and at least provisionally secured; while the costs of patenting and patent maintenance are kept within limits.

7. Contracts with industrial partners

7.1 Various options for outsourcing

Research projects at universities often have application potential that is in line with the goals of industry. Opportunities for partnerships between

R&D working groups at universities and industry may well present themselves. There are many different ways of structuring these partnerships, which differ primarily in the way that contracts are drawn up and thus also in the way that IP is handled.

7.2 Consulting contracts with scientists

A common form of cooperation is where university scientists conduct consulting activities at a company. A consultancy contract – especially if it stipulates extra remuneration for the scientist – requires formal approval by the university management. Unfortunately, this is often ignored by university scientists. Consultancy contracts, which are usually concluded between the company and the individual scientist, should also clarify how IP will be handled: which share belongs to the 'employer' university and which to the company? I fear that the majority of consultancy contracts are unclear on this question (or that this point is circumvented altogether), and that IP often remains exclusively with the company, so that ultimately the university loses out on possible income from the secondary employment of its 'employer' inventors.

7.3 Cooperation agreements between universities and companies

Formal cooperation agreements between R&D groups at the university and a company are another collaboration option. These must be concluded by the university's legal department. The participating university scientists usually work on the joint R&D project in a full-time position (and not in paid part-time employment). For such cooperation agreements, work packages must be defined which outline the R&D tasks on both sides. Such cooperations can be great double wins: the university partner contributes its expertise; often has infrastructure that is helpful for the industrial partner; and in return receives financial means to pay for employees, materials or the possibility to test and validate processes in an industrial context.

Services or contract work is another possibility for partnership. For example, the university partner has access to analytical services that the industrial partner does not have and would otherwise have to buy on the market – if it can even find them at all.

While universities of applied sciences, which are traditionally closer to industry, find it easier to engage in all forms of such cooperation, traditional universities tend to be more reluctant to do so. University administrations and legal departments are often notoriously suspicious of contracts with industry partners. We have also had this experience. All too often, the industrial partner is seen either as an opportunist that is seeking to use public funds for its own benefit or, at the other extreme, as a 'cash cow'. Often, contracts are then drawn up in such a way that makes the cooperation unattractive for the industrial partner, thus depriving the R&D working group at the university of possible research funds.

In principle, our universities should be prepared to cooperate with private third-party funding bodies. This enables them not only to tap new sources of funding, but also to expand their opportunities for attractive research fields. In addition, such industrial cooperations create contacts through which university graduates can subsequently find good jobs.

The modalities of such cooperation possibilities vary significantly from university to university. The university profits from this through the so-called 'overhead' – a surcharge on the cost calculation which, depending on the project, ranges from around 20 per cent for pure R&D cooperation to almost 100 per cent for contract research and services. Although the R&D group at the university is reassigned a part of this overhead, the main part remains with the university (for an overview of how universities deal with private third-party funding, see Heidelberg University (ny)).

8. The 'funding gap' in R&D projects at universities

8.1 Fundraising

Basic research at universities is largely financed by so-called 'third-party funds', which must be acquired competitively by the research groups. These third-party funds are project-bound: their duration is usually two to three years, rarely longer. The so-called 'basic equipment' at universities typically covers only part of the personnel costs, the premises and at least part of the running costs for the operation of a research laboratory. The funds made available by the university to a chair for new research projects are almost always too low to cover the cost of conducting innovative research in the high-technology field. University teachers and researchers therefore spend a significant proportion of their time (at least 20 to 30 per cent) on raising research funds.

8.2 Different donors compared

One of the largest donors in Germany is the German Research Foundation (DFG), which is financed almost exclusively by the federal government and the German federal states. The funding rate depends on the subject and varies between approximately 20 and 30 per cent – only every third to fifth proposal succeeds in getting funding. In 2020, the DFG funded approximately 31100 projects with a total amount of €3.3 billion – that is, approximately €100 000 per project on average.

Although one of the DFG's mottoes is, 'We'll support you all the way to the prototype', the DFG funds basic research almost exclusively. University R&D projects thus quickly reach the point at which an application for funding is rejected because it is 'too applied'. In addition, the DFG is increasingly focusing on collaborative research – for example, with so-called 'collaborative research centres', research units or, within the framework of the Excellence Initiative, 'clusters of excellence'. A small research group that works on the development of innovative processes and devices, patents them and then seeks funding for the technical implementation or construction of a prototype and validation of the process will receive funding from the DFG only in exceptional cases.

The Federal Ministry of Education and Research (BMBF) is also a contact for the funding of R&D projects. Here, new fields of research are regularly defined by means of requests for proposals, in which one can apply for funding. For example, one field of research that has been broadly funded for about ten to 15 years now is photonics. Quantum technologies and more recently artificial intelligence have also been added.

Funding is available for the validation of technologies and for the construction of prototypes. Depending on the type of funding, an industrial partner is needed for this, which will also contribute financially. In this case, it must be carefully considered how the IP of the university research group will be shared with the industrial partner and how new IP created in the course of a BMBF-funded cooperation can be shared and used.

Where cooperation with an industrial partner leads to a funding application to the BMBF, the problem of the university's research group own contribution arises. Industry partners must provide their own contribution (usually 50 per cent of the funding share they apply for), which often leads to a distortion of the shares of the funds applied for by the individual partners. If the university research group has already been spun off, the own contribution to be made can far exceed the financial capabilities of the start-up.

In our own R&D history, we have conducted basic research for many years with 'on-board funds' and funding from the DFG and later received funding from the BMBF, which served as a 'scientific preliminary project' (WiVoPro) for the adaptation of the technologies we developed for medical applications. The aim of a WiVoPro is the further exploitation of the technology with the help of industrial partners or through a start-up.

Within the framework of its science funding, the EU also offers funding opportunities. While EU funding focused on large research consortia for many years, for some years now it has once again been possible to apply for funding as an individual R&D unit – provided that the request for proposal is appropriate for the R&D project.

A major disadvantage of BMBF and EU funding for a newly founded start-up is the long lead time, which can be one to two years. In many cases, this is far too long for a start-up in the initial phase. In addition, there is the effort required for the administration of the funds spent, which can tie up significant human resources in a start-up.

In addition to public funding, it is possible to apply for funding from private or industry-related foundations. These foundations support, for example, R&D work on specific diseases in the medical field.

8.3 The 'valley of tears'

Many innovative research projects that pass the basic research stage end up in the so-called 'valley of tears' (also known as the 'valley of death'), due to the different funding regulations. The funding chain breaks off and it becomes difficult to raise research funds –for example, to build a prototype. At this stage, the risk is often still too great for industrial partners; they would rather wait until a prototype is available and a process is thoroughly tested. This 'valley of tears' appears to be a well-suited phase for the establishment of a start-up, as shown in Figure 4.2.

On the time axis in Figure 4.2, the technology readiness levels (TRLs) are indicated as marks (see Technology Readiness Level). TRL1–TRL3 stand for the phases of basic research up to the demonstration of possible applications; TRL4–TRL6 for the first developments from the experimental setups in the laboratory to prototypes in real use; and TRL7–TRL9 for the first tests of prototypes in real use, the final proof of functionality and product development.

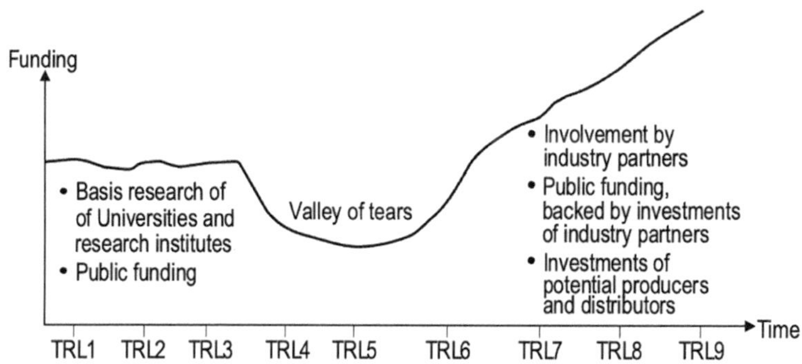

Figure 4.2 *The funding gap between basic research at universities and product development*

The funding gap – the 'valley of tears' – can be of varying width and depth, and in the worst case can lead to a complete discontinuation of R&D work – for example, if the potential for transfer and marketing is unclear. In many cases, the technologies used are still so new and their development and application potential so uncertain that private investors or industrial partners regard the project as 'high risk' and do not want to step in yet. There are no reliable figures on how many R&D projects at universities fail in the 'valley of tears', with the opportunities and possibilities associated with them going unexploited. However, I fear that this is the case for the majority of projects. It is the task of our universities and the public funding of science and technology to help ensure that a large part of university research does not go unused, and that the opportunities for innovation leaps can be seized.

Many R&D teams at universities are also partly to blame for failure in the 'valley of tears'. On the one hand, researchers at universities often have little knowledge of markets and market opportunities. On the other hand, many colleagues lack an objective view of their own developments and the parallel developments of competing groups. This has a lot to do with the basic attitude of researchers at universities towards patenting, which we have discussed above.

9. Establishment of a start-up

9.1 Expectations of industrial companies

The establishment of a start-up is one way to bridge the funding gap and avoid the 'valley of tears'. In our own R&D history, we have been involved in basic research on the spectroscopic analysis of blood parameters for many years and have provided the 'proof of principle' for several applications. Although we had close contact with several companies active in the field of laboratory analysis, determination of blood parameters and point-of-care tests during this time, none of these companies was willing to enter into a partnership at this early stage. In Figure 4.2, this point in time corresponds roughly to TRL 3–TRL 4, where potential partners may claim that the project is 'at a very early stage', 'the risk is too great' or 'the technical requirements are not yet in place'. We also often heard advice (which we found quite cynical) from companies which were involved in our projects to simply continue development, build prototypes and carry out clinical tests – cynical because industry should be aware of the financing possibilities that are available for the various R&D activities at a university. Once this work is done, they will come back and, if the results are positive, they will be happy to provide funding. We have always understood these arguments as indicating that industry is not interested in undertaking its own development, but is happy to wait until others have borne the risk of developing a prototype and then simply take over the innovation.

9.2 Challenges during the foundation process

It is not easy to set up a start-up from an R&D group at a university. From our point of view, the following problems cumulatively present barriers.

First, very few scientists have a network of investors or know of 'business angels' that could provide initial financing – especially since this first step in a technology-driven development easily requires a few hundred thousand euros.

Second, the vast majority of scientists have no experience of business plans, financing, market analysis, organizing a start-up and so on.

Third, for legal reasons, university scientists are not normally allowed to take on the role of managing director, even in the form of a sideline job.

Finally, many start-ups at universities would like to use premises, equipment and possibly even workshops or personnel at their university research facility, and carry out their developments in the 'warm nest' of their facilities. This is advantageous because it initially eliminates the need to purchase expensive infrastructure and rent suitable office and laboratory space for a high-tech start-up. However, this requires closing contracts with the university to regulate the use of the facilities and the corresponding user fees.

9.3 Role of the university administration

Our own experience – and that of many colleagues – is that at this point, there are almost always problems with the administrations and legal departments of our universities. The founders of the start-up are often accused by the administration of wanting to 'enrich themselves with public funds' by taking this step. Unfortunately, this way of thinking all too often leads to unrealistically high expectations on the part of the administration with regard to income from room use and fees for the use of university infrastructure. This, in turn, leads to tough and lengthy negotiations and rarely to consensual contracts. Unfortunately, very few universities run business incubators where start-ups can use office space and possibly also laboratories on fair terms, and which are close to the 'warm nest' of the university.

Another point concerns the use of IP by the start-up. Let us assume that the founders of the start-up submitted invention disclosures to the university during their previous R&D work, and that the university has applied for and obtained one or more patents for this purpose. This was the initial situation for us. According to the law, the university is the holder of the patents. For the start-up, either a long-term licence or an acquisition of the patents is now possible. In my view, this is absolutely necessary for the financing of the start-up in the first and subsequent financing rounds. Investors will seldom be interested – or at least, will be much more reluctant – to finance the start-up if the situation regarding IP is unclear.

However, similar to the negotiations on the use of space described above, there are often disagreements with the university administrations and legal departments responsible for the negotiations on the use of IP. This may be due to the attitude of university management towards the transfer; but it is often also due to a lack of experience among university administrations and legal departments with financing by non-public funds. Some universities have started to grant their spin-offs favourable conditions when licensing IP. This is very helpful in the initial phase of a start-up. In very many cases, however, the university's expectations are unrealistically high: a start-up is not yet an established company and urgently needs the funds from the first financing rounds to conduct the actual development work.

In our own start-up history, we were able to secure, through very tough and protracted negotiations, permission for our start-up to use premises and infrastructure at Goethe University for a fee. This was not only a financial gain for the university: employees of the start-up were doctoral students at the university and helped to supervise the theses of bachelor's and master's students or to offer internships for students, mostly using expensive equipment financed and operated by our start-up. In this way, a range of courses were created which were used very intensively by students, but whose advantages were not recognized by the university.

Overall, however, we found the connection between the start-up and our research institution to be very positive – a real win-win, which manifested itself in development work, scientific productivity, publications and teaching.

In consultation with our investors, our start-up acquired the relevant IP from Goethe University. Again, this involved very lengthy negotiations, as the university's expectations were unrealistically high; and the cost of acquiring the patents represented a sizeable chunk of our initial funding. However, it has paid off in the long term: investors always asked about the

IP and indicated that our strategy of holding it completely (and not just through licensing) in our start-up was the right decision and an important factor in securing investment.

RECOMMENDATIONS

How should one proceed when establishing a spin-off from a university?

The scientists, as founders, should secure the IP necessary for the implementation of the R&D work in advance through patent applications, together with their university.

It is highly recommended to involve partners who already have experience in setting up a business and who have their own network of business angels and investors. These partners need not be scientists themselves. They can, however, contribute significantly to the market analysis and the business plan.

The managing director should have experience in the field of start-ups, allowing the participating scientists to focus on the R&D tasks. A well-functioning team of business expert(s) and scientists creates a good impression for investors.

The founders should enter into negotiations with the university at an early stage to clarify the question of licensing or acquiring IP.

Depending on the project, the founders should consider whether it is advantageous to initially locate the start-up at the university in order to use its facilities and infrastructure.

It is possible for the university to participate financially in the start-up. However, this need not necessarily be advantageous for the founders. The founders should nonetheless consider this possibility in order to obtain favourable conditions for the use of IP or, if necessary, use of university infrastructure.

5 IP rights in start-ups as support when approaching investors in financing rounds

Thorsten Lubinski

1. Introduction

Start-ups must perform many tasks simultaneously upon establishment: defining their business model; hiring employees; renting office space and so on. Due to the limited resources available, the founders must concentrate on their core tasks.

One issue that is often neglected as a result is the creation and management of IP rights. Simple IP rights such as trademarks are often registered during the foundation process, while more extensive property rights such as patents are often overlooked. Either patents already existed before the foundation of the start-up and are brought into the start-up by transfer/licensing; or they arise rather accidentally and unstructured from the start-up's business operations. In the case of software start-ups, there are often no patents at all, as the actual software code is protected by copyright and patent protection is thus unavailable. Nevertheless, it is often possible to patent the concepts on which the software is based.

The founders must often spend considerable time on attracting capital in order to realize the start-up's vision. In most cases, external investors must be convinced of this vision in order to invest.

IP rights are a powerful tool to convince investors of the quality and professionalism of a start-up. In this respect, the development and maintenance of IP rights should be a high priority for the start-up. This chapter discusses the benefits and opportunities that IP rights – in particular, patents – afford for start-ups. It also presents the basic principles and a simple process for the structured creation and monitoring of patents that start-ups can follow.

2. Definition of a 'start-up'

There is no clear definition of a 'start-up'. However, a good starting point is the *Gabler Wirtschaftslexikon*, which defines 'start-ups' as:

> young, not yet established companies which are founded with little seed capital to realise an innovative business idea (often in the fields of electronic business, communication technology or life sciences) and are usually dependent on receiving either venture capital or seed capital (possibly also from business angels) at a very early stage to expand their business and strengthen their capital base. Due to the raising of external funds such as venture capital, the company is dependent on an exit in the course of which the investors realise their investments (*Gabler Wirtschaftslexikon* 2017).

This definition can be modified as follows:

DEFINITION

Start-ups are young companies that have the potential for exponential growth. To realize this potential as quickly as possible, start-ups depend on external cash inflows.

It follows from this description that not every newly created company is a start-up – only those with high growth potential. For this reason, individual restaurants, for example, are not start-ups, as growth very quickly reaches its limits. If a restaurant is very successful, queues form out the door or reservations must be made up to several months in advance; this means that the increased demand cannot be satisfied after a certain point. The same applies to consulting firms, where the service provided is closely linked to the number of hours that consultants work. There is a maximum number of hours that all consultants can work, after which new orders can no longer be served. The potential for growth is thus limited.

This contrasts with, for example, internet companies, where growth is limited only by the number of servers currently available and where it is relatively easy to increase this number. Social network Facebook now has almost 1.9 billion active users worldwide, of whom about 349 million are in Europe, as there are practically no limits on the potential number of users and no local restrictions on where its service can be offered. The listed company had a market capitalization of over €500 billion as of December 2019.

Online search engine Google processes around 3.5 billion search queries per day. Alphabet (Google's parent company) had a turnover of around $137 billion in 2018 and is one of the most valuable companies in the world.

Facebook was founded in 2004 and Google in 1998; and both have quickly become dominant global brands.

3. Forms of financing

Start-ups need capital to realize their vision. In the early stages, growth-oriented companies usually have no revenue, because they need a start-up period to develop products, processes and technical infrastructure. This start-up period requires financing.

There are basically three types of financing: equity capital, borrowed capital and subsidies/grants. In the case of equity capital, part of the company is usually transferred to an investor in return for a sum of money; while debt capital is debt that must be repaid with interest. The best form of financing for entrepreneurs is a grant or subsidy that does not have to be repaid. Often there are mixed forms of financing, in which subsidies are granted only if, for example, equity capital is raised at the same time.

Borrowed capital does not normally play a major role in financing start-ups, as in most cases newly founded companies do not have the necessary collateral to be able to take out a loan. Grants and subsidies usually cannot cover the necessary capital requirements on their own, so most start-ups depend on equity financing.

It is interesting to note the different views on equity financing in Anglo-Saxon countries compared to Germany. In the US, this form of financing is called 'venture capital' – in other words, a risk is taken in order to seize an opportunity. In Germany, on the other hand, the term 'risk capital' is commonly used, emphasizing the risk of losing the capital.

In principle, there are numerous sources that can provide the necessary capital for a start-up. Since the Middle Ages, patrons from wealthy families have been known to support artists and scientists in their work. Since the 1980s, a professional industry has developed that deals exclusively with the financing of start-ups (see also Chapter 10 of this book). Wealthy private investors are called 'business angels'. Professional investors can be divided into financial investors and strategic investors. These investor groups differ in risk profile, investment amount and intention. Business angels often invest in projects that have a personal connection to them; financial investors are interested purely in the risk/return ratio; and strategic investors look for building blocks that fit within a defined portfolio.

4. Case study: SugarLight

In order to illustrate the different methods of financing a start-up, we will examine these methods further using hypothetical start-up SugarLight as an example. SugarLight is a medical device company that wants to develop and produce a novel blood glucose monitoring device. The target group for this measuring device is diabetes patients. More than 450 million people worldwide suffer from diabetes – a globally occurring disease in which patients have impaired blood glucose control and are therefore dependent on regular monitoring of their blood glucose levels. Blood glucose monitoring is performed using a method that is more than 30 years old. People with diabetes must prick their finger and place a drop of blood on a test strip, which is then evaluated by a sensing device. This procedure can be painful and uncomfortable. The market for home blood glucose monitoring devices is approximately $10 billion per year, with an annual growth rate of approximately 6.7 per cent. In the ninth edition of the *Diabetes Atlas*, the International Diabetes Federation estimates that the number of diabetics will increase to 700 million by 2045 (see *Diabetes Atlas* 2019). (See also Figure 5.1.)

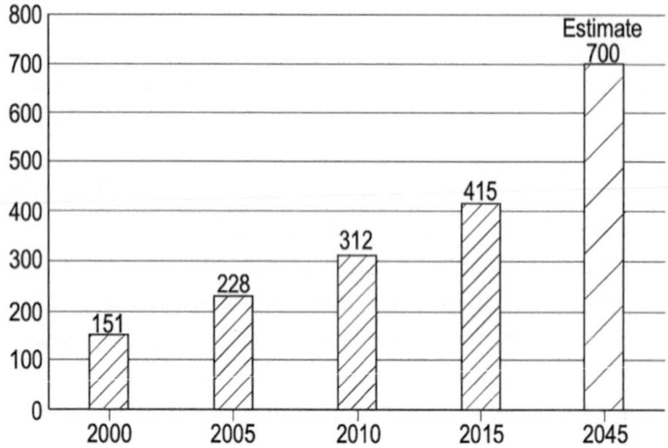

Figure 5.1 *Diabetes as a global problem - number of people with diabetes worldwide in millions*

SugarLight has developed a non-invasive blood monitoring procedure. Instead of pricking a finger to obtain blood, a laser-based technology is used to optically determine the sugar content in the skin and these values are used to determine the blood sugar level. The procedure is just as precise as the conventional method, but works painlessly without drops of blood and requires no consumables. The medical device is a 'non-invasive blood glucose monitor'.

The basic research for the process was carried out at a German university and a patent family has been applied for in the name of the university.

SugarLight is seeking equity capital from private and institutional investors in order to produce a marketable product from the results of the basic research and develop it for mass production. In a first step, SugarLight has acquired the university's patent family and transferred it to the company.

5. IP protection for risk minimization

From an investor's point of view, an investment must be checked for possible returns and risks. Our definition of a 'start-up' factors in high earnings potential, so the risks that exist before sales and profits are realized are a key part of this examination – the so-called 'due diligence'. IP rights, and patents in particular, can play a major role in minimizing the risks.

Eight core risks play a role in all investment decisions in the start-up sector. Depending on the size of the start-up and the type of investor, these risks may be weighted differently; but a start-up should have strategies for all of them.

In working out the risks to be addressed, I took the blog post 'How to De-Risk a Startup' from Coding VC as a guide and adapted it to a technology-driven company (see Coding VC 2016).

One point that does not fall under risk, but which is decisive in determining whether a start-up is in a position to consider an investment application at all, is the ability to describe its purpose briefly and clearly. This sounds like a trivial point, but unfortunately start-ups often lose themselves in flowery descriptions of their vision in order to appear more 'professional' and not be rejected for an investment because of an overly narrow idea. In fact, the first one or two sentences of the company description should create the right image in the minds of investors so that they have a clear idea of the start-up's purpose.

Professor Scott Galloway teaches marketing at the Stern School of Business at New York University. In his not-so-serious blog post 'Yogababbel' (see Galloway 2019), he qualitatively assessed the corporate purpose of several companies and awarded them a 'Bullsh*t Rating'. The lower the rating, the clearer and more concrete the purpose was formulated. A very good rating was given to video conferencing provider Zoom, which states that its purpose is to 'make video conferencing easy'. A bad rating was given to fitness equipment manufacturer Peloton, which states that its corporate purpose is to 'sell a feeling of pleasure'.

A technically correct, but overly abstract formulation for our start-up would be, for example: 'SugarLight has developed a photothermal process to detect molecules in liquids and soft matter. It can be used to implement many novel detection methods.'

Start-up founders are often proud of their technical achievements ('new photothermal process') and want to open up practically infinite new markets ('many detection methods'); but they often forget that it is much more convincing to implement a real application.

An alternative description could look like this: 'SugarLight has developed a medical device that can measure blood sugar without the patient having to prick their finger. It uses a new and patented process developed independently.'

From this description, investors can clearly see what the product is about ('a medical device'); the benefit of the product ('no pricking'); and that it is a new and exciting technology ('patented'). Thus, the first hurdle to investment has been overcome.

In order to assess the overall risk of a start-up, the individual risks set out in Table 5.1 should be surveyed in a more or less structured manner.

These risks are examined in more detail below and the ways in which IP rights can help to minimize them are outlined.

Table 5.1 Overview of the individual risks of a start-up

Risk	What must be proven?
Product requirements ('product/market fit')	Do customers really want the product?
Product quality	Can the start-up produce a high-quality product?
Team	Can the start-up build a powerful team?
Distribution	Can the start-up build the necessary sales structure?
Market size	Is the market big enough?
Funding	Can the start-up raise enough capital to reach milestones?
Competition	What differentiates the product from the competition? Is the differentiating feature sustainable?
'Unfair advantage'	What advantage does the start-up have that nobody else has?

5.1 Product requirements (product/market fit)

A lack of product demand or inappropriate product/market fit is by far the most common reason why start-ups fail. Market research agency CB Insights evaluated more than 100 field reports of failed start-ups and found that in 42 per cent of cases, the cause of failure was a non-existent product requirement (see CB Insights 2019b).

There are innumerable examples of products that have been developed without taking into account the target group, such as fruit and vegetable juicer the Juicero Press. Start-up Juicero was founded in 2013 and received venture capital of $120 million in 2014. The Juicero Press was launched on the US market in early 2016 as an internet-connected juicer that could press small pre-produced packages of fruit and vegetables into fresh juices. The basic business model was similar to the model for coffee capsule machines, which has been very successful. The machine cost $699 on launch and the packages of fresh fruits and vegetables between $5 and $7. In January 2017 the price of the machine was reduced to $399; and a little later, the machine was tested by a journalist from *Bloomberg News*. During the test, the journalist tried simply squeezing the packages by hand and succeeded in producing a juice of practically the same quantity and quality as that produced by the expensive device (see Bloomberg 2017). Overnight, the device became virtually obsolete after several years of development. At the end of 2017, sales were discontinued.

In order to obtain early market feedback, it makes sense to deliver early versions of the product to customers and study the usage behaviour. Compared to classic market research, this method has the advantage that customers do not need to be asked about possible product features in an abstract way; instead, the start-up can observe how they deal with the product and draw its own conclusions. This approach is particularly helpful with new technologies, as many customers must experience a product first hand before they can evaluate it.

The disadvantage of this approach is that the product becomes known to the public at a very early stage of development. Competitors and potential imitators can easily monitor its development and develop their own products if necessary. SugarLight works in short development cycles, each ending with a demonstrator. Demonstrators need not be fully functional, but they must implement a partial aspect of the product, at least superficially. In the initial development stages, for example, it is not necessary to measure precisely; but the process of measuring should be testable for an end customer, including possible operating errors. In this way, end customers will get an early impression of how this non-invasive glucose measurement works. It also makes it possible to detect operating errors. For example, as the measurement is painless, some customers may remove their finger from the sensor before the measurement cycle has ended. This knowledge can be passed on to the development department and addressed in the next product iteration.

IP rights help to secure this process with the involvement of external third parties and thus bring a better product to market. If new developments are consistently protected, it is difficult for imitators to copy them.

5.2 Product quality

Once product/market fit has been confirmed, the question arises as to whether the start-up can produce the developed product at high quality, even if the number of users or units increases. Small design errors in the prototype can lead to major difficulties, especially when it comes to the mass production of hardware products. In addition, SugarLight is manufacturing a medical product; so in addition to the usual requirements, regulatory specifications must be observed and appropriate processes implemented.

Well-designed IP rights can serve as a basis for the specifications of the finished product. These specifications can then be discussed and improved with external specialist partners, all under the protection of existing rights.

5.3 Team

The success of start-ups depends largely on the quality of the team. Especially in the early stages, individual team members must take on many different tasks and find, define and implement processes. Many core aspects of the technology are in the minds of individual employees and must be gradually incorporated into the organization.

IP rights help with both recruiting new employees and retaining existing employees. For new employees, IP rights are an indication of the sustainability of the technology in the market. Like investors, employees will also consider how their new employer is seeking to minimize typical start-up risks, and all the arguments presented in this chapter naturally apply to new employees as well.

Existing employees benefit from the registration of new IP rights. It is important for the start-up that employee know-how is documented and bound to the company – for example, by applying for patents. Employees can be named as inventors when the patents are filed and participate in later successes (eg, in Germany, through the Employee Invention Act; see also Chapter 3). As patents are published, a link between the inventor's name and the technology is created for the outside world, and employees are thus increasingly identified with the technology and the company. However, it is worthwhile for the start-up to pay attention to the clear transfer of IP rights from employees to the company.

IP rights are therefore a very elegant method of recruiting and motivating employees.

5.4 Distribution

The basic motivation of all private sector companies is to make a profit – that is, to sell services or products with a profit margin. The way in which the money will be earned is known as the 'business model'. In the case of SugarLight, the business model consists of selling the non-invasive blood glucose monitor to patients. A peculiarity of medical devices is that the users are not necessarily also the buyers of the product. In Germany, for example, customers often expect a health insurance company to cover the costs. SugarLight would like to take care of marketing itself in Germany, but would like to work with distribution partners in other regions of the world.

In this constellation, patents in different regions of the world are helpful in order to be able to prohibit the sale of copied products. Patents are prohibitive rights through which the patent holder can prohibit the manufacture, marketing and advertising of products covered by the IP right. It is not necessary – and usually also not useful – to apply for patents in all regions and countries of the world, but only in those regions where a particularly large market can be addressed or where high production capacities are available.

In addition to classic distribution agreements, IP rights can be used to create licensing models through which an external partner is granted the right to use the patented technology in its own products.

5.5 Market size

While the preceding risks are mainly concerned with assessing whether the start-up is capable of producing a product that is capable of mass distribution, the size of the addressable market and thus the growth potential of the start-up is another key factor to consider. If the developed product is only intended for a niche market that is expected to generate rather small revenues, even with a 100 per cent market share, the return potential will not be large enough for most investors. Many institutional investors have internal guidelines for minimum returns. If these cannot be achieved even under optimal conditions given the size of the existing market, the investor will refrain from investing.

This risk is also an opportunity for start-ups which can show that a very large market can be addressed, which in turn can lead to increased willingness on the part of investors to accept risks on other points.

SugarLight serves the market for blood glucose monitors in the private environment. The current size of this market is $10 billion worldwide per year, with an expected size of $16 billion in 2025. It is very easy to show that, even with a small market share, very large sales can be expected.

In principle, IP rights do not influence the size of the market; but when it comes to estimating the share of the market that a start-up can secure and maintain for itself, the prohibitive effects of IP rights on other market participants play a major role.

In addition, IP rights may be of interest for other fields of application that do not fall within the core area of the start-up and are not pursued further, but are of importance to other companies. Here, licensing models can be used to generate new revenue streams that would not otherwise have materialized.

5.6 Funding

This point often causes surprise during the financing process. Why do investors see financing as a risk when they should be responsible for it themselves? The answer is amazingly simple: investors only want to invest in good and successful start-ups, and the best validation of the quality of a start-up is the existence of another investor. This creates a dilemma for the start-up, as it is extremely difficult to convince the initial investors to invest; but at a certain point, there will be more interest than investment opportunities. Many start-ups have observed this trend, so that in start-up circles there is talk of the 'lemming behaviour' of investors.

Patents constitute an external validation of the technology by experts. A granted patent fulfils at least the requirements of novelty and inventive activity. The search reports prepared during the patent examination process also give external investors a good overview of the current state of the art. For the start-up, it is advisable to have an independent service provider conduct a freedom-to-operate search at regular intervals, to check both whether the developed product is covered by the company's existing IP rights and whether the product infringes the IP rights of other companies. The results of this search can be presented to investors during the technical examination.

5.7 Competition

The start-up's competitive position should be assessed for both short and long-term periods. SugarLight is entering a large market with longstanding, highly successful competitors. However, given the advantages of its novel non-invasive technology, a successful market entry seems very likely and SugarLight can prove demand through pre-orders. However, SugarLight must also be able to show that it can grow continuously after market entry, and that it can take market share away from the competition over longer periods of time. Building up a portfolio of IP rights helps start-ups to overcome the market entry hurdle and at the same time makes it more difficult for competitors to develop existing systems into competitive products.

In addition to the prohibition aspect, IP rights can be used as a powerful negotiating tool. If several companies want to use the IP rights of others, it may be easier to set up a common IP rights pool and grant each other the use of the rights instead of having to conclude licence negotiations with all market participants. Today, every smartphone contains over 100 000 different patents (eg, see Süddeutsche Zeitung 2011), making it practically impossible to manufacture a mobile phone without infringing a patent. However, if the company's own patent portfolio in this area is sufficiently valuable, it is in the interests of all manufacturers to agree on a compromise. And this is not only applicable to patents: other IP rights, such as designs, can also strengthen your negotiating position.

5.8 'Unfair advantage'

The 'unfair advantage' in risk assessment is the joker card for start-ups. In the context of this chapter, an 'unfair advantage' is an opportunity or characteristic of a company that cannot easily be copied by other market participants. This might include, for example, exclusive access to distribution channels, cooperation with large companies on special terms or a particularly good relationship with future customers.

SugarLight benefits from years of experience gained from research that took place before the company was founded, and from a very broad patent that protects the technology far beyond the scope of the actual product and also includes other areas of application.

A hard-to-control but powerful unfair advantage is an IP right to a standard or a *de facto* standard. The music encoding method MP3 is the most common method for the digital storage of music and is covered by several patents. Virtually every software and hardware manufacturer had to pay royalties to the rights holders until 2017, when the patents on the MP3 standard expired. In 2017, however, the patents on the MP3 standard expired.

6. IP management in start-ups

In order to benefit from the risk-reducing properties of IP, start-ups must establish a process at an early stage to create and obtain IP rights. It makes sense to define a catalogue of values that reflects the strategic character of the IP rights and thus also makes clear to employees the significance of IP rights to the company.

The value catalogue for SugarLight defines the following points:

SugarLight:

- considers its own strong IP rights as a strategic instrument;
- strives to be the owner of all IP rights used in the company, especially in cooperation with other companies;
- continuously monitors its own development work through a structured process to search for possible IP rights;
- focuses its efforts on value-oriented IP rights that keep the interests of its customers in mind (quality before quantity also applies to IP rights);
- ensures that developed products are covered by IP rights;
- regularly checks whether in-house developments infringe third-party IP rights;
- aims at broad coverage of the content of IP rights in order to prevent circumvention;
- is geographically broad, with IP rights in many parts of the world;
- strives to use all kinds of protective rights (patents, utility models, trademarks, copyright) in order to be optimally positioned;
- tries to keep IP rights in the approval process for as long as possible, in order to be able to react to new developments by adapting an IP right (eg, a patent application) if necessary; and
- examines on a case-by-case basis whether it is advisable to achieve a quick grant with limited scope of protection and subsequently pursue broader claims.

This catalogue provides employees with a tool that they can use in their daily work. In contract negotiations, IP right clauses are perceived differently and negotiated in the interests of the company. Developers are sensitized to check their progress for elements that are suitable for IP protection and report these to their superiors. Team leaders can hold regular workshops with their teams to identify or develop patentable ideas. It is also a good idea to monitor the IP strategies of competitors and respond to current developments in the market.

SugarLight has defined a simple process for living its IP values. Once or twice a year, it holds a patent workshop, to which a representative from each area of the company is sent to consider developments since the last workshop, preferably together with a patent attorney. In addition to a presentation on actual new developments, participants are encouraged to ask themselves and their staff about new patent ideas.

A member of staff is also instructed to review the search reports on the company's own patents, to conduct a brief search for new academic findings and to look at publications of IP rights and product launches by competitors.

Patentable ideas are then developed from these individual building blocks in presentations and discussions. A patent attorney, in cooperation with a designated employee who acts as an interface between the attorney and the start-up staff, translates these ideas into fully fledged patents. Through this process, alternative ways to patent the actual solution are also sought, in order to effectively block possible circumventions of the first implementation. The aim is to formulate a patent that is as broad as possible, even if a very concrete implementation is to be patented, in order to secure the strongest possible protection.

Some companies consciously seek narrow patents in order to enable a quick grant; this can be a very good strategy where a company has few or no patents. However, SugarLight takes the opposite approach and tries to keep the granting process open for as long as possible with broad claims, so that the patents can be adapted to new circumstances if necessary.

In individual cases, narrower divisional applications are separated from the broad patents of origin in order to be able to show investors that the patent applications are in principle eligible for grant. However, the original patent application remains as broad as possible in order to achieve maximum patent protection. It is also accepted that the first application will be rejected by the patent examiner, so this application must be restricted.

For practical implementation, SugarLight opts for applications under the Patent Cooperation Treaty (PCT), which are filed and managed by an external patent attorney. A PCT application offers provisional protection in over 150 states that have acceded to the treaty and gives the start-up the opportunity to decide on the regions and countries of the world in which patents should be filed, usually at least 30 months after the priority date. Unfortunately, there is no single worldwide patent, so individual patents must be filed per region/country; although national rules on patents may differ. With a PCT application, the applicant gains the possibility of deferring the decision on the countries in which patents should be sought.

In selecting these countries, SugarLight is guided by the economic importance of the markets and the available production capabilities in the relevant countries. Core patents are registered in the ten largest nations/regions of the world, and patents of lesser importance only in the five largest regions (Figure 5.2).

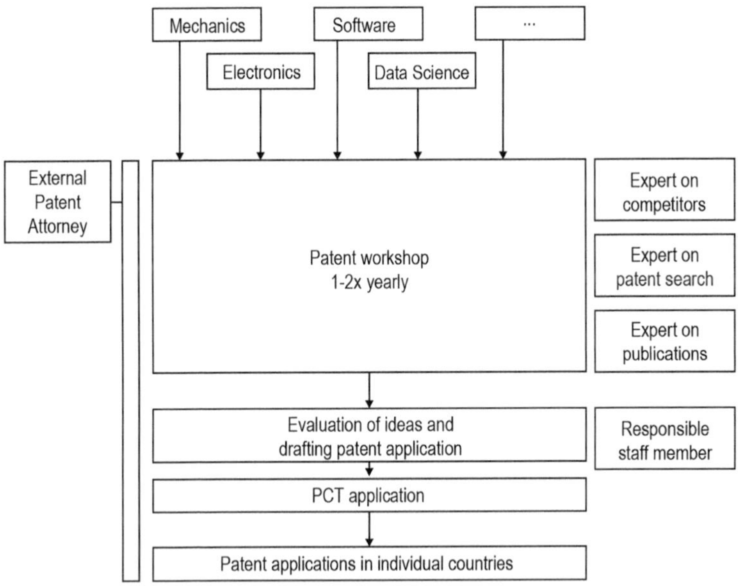

Figure 5.2 Structured process for patent development

All in all, this results in a more complex granting process, which costs time and money, but results in high-quality patents. Through this procedure, SugarLight has applied for new patent families every year since its foundation, thus compiling a high-quality patent portfolio.

7. Summary

The founders of a start-up must solve many different challenges and pay particular attention to good capitalization of the company, as without the necessary resources, the steps for success cannot be implemented.

In deciding whether to invest in a project, external investors will review the company's substance and evaluate various risk factors in order to create a risk profile. Their decision will be based on the risk and the expected return.

IP rights are a powerful instrument to reduce the risk of investment and thus facilitate positive investment decisions. For the founders/managing directors, the creation and management of IP rights are of vital strategic importance, which can be codified through a common set of values. Based on a clear catalogue of values, a pragmatic process can be established which implements the IP rights strategy and ultimately leads to new IP rights.

Ultimately, this approach will also benefit the start-up. If the risk of investment is reduced, the overall risk for the company and its founders will also be reduced!

6 Contract drafting for start-ups with a focus on IP rights

Rainer Gith

1. Introduction

The start-up phase, capital increases and exits, IP and its allocation to the company, and freedom from third-party rights are all issues of central importance when drafting contracts for a start-up. This relates in particular to important aspects such as the correct identification of the inventors; the correct indication of the holder of the IP rights; and the legal validity of the IP rights. Either these are checked by the purchasing side ('IP due diligence') or guarantees are given by the seller. It is also important that any royalty payments and employee invention compensation are handled transparently.

IP rights are often an important component of the business model – and not only for technology-driven start-ups. IP rights, especially patents, can shield the start-up from competition and thus make it more attractive for investors. IP rights – especially patents, utility models, trademarks, copyright and designs, as well as domain names and know-how – can be important drivers in determining the start-up's value. This applies both to the financing rounds within the scope of the start-up's establishment and to possible sale (exit).

Founders should therefore consider transferring IP rights to the start-up at an early stage, as these rights usually originate not with the company, but with people (eg, authors or inventors). The transfer process should be carried out in a legally effective manner and should be documented transparently, so that investors and prospective buyers can easily check the start-up's ownership of rights without any gaps.

It is not possible to present all possible constellations of contract design in this chapter. The focus is thus on particularly important contractual areas in the typical phases of a start-up. The aim is to sensitize company founders to the importance of this contractual area. In order to narrow this presentation further, the following remarks refer only to patents and utility models and the related know-how. Thus, to the extent that the term 'IP' is used in this chapter, it is synonymous with patents and utility models and the related know-how. The principles described in this chapter apply to a large number of countries, particularly in Central Europe (the examples mostly refer to the legal situation in Germany).

2. Acquisition and use of IP rights by the start-up

2.1 Initial situation

As outlined in the introduction, if the founders of the start-up are themselves the holders of IP rights, they should transfer these rights to the start-up immediately after its establishment. The transfer is effected by way of a transfer agreement and the transfer of the IP rights to the start-up. In this case, a careful examination of the patent or the seller's ownership of the rights is generally unnecessary, as all information about the IP rights in question should already be known and there is usually no doubt about their ownership.

However, where a start-up requires third-party IP rights to implement its business model (eg, in the case of spin-offs from larger companies or from university projects), the examination of the IP rights prior to an acquisition is an important prerequisite to ensure the legally secure contractual transfer or licensing of these IP rights. In later financing rounds, investors will examine the quality of the existing IP rights and the contractual regulations very carefully in the context of their IP due diligence. If the contractual IP position is not bulletproof, this can put considerable pressure on the company valuation or even deter investors from investing.

2.2 Differentiation purchase/licensing

In order to be able to use the requisite IP of a third party, the first step is essentially to purchase or license the corresponding rights. A purchase or full transfer of IP rights occurs upon a complete and final change of ownership.

In contrast to a purchase, in the case of licensing, the start-up does not become the owner of the IP rights. From an economic point of view, the licence opens up access to third-party technologies. Legally, licences are rights of use and enjoyment of technical IP rights (see Henn/Palow 2017).

It is difficult to give a general answer to the question of which variant is preferred. Too many individual factors are important in answering this question. In the case of technology-driven start-ups with high capital requirements, I would nevertheless recommend in principle that IP rights be acquired wherever possible. Venture capital investors like to see all rights held by the company they invest in. This presents fewer dependencies and legal uncertainties – for example, due to the insolvency of the licensor or the extraordinary termination of the licence agreement for good cause by the licensor. In addition, having its own IP rights will generally increase the enterprise value of the start-up.

2.3 Sales contracts

2.3.1 IP due diligence

If the rights are to be acquired from a third party, it is important to obtain as much information as possible about them before concluding the purchase contract. In contrast to professional investors, which spend a lot of time and effort on examining the IP situation of the start-up in the course of IP due diligence before making an investment, newly founded companies often have only limited funds available, especially in the early phase. Nevertheless, the founders should try to gather as much information as possible in advance, in order to realistically assess the quality and value of the relevant IP rights.

It is very important to consult an experienced IP expert before buying a patent. If there are insufficient financial resources to engage a competent expert (usually a patent attorney), participation of the IP expert in the start-up may also be an option. Having IP competence in the company is a valuable resource for the founding team.

The first step in examining the IP rights to be acquired is to draw up a complete list of the IP rights, divided into applications and granted IP rights. Based on the information provided, it should be determined whether the IP rights in question exist in law and whether all fees previously incurred for the IP right have been paid to the patent office. Special focus should be placed on the seller's right of ownership: the buyer should be as certain as possible that the seller is actually the entitled owner of the IP right. In certain countries (eg, Austria), ownership can be reliably verified by consulting the patent register maintained by the respective patent offices. In other countries (eg, Germany), the IP rights can be transferred (change of ownership) without this being reflected in the patent register (see Beck's Mandatshandbuch Due Diligence 2017). The mere indication of the patent owner on the patent specification or in the register is thus not conclusive proof of the true ownership of the rights. In this respect, the guarantees and corresponding compensation provisions included in the patent purchase agreement have an important protective function for the purchaser.

Caution

Always conduct a thorough examination of the IP rights prior to the conclusion of the contract. Possible contractual claims for damages against the seller are of little help if the business model cannot be implemented due to previously unknown third-party rights. Claims for damages can also be in vain if there is nothing more to be gained from the seller. The best protection is achieved through thorough IP due diligence in connection with a carefully and professionally drafted transfer agreement.

There is no generally applicable IP checklist for the examination of IP rights prior to the conclusion of a sales contract. The list set out in Table 6.1 serves as a guide and should be adapted accordingly to the individual case.

Table 6.1 *Checklist for the examination of IP rights prior to the conclusion of a sales contract*

Patents/utility models	Patent applications	Conflicts	Employee inventions*
- Who is the owner? - What is the application date? - What is the claimed priority date? - When was the renewal fee last paid? - How long is the remaining term of protection?	- Who is the applicant? - What is the application date? - What is the claimed priority date? - What are the chances that the property right will be granted (decision to grant; oppositions)?	- Types of proceedings; - Parties involved; - Status of proceedings; - Outcome of proceedings or prospects of success; - Economic significance of the process output or possible process output; - Cease and desist declarations.	- Description of the operational practice of the vendor; - Invention report/ claiming of right (in due form and time); - Inventor remuneration (proper determination; remuneration regulation; current payments); - Allocation of property rights to the reported inventions.

Note: * Depending on the respective regime governing the allocation of employee inventions in the country in which the start-up is based.

All items on the IP checklist that are not relevant to the specific case can be deleted accordingly. If the IP right belongs to more than one party (patent community), the property right can only be sold 'as a whole' with the consent of all entitled parties. In this case, care must be taken to ensure that all declarations of consent of the entitled parties are available.

2.3.2 *Freedom-to-operate search*

In order to be able to assess the value of the IP rights to be acquired as comprehensively as possible, the start-up should have a so-called 'freedom-to-operate' (FTO) search carried out before the conclusion of the purchase agreement. This aims to determine whether a product to be marketed infringes the IP rights of third parties. Such IP rights can concern the entire product as well as components, production methods, technical details or design and brand elements of the product. The owner of an infringed IP right can demand not only compensation for damages, but also an injunction to cease marketing the product. If a court grants the competitor a cease-and-desist order, in the worst case the entire business model of the start-up may be unfeasible.

Thus, the results of the FTO search may prevent disputes about IP claims with competitors from arising after the product launch. Such IP claims disputes entail considerable cost risks and could jeopardize further financing rounds with investors.

The more effort and costs that are invested in the search, the more accurate the results. However, it is almost impossible to find all relevant documents, even with a comprehensive and careful search. For example, it is impossible to search for patent applications that have not yet been published. Furthermore, it is very time consuming to search for international patent applications in Asian languages and to determine their exact content. Therefore, after consultation with an experienced patent expert, a reasonable trade-off should be found between search costs and the residual risk presented by unsearched documents. The results of an FTO search are not self-explanatory, but must be analysed and legally evaluated together with a patent attorney.

2.3.3 Important regulatory areas

IP due diligence primarily aims to obtain as much information as possible about the IP right to be acquired so that its existence and value can be assessed. The patent purchase agreement aims to effect the transfer of the IP right and to minimize possible risks with regard to untrue or incomplete information on the part of the seller.

It should be checked in advance whether the patent purchase agreement must fulfil certain formal requirements in order to be effective. This is regulated differently from country to country. In most countries, such as the UK and Germany, the patent purchase agreement does not generally require a special form (freedom of form). By contrast, the transfer of European patent applications must be documented in writing (Article 72 of the European Patent Convention). However, even if it is possible to conclude the patent purchase agreement without any formalities, the agreement should always be concluded in writing, to provide proof of its conclusion and to document its individual provisions.

The IP rights to be transferred must be specified precisely in the contract. Patents or patent applications can be clearly identified by the corresponding patent number or publication number. If patent families or patent portfolios are being acquired, it is advisable to clearly list the relevant rights in a separate annex to the contract and to refer to them in the text of the contract itself. A typical clause on the subject matter of the contract in the purchase contract could read as follows:

> The seller shall transfer the goods specified in annex … on the due date … existing or pending patents and utility models (contractual property rights) with economic effect on the effective date to the buyer; the buyer accepts the transfer. (Henn/Pahlow 2017: 367)

Insofar as the use of the IP requires the transfer of supplementary know-how by the seller, the obligation to transfer the know-how should be included in the purchase contract as the seller's main obligation. Unless there is an express provision to this effect in the purchase agreement, it is not one of the main performance obligations of the seller to transfer this know-how to the start-up as buyer. In exceptional cases, an obligation to transfer know-how may arise if the purpose of the contract cannot be achieved without this supplementary know-how. However, this is a matter of interpretation and involves risks which should be avoided. In such cases, the patent purchase agreement should also extend the obligation to transfer the know-how. If necessary, the seller will agree on additional remuneration for this.

The determination of the purchase price is subject to the freedom of contract. General statements regarding the amount of the patent purchase price are unhelpful. The value of the patent and, based on this, the determination of the purchase price will depend on many factors and are particularly difficult to predict when it is not yet possible to determine whether a product can be successfully developed from the patented technology (eg, technical development risks; lack of proof of concept of the innovation).

There are different quantitative valuation methods to determine the value of a patent – for example, in Germany, standards DIN 77100, IDW S 5 and DIN ISO 10668. Other factors such as the remaining term of the IP right and its legal validity should be taken into account in determining the purchase price. The marketability of the start-up's products is also of paramount importance and another key factor in determining the purchase price. Patents that establish a new technical standard (so-called 'standard-essential patents') are particularly valuable.

Special features apply to the purchase of a patent application, as in most cases the abovementioned factors cannot yet be ascertained. There is also uncertainty as to whether and to what extent the patent will ultimately be granted. In case of significant doubt, it is advisable to obtain an expert opinion on the patentability of the invention.

Regardless of the many uncertainties – especially in the early phases, when a product may still have to be developed – it is often a wise strategy to acquire the IP right by paying a one-off fee. This provides planning security and increases the value of the start-up both in future financing rounds and in the event of an exit. Possible development risks of the product and other uncertainties can be introduced into the negotiations in order to reduce the purchase price. If the start-up cannot or does not want to pay the required purchase price due to the amount and/or technical risks, the purchase price can also be linked to 'milestones'. Usual milestones could include the grant of patents in different countries or the market entry of a product. The purchase price can also be linked to a sale and/or exit participation of the patent seller. In the latter cases, it is important to agree on maximum limits and to document the calculation of the participation amounts transparently in the patent purchase agreement. Calculation examples, which can be attached to the purchase contract as an annex, are recommended.

As previously mentioned, proof of patent ownership by the seller is a central component of IP due diligence. In the purchase agreement, the results of the due diligence should be backed up by guarantees from the seller. The seller should therefore at least be obliged to guarantee that the IP rights in question are legally valid, and that the fees previously incurred for the IP rights have been paid. It should also guarantee that no third-parties have rights in the IP rights, and that no dispositions or encumbrances have been made in respect of the IP rights.

This simple contractual clause could take the following form:

> The seller assures that
>
> he is the sole owner of the property rights and contractual know-how which are the subject matter of the contract, that he has not otherwise transferred these or otherwise granted third parties rights to the contractual property rights and that he can freely dispose of the contractual property rights without restrictions,
>
> he is not aware of any rights of third parties which could conflict with the use of the contractual property rights, nor of any other reasons for cancellation, nor of any threats of cancellation made by third parties,
>
> he has not granted any licence rights to the property rights or contractual know-how covered by the contract to third parties ...

These are minimum guarantees that should be included in any transfer contract. The seller should provide these guarantees in the form of an independent no-fault guarantee commitment. In addition, depending on the results of the IP due diligence, it may be advisable to contractually agree on further guarantees of the seller – for example, that all fees for maintaining the IP rights have been paid so far; that no legal disputes with regard to the IP exist or have been threatened; and/or that the seller is not aware of any legal or material defects in the subject matter of the contract.

The contract should also oblige the seller to cooperate with the necessary formalities to secure or implement the transfer of IP rights and, if applicable, the registration of the start-up as their new owner; and to make all necessary declarations for this purpose without delay.

In addition, the publication of all documents relating to the IP rights should be regulated. These include, among other things, registration certificates, renewal certificates, deadline calendars (regarding renewal of the IP rights, especially trademarks), and correspondence with the authorities, courts and surveillance services.

If the seller is to be excluded from further use of the IP rights after the sale, the contract can clarify that the seller will not be granted a re-licence. The seller is therefore no longer entitled to use the IP rights and contractual know-how after the transfer, whether in its name or for or through third parties.

2.4 Licence agreement

2.4.1 General information

Where it is not possible to acquire the IP rights or where those responsible for the start-up have decided not to acquire them, it is usual to obtain a licence to ensure the lawful use of the technology. From a legal point of view, licences constitute usage rights of technical IP rights (Henn/Pahlow 2017: 187). The licence agreement regulates the use of patents and technologies, and determines the type, scope and licence fee. The drafting of a licence agreement is complex and requires the assistance of an experienced contract lawyer. Some important aspects of a licence agreement are briefly outlined below.

Before concluding a licence agreement, the licensor's ownership of the rights should be carefully examined, as for a patent purchase agreement. An FTO search is also useful to better estimate the value of the licence.

A licence agreement can be concluded without any formal requirements. However, a written contract is strongly recommended for documentation purposes and to avoid disputes about the content and scope of the agreement. The parties are largely free to determine the content and scope of the licence agreement.

The subject matter of the licence agreement must be defined very precisely. The IP rights which are the subject matter of the agreement must be precisely designated and a copy attached to the licence agreement as an annex. Necessary know-how, such as development results and designs, should also be made the subject matter of the licence agreement and should be continuously supplemented by the licensor during the term of the agreement.

2.4.2 Licence types

The type of licence – simple, exclusive or semi-exclusive – can be freely agreed between the parties. It is also important to consider whether sub-licences can be granted to third parties or whether use should be limited to the start-up only. Distinctions between manufacturing, distribution and use licences are also possible. Those responsible for the start-up should carefully examine the extent to which the licence is required. Spatial and temporal restrictions of the licence can also be freely agreed. A licence for an IP right cannot extend geographically beyond the territory for which the IP right has been granted. A licence ends at the latest when the IP right expires. In principle, the aim should be for the start-up to allow the contract to run until the expiry of the last contractual IP right. The possibility for unilateral ordinary termination of the licence agreement by the start-up offers it a certain degree of flexibility. It will become apparent in the contract negotiations whether this can be enforced.

2.4.3 *Licence fees*

An essential component of the licence agreement is the amount of the licence fee. The type, scope and amount should be agreed very clearly in the contract, in order to avoid any misinterpretation. Calculation examples can avoid subsequent discussions and can be attached to the contract. In practice, the turnover licence fee is one of the most common types of licence fees. A unit licence (where the basis of assessment is the number of licensed products produced or sold) or even a one-off payment (flat-rate licence) for the contract period may also be interesting to consider. Especially in the case of the turnover royalty, it is important to precisely regulate the content of the turnover or revenue in the contract. During the negotiations, it is important to ensure that the supply or manufacture of the products based on the contractual IP rights is not already subject to a turnover licence fee, but only the proceeds that actually accrue to the start-up. A minimum licence fee, which is often found in licence agreements, can be dangerous for the start-up, as this is generally incurred even if the start-up becomes unable to manufacture and market the licensed products through no fault of its own. In practice, it is often difficult to avoid a minimum licence fee. However, it is always worthwhile negotiating hard on this point. Conversely, if the start-up will be a licensor, a minimum royalty from the licensee is an important negotiation objective.

Those responsible for the start-up must ensure that in the event of a conflict with third-party rights, all rights and obligations are precisely regulated in the licence agreement. In particular, the economic risk of being unable to use the licensed object (any longer) due to conflicting third-party rights represents a danger for the start-up as licensee. Even a very careful examination in the run-up to the conclusion of the agreement does not afford 100 per cent security. It should therefore be ensured that the licence agreement contains warranty provisions.

The licensor should at least guarantee the start-up that it can freely dispose of the IP rights, and that it is not aware of any facts which could affect the validity of the IP rights at the time of conclusion of the contract. In the event of breach of the guarantee, the licensor should compensate the start-up for lost profits as well as for any other damages – for example, if the IP rights are lost due to an action for annulment.

As a rule, the licensor will not assume any guarantee for the commercial exploitability of the contractual IP rights or the underlying inventions.

2.4.4 Insolvency of the licensor

The insolvency of the licensor is one of the most difficult issues in the field of licensing contract law. In essence, the question is how the fate of the licence and the licence agreement is to be assessed once insolvency proceedings have commenced in relation to the licensor. Depending on the insolvency regime in the country in which the licensor is located, an insolvency administrator generally has the choice of continuing the licence agreement or refusing to fulfil it. Problems can thus arise where the insolvency administrator refuses performance. In principle, it will refuse performance if the costs of performance or the risks to the insolvency assets exceed the income expected from the licence agreement. In this case, the start-up's right to use the IP rights will expire. Claims for damages against the insolvent licensor are largely worthless in most cases.

Those responsible for the start-up should take this point into account when considering whether to purchase or license. If there are justified doubts about the economic power of the licensor, purchase of the IP rights will be the safer option.

Nonetheless, it is advisable to regulate this aspect in the licence agreement. There are no general contractual formulations or principles in this regard. Case law considers the respective contracting parties, the type of licence and the specific contractual construction in the individual case (see Henn/Pahlow 2017: 236). Those responsible for the start-up should at least discuss these issues with an experienced lawyer during the contract negotiations.

2.5 R&D contract

Technology-driven start-ups, especially in the initial phase, must often work with specialized companies or award development contracts to them because they themselves do not yet have the necessary expertise and experience. In practice, this cooperation often takes place through the conclusion of an R&D contract. While 'research' is basic research, 'development' is regularly focused on the production of a technical or application-ready prototype. A clear distinction between research and development activities is not always easy to draw, as they often coincide.

2.5.1 Background IP

In order for the commissioned party (contractor) to provide the agreed development service/research service, it is often necessary for the start-up to provide the relevant background IP. If the background IP contains company secrets, this should be secured by a clear contractual obligation of the contractor to maintain secrecy, such as the following:

> Insofar as the Customer's Background IP is required for the performance of the research and development work, the Customer shall grant the Contractor a simple, non-transferable and non-sublicensable right of use to this background IP during the term and exclusively for the purposes of this Agreement. (Henn/Pahlow 2017: 454)

It is important to describe the start-up's background IP as precisely as possible and attach it to the contract. If the persons responsible for the start-up are aware that the development work commissioned is restricted by third-party rights (FTO), the developer should be informed of this in writing.

2.5.2 Foreground IP

For the start-up, provisions on the protection and exploitation of emerging inventions should be included in the R&D agreement as an IP right. If the contractor is a company, it should always be determined whether there are specific legal provisions on the assignment of invention rights in the country in which it is based. For example, in Germany, this is the Employee Invention Act (ArbnErfG). Further details on the German

ArbnErfG are presented in Chapter 3. The relevant clause could read as follows:

> The Contractor has made valid and sufficient agreements with its employees (including researchers, representatives, consultants and subcontractors) or will take all necessary measures to ensure the transfer of the Foreground IP created by this group of persons to the Contractor. In particular, he will make unlimited use of the inventions – patentable and/or utility modellable – created by his employees. (Henn/Pahlow 2017: 454)

From the perspective of those responsible for the start-up, the central elements of the drafting of an R&D agreement are the provisions under which the start-up, as the customer, is exclusively entitled to all IP rights, copyright and know-how ('foreground IP') created by the contractor in the execution of the R&D work and during the term of this agreement. A contractual clause for the allocation of the IP rights may be formulated as follows:

> The intellectual property Rights and Copyrights as well as the Know-How ('Foreground' IP) created by Contractor in the course of the research and development work and during the term of this Agreement shall be the exclusive property of Customer and are hereby or in accordance with the following provisions transferred in full by Contractor to Customer.
>
> Insofar as the Foreground IP consists of works protected by Copyright, the Contractor hereby assigns to the Customer the exclusive, temporally and spatially unlimited, transferable and sub-licensable right of use. This right of use includes in particular the duplication, distribution, public reproduction and making the Foreground IP publicly accessible in all known types of use, including the right to edit and further develop the Foreground IP and to use the results arising from this to the aforementioned extent.
>
> The contractor and its employees (including researchers, agents, consultants and subcontractors) will take all necessary measures to transfer the Foreground IP created by this group of persons to the Customer. In particular, the Contractor will make unlimited use of the inventions – patentable and/or utility modellable – created by his employees (Henn/Pahlow 2017).

It is recommended that a provision be introduced which allows the start-up as the customer to file the patent applications. This avoids the risk of a later transfer.

It is usual to grant the contractor a simple, non-transferable and non-sub-licensable right to use the foreground IP. However, use of the foreground IP by the contractor in the context of research for any third parties should not be permitted.

2.6 Contracts with freelancers

2.6.1 Initial situation

It is not uncommon for start-ups to engage freelancers for development work, especially in the early stages of the company. A freelancer is a self-employed person who carries out orders for a company under a service or works contract without being a member of the company himself. He is not subject to the generally applicable provisions of labour law. This means that the regulations on the assignment of the work results of employees do not apply to freelancers. In order to gain access to IP rights that may arise from the work of the freelancer, it is thus very important for the start-up to address this in the contract.

The contract should provide that the work results created by the freelancer under the contract – whether they are inventions, copyrightable work results or know-how – are entirely owned by the start-up as the customer, and that the start-up can freely dispose of them.

2.6.2 Important regulatory areas

In order to achieve this objective, it is necessary – as in the case of R&D contracts – to agree precisely when and to what extent the start-up's rights to the work results will arise, and how these rights will be transferred to the start-up.

A contractual clause in a contract with a freelancer could read as follows:

> The Freelancer grants the Customer the spatially, temporally and contentwise unrestricted, exclusive and irrevocable right to all known and unknown types of use of the work results at the time of their creation, as well as the sole and unrestricted right of ownership of those work results to which such a right can be established and transferred. In particular, the Customer is entitled without restriction to reproduce the work results, to process them, to transfer them into other forms of presentation and to change, continue and supplement them in any other way, to distribute them in unchanged and changed form, to reproduce them publicly in wired and wireless form, to grant sub-licences and to transfer, both against payment and free of charge, all rights of use granted within the scope of this contract.

Insofar as the resulting work results can be protected by IP rights, the start-up alone should be entitled to apply for these IP rights. It is recommended that the start-up apply for and register the IP rights directly by the start-up in its own name. If the freelancer applies for the IP right in his own name, there may be uncertainties as to whether the intended transfer to the start-up has actually taken place. The relevant contractual clause could read as follows:

> Insofar as work results are created which can be protected by IP rights, the Freelancer shall immediately notify the Customer in writing. The Customer is free to apply for or have these IP rights registered in his name at home and abroad, to maintain or withdraw them or to proceed with them in any other way. The Freelancer will provide the Customer with comprehensive support in this respect, in particular he will transfer the rights to these work results including the rights to inventions to the Customer. The Freelancer shall provide the Customer with the information required for this purpose and make all necessary declarations and take all necessary measures. The Freelancer is not permitted to make a corresponding entry in his own name or that of a third party or to support third parties directly or indirectly in doing so.

The above example provisions represent an attempt to allocate the rights to the work results to the start-up as far as possible. Given the importance of IP for potential investors and buyers of the start-up, this should also be the contractual objective. Of course, this position cannot always be asserted unequivocally in negotiations with the freelancer. Details and potential compromises (eg, the freelancer retaining a simple, non-transferable right of use to the work results) must be sounded out in the negotiations. Those responsible for start-ups must be aware of the importance of these issues from the very beginning when working with freelancers. An exact definition of the purpose of the contract (service description) and the remuneration, and provisions on the rights to the work results, should be central components of contracts with freelancers.

2.7 Employee inventions

2.7.1 Scope of application

It is possible that inventions which are eligible for protection may be made by employees of the start-up within the framework of the employment relationship. The assignment of these inventions is regulated differently from country to country. The start-up must thus determine under this law whether it is entitled to the rights to the invention or whether the rights must be transferred to it; and what compensation payments (if any) for claiming the invention must be made to the respective employee(s).

As an example, in Germany, the ArbnErfG aims to strike a balance between the interests of the start-up as employer and those of the employee where the latter has made a patentable invention in the course of his work (see also Chapter 3). An employee inventor is entitled to reasonable compensation where the employer claims his employee invention.

The amount of compensation is based on official compensation guidelines for employee inventions.

The ArbnErfG regulates the transfer of an employee's invention to the company. It is thus very important for technology-oriented start-ups to follow the formal procedure regarding employee inventions set out in this Act (see also Chapter 3). This covers matters such as the type of notification procedure within the start-up; the formal and timely claiming of the invention by the start-up; the proper determination and payment of compensation to the inventor; the clear assignment of possible IP right applications; and the avoidance of pitfalls in the abandonment of rights by the start-up. (These aspects are highlighted by Reitzle/Karge/Golkowsky 2020 with regard to Germany and other countries – in particular the US, China and a number of European jurisdictions).

2.7.2 Rights and responsibilities

The essential rights and duties of both the start-up and the employee (inventor) with regard to employee inventions in Germany are set out in Table 6.2.

To secure the rights to an employee invention, it is important that the process set out in Table 6.2 is followed and well documented. For this reason alone, all declarations in connection with the notification and adoption of the invention should be made in writing. It is recommended to include provisions that clarify how employee inventions will be handled in the employment contracts concluded with employees of the start-up. In doing so, the persons responsible for the start-up must bear in mind that the rights and obligations may not be regulated in the employment contract to the detriment of the employee (Section 22 of the ArbnErfG).

Table 6.2 *Rights and duties of a start-up and its employee inventor*

Employee (EY)	Start-up (SU)
EY must report the invention in text form (eg, by email, fax or letter) immediately after completion (Section 5 of the ArbnErfG). In the invention disclosure, EY must describe the technical task, its solution and the making of the service invention. EY must also report free inventions to SU (Section 18 of the ArbnErfG). In doing so, EY must provide enough information to enable SU to assess whether the invention is indeed a free invention. If a free invention falls within the scope of work of EY, EY must offer it to SU for the duration of the employment relationship on reasonable terms (Section 19 of the ArbnErfG). EY retains the inventor personality right. In particular, he has the right to be named as inventor. In return for exploitation by SU, EY is entitled to appropriate remuneration from SU (Section 19 of the ArbnErfG).	SU must immediately confirm the date of receipt of the invention disclosure to EY in text form. A report that does not meet the requirements will be deemed to be in order if SU does not object to it within two months, stating the objection and the respect in which the report requires amendment. From receipt of the proper inventor's notification, SU has four months to decide whether it wishes to claim or release EY's invention. If SU does not wish to claim the invention, SU must declare the release to EY in text form. If SU does not do so within the four-month period, the invention is deemed to have been claimed (Section 6(2) of the ArbnErfG). With the claim to the invention, all rights to the invention are transferred to SU. In particular, SU alone is entitled - and obliged (Section 13 of the ArbnErfG) - to apply for patents. For foreign countries in which SU does not wish to acquire any IP rights, SU must release the invention to EY (Section 14 of the ArbnErfG).

An employment contract could include the following provisions:

> Employee inventions
>
> All results of the official work (including suggestions for operational improvements with all rights resulting from them), which are achieved alone or together with others, must be immediately notified to the employer and – beyond the termination of the employment relationship – be made available for exclusive use without any restrictions in terms of time, subject matter or location.

> This also applies to work results that are not attributable to a specific work order, provided they are related to the business activity. Such a connection is also given if the results can be traced back to official suggestions.

The employee grants the employer the exclusive and unrestricted right of use for all types of exploitation of all copyrightable works created in connection with the official activity or based on official suggestions.

This includes, among other things, the right to reproduce the aforementioned works, to transfer them to image, sound and data carriers, to process, distribute, redesign or translate them and to publish and exploit them in modified form or in the original. The employer is also entitled to transfer this right in whole or in part to others or to grant rights of use to others.

There is no obligation for the employer to name the author when exercising the right of use.

All claims of the employee for the transfer of these rights to the employer are settled with the remuneration. This agreement remains valid even after termination of the employment relationship.

The law on employee inventions applies to inventions.

2.7.3 Service inventions of managing directors/executives

Special features apply to the inventions of managing directors. Managing directors and board members are organs or members of organs of the respective start-up, and are not generally its employees. Therefore, the inventions of managing directors are not usually employee inventions, so – depending on the legal situation in the country where the start-up is based – the applicable legal regime on the assignment of employment inventions will not apply to such inventions. Again depending on the applicable law in the country where the start-up is based, in particular cases the inventions of shareholders may be subject to the rules on the assignment of employee inventions. This should be checked by an expert in this area of law in the respective country. In other cases, such inventions must be treated in the same way as the inventions of managing directors. In order to ensure that the inventions of managing directors, board members and shareholders will become the property of the start-up, the contracts of managing directors, board members and assisting shareholders should contain an express provision stating that the company is entitled to all possible inventions made by such persons and whether additional compensation will be due for them. The relevant provisions could read as follows:

> Inventions
>
> All rights to inventions, irrespective of their patent or utility model protection, to technical and organisational improvement proposals and to computer software made by the Managing Director during the term of this Agreement (hereinafter referred to collectively as 'Inventions') shall be the exclusive property of the Company, without any additional remuneration being paid. The Managing Director shall inform the Company or a person designated by the Company without delay about inventions and, upon request, provide the Company with the best possible support in obtaining patent protection or other IP rights.
>
> All written documents and all copyrightable works prepared by the Managing Director during the term of this Agreement that relate to present or future business activities of the Company or its affiliates shall be the sole property of the Company or any of its affiliates without additional compensation. The Company or its affiliated companies have the worldwide exclusive, unlimited exploitation right. The same applies to essential ideas, formulas, applications, methods, developments, improvements and discoveries relating to the Company or an affiliated company.

Without such contractual provisions, the start-up risks losing access to the invention. They should therefore be included in every contract with such persons.

In summary, effective assignment clauses in the respective contracts are extremely important to ensure that the start-up will own the relevant IP rights. This applies not only where the acquisition or use of IP rights is directly concerned (eg, purchase or licence agreement), but also where IP rights may arise from a contractual cooperation of the start-up with third parties. If assignment clauses have not been included in the relevant contracts (eg, in the case of freelancers), the persons responsible for the start-up should try to conclude subsequent assignment agreements as soon as possible.

3. Investment agreements with investors

In the first round of financing with professional venture capitalists at the latest, the rights chain – that is, the contracts for the transfer of IP rights from the inventor or originator to the start-up – will be examined in the course of the IP due diligence. Existing patent transfer agreements and licence agreements are usually attached to the investment agreements concluded with investors.

3.1 Guarantees of start-up shareholders

Investors usually demand quite extensive guarantees from the founders of the start-up with regard to IP. From the perspective of the founders, caution is required here, as in the event of a breach of guarantee, in addition to the investors bringing damages claims against the start-up, the founders may be held personally liable under the investment agreements, with substantial amounts of compensation being due.

In simplified terms, a distinction is made between an independent, no-fault guarantee for the objective correctness of the guarantees given in the participation agreement on the one hand, and guarantees which the founders give to the best of their knowledge on the other. In the latter case, the subjective knowledge of the start-up's shareholders and managing directors is decisive. In the absence of any provision to the contrary in the participation agreement, the investor bears the burden of proving that the founders were aware of the breach of guarantee.

In contract negotiations, investors try to extend the guarantees as far as possible into the area of objective no-fault guarantees. A typical (and for the start-up shareholders, very bad) clause in a term sheet in the run-up to due diligence and a participation agreement could read:

> As part of the investment, guarantees will be given to the investor after completion of the due diligence process regarding entitlement to all relevant IP and full compliance with all applicable legal requirements.

Such a provision is dangerous, as the founders cannot objectively know whether this guarantee is applicable – at least with regard to the guarantee of full compliance. The founders (and their legal advisers) will need to sound out how much contractual leeway there is. Naturally, their negotiating position will improve if several investors are interested in participating. In such case the clause mentioned in the above example should not be accepted in the term sheet.

In order to enable the investors to conduct IP due diligence, the start-up management must place all documentation relating to the IP rights in the data room in chronological order. In practice, professional investors will send the start-up's management a catalogue of requirements stating the desired information and documents in advance of the IP due diligence. These catalogues of requirements vary in detail from case to case, but the checklist presented in Table 6.1 can be used for general orientation.

In addition to the catalogue of requirements sent by the investors, the start-up management should always check whether further relevant information and documentation on the IP situation are available. All documents deposited in the data room must be presented to the investor as known. Therefore, the rule of thumb is to place as much information about the IP situation as possible in the data room. In this context, it makes sense to have an up-to-date FTO search carried out by a recognized provider, deposit the search report in the data room and attach it to the participation agreement. This ensures that investors are aware of the results of the FTO search. The liability potential for the management and shareholders of the start-up is reduced by these measures.

3.2 Provisions in the participation agreement

As outlined above, investors are anxious to obtain as far-reaching a guarantee on the IP rights as possible from the start-up's shareholders in the participation agreement. The clause on guarantees in the participation agreement could read as follows:

> B is the owner of the assets ... including technical and operational know-how, intellectual property rights (in particular patents, utility models, registered designs, trademarks, etc.) and copyrightable works, such as in particular software (collectively 'IP Rights'), and thus possesses all rights with regard to IP which are necessary for the continuation of its current and planned business operations. The founding shareholders are not the owners of any other IP Rights related to the business operations of B. To the extent an IP Right is not transferable, B ... is entitled to an exclusive, royalty-free, unrestricted and irrevocable right of use for the duration of the IP Right and for all types of use. The IP Rights are free of any contractual or statutory rights of the founding partners or third parties; there are no claims for employee invention compen-

> sation. The IP Rights are not the subject of any pending proceedings to contest, delete, revoke or correct them that could have a negative impact on B's business operations, nor are they infringed by third parties to the best knowledge of the Founding Shareholders, nor do the IP Rights infringe any intellectual property rights of third parties. (Weitnauer 2016: 615)

In the event of breaches of guarantee – that is, if it later turns out that a statement made by the persons responsible for the start-up regarding IP rights was incorrect – the investors in the corresponding financing round can usually demand a legal consequence from the founders or the other shareholders (ie, shareholders who are not founders), insofar as they have assumed the breached guarantee. The usual demand would be to immediately restore the situation to that which would have existed had the guarantee in question applied (so-called '*in rem* restitution'). If *in rem* restitution is not possible or not sufficient, usually damages must be paid instead.

It is thus crucial that the persons responsible for the start-up clearly document its IP situation in the contract and, when issuing guarantees in the investment contract, take special care to issue certain guarantees only to the best of their knowledge.

The investors will be entitled to demand the inclusion of an objective and independent guarantee from the founders or other shareholders in the investment contract where the start-up shareholders know or should know the subject of the guarantee. This applies, for example, to the question of whether the start-up has granted licences to third parties; or whether third parties have asserted or threatened to assert claims against the start-up due to the infringement of IP rights.

However, the situation is different when it comes to the question of whether the start-up has infringed third-party IP rights or know-how through its current business activities. In this case, the founders cannot know for sure whether there are third-party IP rights somewhere in the world which they may have inadvertently infringed. Even careful FTO searches cannot completely rule out this risk. A contractual guarantee in this respect should therefore always be given only to the best of one's knowledge.

In addition to the careful differentiation of contractual guarantees, it is important for the founders or shareholders to limit the legal consequences of breach of guarantee in the investment contract to maximum amounts. The absolute limit of contractual liability should not exceed 100 per cent of the investors' investment in the respective financing round. It is common practice to limit the liability amount to a certain percentage of the investors' investment (eg, 20 per cent), as long as the guarantors do not act intentionally or with gross negligence on the part of the start-up.

Furthermore, a contractual limitation of the founders' personal liability for breach of guarantee to absolute maximum amounts (cap) is highly recommended. Otherwise, in the worst-case scenario, the guarantor may even face insolvency. Depending on the amount of the investors' investment, the maximum liability should not exceed €100,000 per person.

Again, whether and to what extent limitations of liability can be included in the investment agreement will depend on the negotiating skills of the founders and the investors' interest in participating in the start-up. However, it is always worthwhile to negotiate hard for the guarantee restrictions and not to be too hasty or too extensive in meeting investors' demands with regard to contractual guarantees and their legal consequences.

4. Sale of the company (exit)

An important exit channel for venture capital-financed start-ups is the sale of the company. If an initial public offering is out of the question (in Europe, as compared to the US, this route has been reserved for relatively few start-ups in recent years), a trade sale is often the only way for investors to withdraw their investment from the start-up within a manageable timeframe (three to five years is the average investment horizon for professional investors). Therefore, a so-called 'drag-along' clause is regularly included in investment contracts. This clause obliges all shareholders of the start-up (including the founders) to sell their shares if a certain number of shareholders (eg, who alone or together hold more than 50 per cent of the shares in the start-up), as defined in the investment agreement, advocate a sale.

4.1 IP due diligence of the buyer

In the run-up to a company purchase agreement, the potential buyer will thoroughly examine the IP situation of the start-up in the course of the due diligence, just like the investors in the previous financing rounds.

The checklist for examining the IP rights to a company acquisition is similar in many respects to that presented in Table 6.1 in the context of a patent purchase. It is set out in Table 6.3.

Table 6.3 Checklist for the examination of IP rights in the case of company acquisitions

Nature of the property right	Audit points and information
- Patent - Utility model - Know-how	- Owner of rights - Registration or application number - Status (application/registration) - Priority - Term of protection, remaining term - Country of protection - Property right management - Licences - Property right history - Legal disputes or imminent legal disputes - Third-party security interests

Due diligence documents the IP situation of the start-up. In order to minimize the liability risks for the start-up or the shareholders for possible breach of guarantees included in the company purchase agreement, all documents relating to the IP rights should be clearly and completely deposited in the data room for the potential buyer. In the case of a company purchase, the buyer in principle must accept all information stored in the data room as known. All information which the buyer or its advisers knew or could have known as a result of the IP due diligence or otherwise is deemed to be known to the buyer. This includes in particular all information resulting from the documents deposited in the data room. It is therefore also recommended that an up-to-date FTO search report be deposited in the data room.

It should be made clear in the company purchase agreement that the buyer has thoroughly examined all IP documentation as part of the due diligence; and that the buyers and its advisers have been given the opportunity to inspect all existing documents relating to the IP rights in a data room set up by the seller specifically for this purpose.

4.2 Warranty provisions in the company purchase agreement

Agreements on liability for defects are an essential component of a company purchase agreement with regard to IP rights, whether the purchase is a share deal (ie, the purchase of the start-up's shares) or an asset deal (ie, the purchase and transfer of the start-up's assets and rights). In almost every company purchase agreement, the guarantees and warranties are negotiated individually between the contracting parties. In the negotiations, the buyer will regularly demand the inclusion of a so-called 'no-fault' guarantee promise from the seller in the company purchase agreement. In the case of an independent guarantee promise, the rights of the buyer arise directly from the agreed guarantee itself. The parties are largely free to agree on the prerequisites and legal consequences of the guarantee. This is to be distinguished from guarantees which are given only to the best of the seller's knowledge. In the case of guarantees which have been given to the best of the seller's knowledge, the buyer must prove that the seller or the shareholders had or could have had knowledge, unless otherwise stipulated in the contract.

Based on the results of the IP due diligence, the buyer will negotiate the guarantees for the purchase agreement. A typical regulation on guarantees in company purchase agreements could read as follows:

> The Seller guarantees to the Buyer in the form of an independent and no-fault guarantee promise at the time of the notarisation of this contract as well as at the time of the transfer in rem of the shares in the company (unless otherwise regulated below) that the following information is correct and complete:
>
> Intellectual Property Rights
>
> The Company is the unrestricted owner of the patents, utility models and designs, trademarks, business names, trade names and domain names and addresses (hereinafter collectively referred to as 'Intellectual Property Rights') listed in the ANNEX attached to this document and is the unrestricted licensee of the licenses to such Intellectual Property Rights listed in the ANNEX attached to this document. The licenses are not terminated. The fees due

> for the acquisition and maintenance of the Intellectual Property Rights and licences are paid in full. Third parties are not entitled to any licence or other rights to the Intellectual Property Rights or contractual know-how.
>
> To the best of its knowledge, the Company does not infringe any Intellectual Property Rights or rights to a name of third parties with its current business activities at the time of notarisation of this contract. No claims for injunctive relief or damages have been asserted or threatened against the Company in this respect.

As for guarantees issued in the context of the financing rounds, care must be taken to issue guarantees for the non-infringement of third-party IP rights only to the best of one's knowledge. Despite conscientious FTO research, the people responsible for start-ups cannot be 100 per cent certain that no third-party rights have been infringed.

In addition to these standard guarantees, further guarantees on IP rights may be required from the buyers, the details of which will depend on the individual case. These must be carefully drafted together with an experienced M&A lawyer.

Should it later transpire that one or more guarantees are not applicable in whole or in part, the buyer can demand that the start-up restore the situation to that which would have existed had the guarantee in question not been breached within a timeframe specified in the contract (*in rem* restitution). If this is not possible in whole or in part, the buyer will be entitled to compensation.

As for participation agreements, it is common practice to limit the seller's liability in terms of amount to a percentage of the purchase price if the seller has not acted intentionally or with gross negligence.

Finally, an exclusion of liability should be agreed for guarantees in the company purchase agreement whose incorrectness was or should have been known to the buyer (eg, from the documents deposited in the data room). A typical clause could read as follows:

> The liability of the seller is excluded if the buyer is aware of the incorrectness of the declarations made at the time of signing this sales contract. The buyer has thoroughly examined the legal and economic circumstances of the seller prior to signing this purchase contract within the scope of a so-called due diligence. The buyer and the advisers and persons engaged by him had the opportunity to inspect documents in a data room set up by the seller especially for this

> purpose. Therefore, all information and circumstances which the buyer or the advisers or persons engaged by the buyer knew or could have known as a result of the due diligence or otherwise are deemed to be known to the buyer. In this respect, in particular all information resulting from the documents in the data room shall be deemed to be known. (Beck'sche Online-Formulare Vertrag, 20.3 share deal, § 6 paragraph (5))

The areas of regulation in the context of the sale of a start-up form the conclusion of the contractual case constellations with regard to IP rights in the lifecycle of a start-up presented in this chapter. The isolated sale of IP rights by the start-up and the licensing of its own IP rights to third parties have not been addressed in this chapter. However, the review process and the contractual provisions in the case of an isolated sale of IP rights will not differ significantly from those in the case of a company acquisition. In the case of licensing by the start-up to third parties, the contractual areas should be carefully defined. In particular, the start-up should be very cautious when granting exclusive licences; and should contractually link possible exclusivity to clearly defined conditions which, if not fulfilled, will result in the loss of exclusivity.

7 Protecting future business with a value-driven IP strategy

Rudolf Freytag

1. Introduction

New business and innovative growth are high on the agenda for many companies. Technical developments, especially digitization, are releasing creative impulses and opening up new opportunities. But they also present risks for existing businesses.

Many companies proudly refer to the number of invention disclosures made and the number of IP rights they hold as a measure of their innovative strength. This is why they invest a lot of money and manpower in filing patents for as many inventions as possible, originating from their R&D departments.

For a company, however, the value of an IP rights portfolio becomes apparent only when it is necessary to actually use those IP rights against a competitor in order to prevent that competitor from impairing its own appearance on a market. Such cases are often a cause for disillusionment, because the supposedly robust IP portfolio proves to be unhelpful or difficult to enforce in practice.

For companies, it is therefore not a question of having as many IP rights as possible, but rather having exactly the right ones. The criterion for this is that these IP rights should optimally protect the company's existing and future business.

The more uncertain the business development is, the more difficult – but also the more important – it is to build up an IP portfolio to protect future business. New technical developments, changes in customer requirements and the market entry of new competitors are just a few examples of factors that are difficult to predict and can have a significant impact on the business development of a company.

However, the effective protection of future business in this sense is possible through IP rights. The author is convinced of this because of his decades of experience, from the perspectives of both established companies and start-ups.

The solution is a systematically pursued value-driven IP strategy (Freytag/Weibel 2019). In this chapter, we will look at what a 'value-driven IP strategy' means in theory and practice; how it can be implemented; and which aspects demand particular attention.

For start-ups, the question of effective protection of the future business has special significance. On the one hand, a start-up is usually just beginning in its search for a suitable business model and may have to make abrupt changes in its business approach at this stage. On the other hand, the start-up must prove to its investors from the very outset that the future business is well protected by IP rights, because such protection is a key factor for investment decisions.

Although start-ups are the focus of this book, all of the following statements can easily be applied to established companies. This is unsurprising, since the protection of future business is a fundamental issue that does not depend on the size of a company. But for newcomers to the market, this insight is important because it means that the basic approach of a value-driven IP strategy needs not be abandoned once the start-up grows into a larger enterprise.

In this chapter, we will deal in detail with the IP strategy and its implementation. We will focus on the strategic and entrepreneurial dimensions of the IP strategy, and examine it both from a theoretical point of view and using a practical example. These strategic-entrepreneurial dimensions then provide guidelines for the development of the legal dimension of the IP strategy, which determines how to develop, apply for, maintain and defend IP rights in different jurisdictions. For further discussion of these legal aspects, please refer to the other chapters of this book – in particular, Chapter 1. The term 'IP' in this chapter is synonymous with 'protective rights' – more precisely, with any form of protective rights. This means not only patents, but also utility models, designs, trademarks and copyrights (see especially Chapter 1, section 2).

In order to explain the general considerations and concepts in this chapter in a clear and practical way from the perspective of a start-up, we will present a case study of an e-scooter start-up. The example is fictitious and has been chosen in such a way that it comes as close as possible to the economic reality in the 'real life' of a start-up.

2. E-scooter case study

'E-scooters' are pedal scooters driven by a battery-powered electric motor. Conventional scooters – which are driven purely mechanically, by pushing with one leg – have been around for centuries. Recently, they have become increasingly popular for children and young people on their way to school or to the subway stop, because they are easily manoeuvrable and can easily be folded up and carried.

Equipping conventional scooters with electric motors has made them an increasingly attractive option for adults to travel short distances. In combination with public transport and car-sharing services, electric scooters could help to keep people in cities mobile from their front door to their destination and back in a seamless, environmentally friendly way. They bridge the 'last mile' between the front door or destination and other means of transport.

These types of scooters are assigned to the 'micro-mobility' market. Other micro-mobility solutions include personal bicycles, rental bicycles, personal cars in combination with park and ride services, taxis, minibus lines, walking and much more. The dynamics in this market are great and the competition will reveal which approaches will be most successful. E-scooters will certainly play an important role here, as reflected by their current rapid spread in large cities.

However, the worldwide boom in e-scooters has also quickly revealed their problems. E-scooters have a limited range, because only relatively small batteries can be installed, as there is little space under the running board. In addition, e-scooters often have unacceptably long braking distances because the small wheels make it difficult to install powerful braking systems.

The founders of our fictitious e-scooter start-up have addressed these disadvantages. As part of their master's thesis at university, they developed a highly innovative electric wheel hub motor that can be installed directly in the rear wheel of the scooter to save space. This drive concept differs significantly from the drive with a classic electric motor, which requires a chain and a gearbox to transmit power from the motor to the rear wheel. Both are maintenance-intensive components that also require installation space.

A wheel hub motor has two modes of operation: it acts either as an energy-efficient drive, which affords greater range than a classic electric motor with the same battery capacity; or as a powerful braking system, which additionally converts braking energy back into the battery, thus further increasing the range of a battery charge.

The founders of our e-scooter start-up recognized that with their wheel hub motor, they have addressed the two main problems of electric pedal scooters: the range and the braking system. They hope to revolutionize the market for e-scooters with their invention. They envisage three different business models for their future start-up, which differ significantly in terms of their range of products, customer benefits and competitive situations:

- Business Model 1 – e-scooter sales: One option for the start-up is to develop, manufacture and sell e-scooters. In order for the innovative wheel hub motor to become the decisive purchasing criterion for customers in the market for an electric scooter, potential buyers would have to perceive the advantages of the wheel hub motor in terms of range and braking system as customer value of particular importance, and evaluate these advantages as superior to the range and braking systems of electric scooters from other suppliers with alternative drive concepts. Competitors to our e-scooter start-up include not only other suppliers of e-scooters, but also all other micro-mobility solutions (eg, bicycles, taxis, park and ride services and walking).
- Business Model 2 – e-scooter sharing: As an alternative, the start-up could offer scooters for spontaneous rental in city centres. The

customer value of this micro-mobility service with e-scooters is completely different from that in Business Model 1: customers are mainly interested in whether rentals and payments via smartphone work; whether sufficient numbers of functional scooters are available throughout their cities; and whether the scooters' batteries are charged. The two advantages in the case of purchase – the powerful braking system and long range – are less important in this business model. Competitors in this market – and thus competitors of our example start-up – are mainly providers of rental bicycles.

- Business Model 3 – e-scooter wheel hub motor supply: The start-up could concentrate on the core competence of wheel hub motor development, develop such motors and sell them to different manufacturers of e-scooters. This customer group sees the value in factors such as size, weight, energy efficiency, braking power and price. The competitors of our start-up are suppliers of classic drives with electric motors and gears in this market.

Once the founders of the e-scooter start-up have clarified, through systematic business strategy development, which business model they wish to adopt, they can derive a tailor-made IP strategy for the effective protection of this future business based on these considerations. We will accompany our example start-up on this exciting journey in the following sections.

3. What is a value-driven IP strategy?

Every function of a company – be it research, development, marketing, production or even IP – has a contribution to make to the current and future business success of the company as a whole.

For this to succeed, all of those responsible in the company must have the same understanding of what exactly is meant by a 'value-driven IP strategy' and how to proceed in a targeted manner. We will examine these questions below.

Figure 7.1 shows how a value-driven business strategy is structured and what contribution the value-driven IP strategy makes to it. The illustration creates a logical basic structure for this chapter and serves as an orientation framework for further considerations.

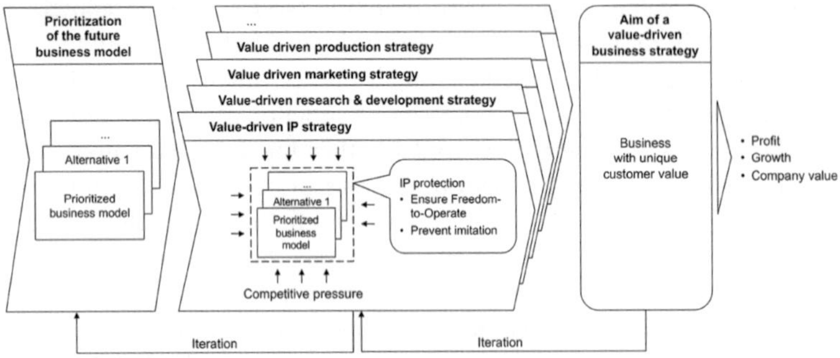

Figure 7.1 *A value-driven business strategy and the contribution of the value-driven IP strategy to this*

3.1 Business with unique customer value as a goal

Customers do not buy a product or service – customers buy a customer value. In return, they bring a certain willingness to pay. The extent of this willingness to pay depends on how great the value of the product or service is in their perception, and how high they estimate this value in comparison to that of competitive offers. From the point of view of companies, this means that they compete with each other for customer value.

The task of a company is therefore to win and retain satisfied customers with a unique customer value that stands out from the competition. As shown in Figure 7.1, this customer value then leads to financial variables such as profit, company growth and increasing company value. A customer value which is unique from those of competitors has numerous advantages for a company. The company can achieve premium prices, will therefore be particularly profitable and can grow rapidly in its market segment. This leads to a particularly high inflow of capital into the company, resulting on the one hand from operating revenues and on the other hand from the fact that financial investors find the company attractive and invest capital in it. This capital is then available for further growth, with the overall result that the company's value increases faster than that of its competitors.

Customer value is therefore the decisive goal for a business strategy (Christensen/Raynor 2003; Dodgson et al 2014; Gassmann/Bader 2011; Narayanan et al 2009; Weibel 2013; Wurzer et al 2016). This is referred to as a 'value-driven business strategy'. Correspondingly, an IP strategy that makes an optimal contribution to this is called a 'value-driven IP strategy'.

In this context, one point is very important: a business strategy must be oriented towards customer value. If this is planned and implemented correctly, the abovementioned financial parameters – such as profit, growth and company value – will generally move in the right direction. While it is also true that mistakes can still be made in strategy and operational implementation when it comes to orientation towards customer value, those mistakes are not as serious as when a company is oriented exclusively towards share price and all measures are aimed at driving the share price upwards. Many companies that are committed to maximizing shareholder value eventually disappear from the market because customers migrate elsewhere; this shows what can happen if a company focuses on financial indicators as the primary management parameters. For this reason, the financial figures themselves are not a direct target of the strategy, but are rather important criteria to measure the operational effectiveness and efficiency of the implementation of the business strategy, which should focus on customer value.

For a company to achieve financial success, it is crucial that customer value leads to the highest possible willingness to pay. Three conditions must be met in this regard. Based on our e-scooter start-up, we will show how these can be fulfilled.

First, there must be a customer value. Whether a customer group attributes a particular value to an offer depends strongly on the needs of that customer group. As shown, the 'long range' and 'powerful braking system' criteria are far more relevant for customers who may want to buy an e-scooter than for customers who only want to rent an e-scooter for a short time and will thus pay more attention to the ease of the rental process and the widespread availability of e-scooters.

Second, the customer value must be perceived. A customer value will lead to willingness to pay only if the customer perceives it as such. In many cases, this is unproblematic – for example, in the case of visually recognizable features. However, invisible properties of products must first be made perceptible. In the e-scooter example, in the 'sales' scenario, it must be immediately apparent to customers that the braking system in the wheel hub motor is particularly powerful. However, this motor is not visually noticeable and could hardly be distinguished from a normal electric drive by a layperson. That is why our start-up founders must think about how they can make the customer value associated with the wheel hub motor so visible that it catches the eye of the potential customer. For example, they might be inspired by sports car manufacturers, whose high-performance brakes shimmer through the spokes in colourful, eye-catching designs. Actively shaping the perception of customer value is thus just as important as providing the customer value itself.

Third, the customer value must be higher than that of other offers. The customer value is not an absolute, but a relative quantity, and is oriented towards the perceived value of comparable competitive offers. The perceived difference determines the purchase decision and in particular, customers' willingness to pay. As offers with very similar customer value ultimately lead to price competition, the goal of the business strategy must be to create a customer value that is so unique, and that the company can defend so well, that the customer is prepared to pay a significant price premium compared to competing products. In the e-scooter example, our founders must therefore consider how they can create such a unique and defensible customer value based on their invention of the wheel hub motor. To this end, they must look at alternative drive and braking concepts that already exist on the market or are under development and that offer similar or even greater customer benefits; and in view of these competitive products, they must highlight the value of their own product even more prominently and defend it against the competition. The problem for our e-scooter start-up is that business ideas based on the use of a specific technology are often difficult to defend, because there is always the danger that superior new technologies will emerge. How to deal with this problem in the course of an IP strategy will be discussed later.

3.2 Prioritization of the future business model

Let's return to Figure 7.1, which presents an overview of the path towards a business with unique customer value:

- First phase: Priority is given to the future business model to be pursued and the available alternatives.
- Second phase: This prioritization is then translated into function-specific strategies in the individual functions within the company, such as the research, development, marketing, production, finance and IP function.

- Iteration: When new insights are obtained, the prioritized business model and the individual strategies of the functions may have to be adapted. To be on the safe side, the prioritization of the business model should be reviewed at least once a year – for example, in the context of budget planning.

We will first turn to the first phase: the prioritization of the future business model.

A business model describes which customer value an organization generates for which customers (customer perspective) and how this customer value is provided by the organization (operational perspective). A business model thus answers the following questions:

- Customer perspective: Who pays for what; why; how much; and in what way?
- Operational perspective: How and at what cost does the organization generate this 'what'?

When prioritizing the future business model, it is necessary to examine within the company which hypotheses there are regarding influencing factors such as customers, markets, technologies and competitors. These hypotheses must then be carefully tested through market studies, customer and expert interviews, product prototypes, pilot sales and similar activities. Based on these hypotheses, the company can finally decide, as shown in Figure 7.1, which future business model to pursue and which business models could be interesting alternatives.

However, this step does not happen in the same way for all companies. There are sometimes significant differences between established companies on the one hand and start-ups on the other.

Established companies have the advantage that they have already been running a successful business for a long time and therefore have a proven business model. They can thus consider the factors that may influence this business model and how they can take advantage of opportunities for further development and avoid risks. Based on these findings, they can then develop the prioritized future business model and its possible alternatives.

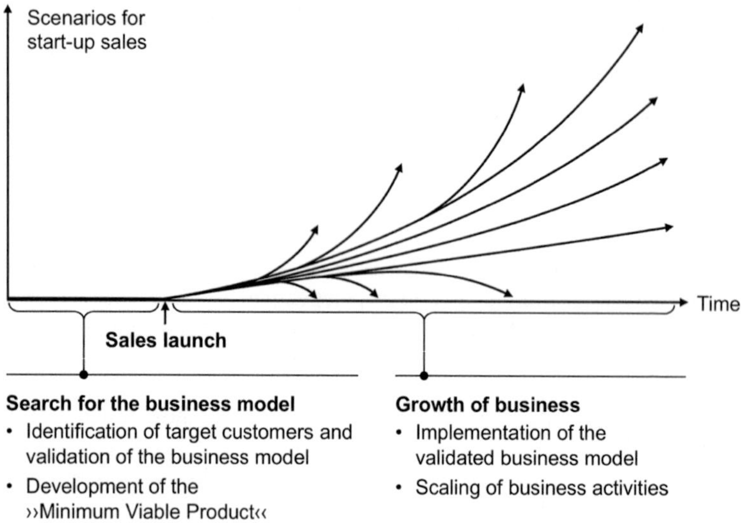

Figure 7.2 Development of start-ups (schematic)

The starting position is more difficult for start-ups because they naturally have no business to begin with and therefore have no proven business model. They go through two main phases in their development, as shown schematically in Figure 7.2:

- Searching for the business model: In this phase, the start-up works on concretizing the business idea in fast and iterative 'build-measure-learn' cycles. The start-up identifies the right customers and their needs, and validates the business idea hypotheses with prototypes in order to arrive at the first marketable 'minimum viable product' as quickly as possible. This can result in significant changes to the original business idea, up to and including a complete rejection and reorientation. Such a drastic 'swing' in the business model is called a 'pivot'.
- Business growth: This phase begins with the sales launch. The start-up now implements the previously validated business model and aims to scale up the business volume as quickly as possible.

The iteration loops for the incorporation of new knowledge, shown in the lower part of Figure 7.1, are important for all types of companies; but they are particularly important for start-ups, because their business is only just developing. In the start-up world, the iteration loops in Figure 7.1 are therefore called 'build-measure-learn' cycles.

Both established companies and start-ups must take account of the following fundamental factors when considering future business models:

- Technical, regulatory and socio-economic trends: One fundamental technical trend that is currently affecting all companies in terms of the opportunities and risks involved is digitization. However, changing regulatory requirements can also change an industry dramatically, as the discussion about pollutant levels in diesel vehicles shows. Socio-economic trends also should not be underestimated, such as the sharp decline in young people's interest in car ownership.
- Market and industry forces: Companies often have a good view of direct competitors in their market segment, but overlook new competitors which have adopted a completely different approach to deliver better customer value. This is what happened to the manufacturers of analogue cameras, for example, which long underestimated the new digital camera suppliers. Questions regarding the basic profitability of certain market segments are also important: in many markets, such as the supplier business for the automotive industry, the price pressure is so high that margins in the double-digit percentage range are hardly possible; whereas double-digit margins for medical products are considered normal.
- Macroeconomic forces: Global conditions in sales markets and capital markets can also have a strong impact on a company's business model. Protectionist tendencies and associated customs duties and other obstacles can quickly turn an attractive sales and manufacturing country into an unattractive region.

All functions in the company – whether strategy, innovation management, research, development, marketing, production, finance or IP – are involved in the development and prioritization of the business models. In established companies, these functions are usually performed by departments; whereas in start-ups – especially in the initial phase – they are performed by the founders. Irrespective of this, it is also important for start-ups to consider the business model from the perspective of all these functions.

3.3 The IP strategy as part of a value-driven business strategy

The result of the first phase – prioritization the future business model – in Figure 7.1 is that all functions of the company have a common and coordinated understanding of what the company's future business model and its possible alternatives will look like.

Based on this, value-driven and function-specific strategies can now be developed in the second phase. The common understanding of the starting position and the end goal established in the first phase is an indispensable prerequisite to ensure that these function-specific strategies are coordinated with each other and geared towards the same goal – namely, the creation of unique customer value through implementing the prioritized business model or its alternatives. Thus, the function-specific strategies should optimally support the overall approach of the value-driven business strategy and should thus themselves be optimally value driven.

So, in phase 2 of Figure 7.1, the R&D department develops a value-driven strategy for technology and product development; the marketing department develops a value-driven strategy for product launch and sales; and the production department develops a value-driven strategy for the provision of production capacity and manufacturing technologies. In parallel, the IP function develops a value-driven IP strategy, which we are now moving towards.

The goal of a value-driven IP strategy is to protect the future business model and its alternatives through IP as effectively as possible and thus contribute to creating a business with unique customer value. Two different tasks must be fulfilled, which are shown in Figure 7.3:

- Ensure freedom to operate (FTO): The goal here is to ensure that the company's implementation of the prioritized future business model does not infringe any third-party IP rights. These activities are a prerequisite to be able to operate the future business.
- Prevent imitation: This is about legally ensuring that the company's own business offers a unique customer value in the market (see Figure 7.1). By establishing IP rights, the company can prevent others from imitating its own offering and thus appearing as competitors in the market.

As Figure 7.3 shows, 'Prevent imitation' has a retroactive effect on 'Ensure FTO', as IP protection for a company's implementation of its business model may also support its own future FTO.

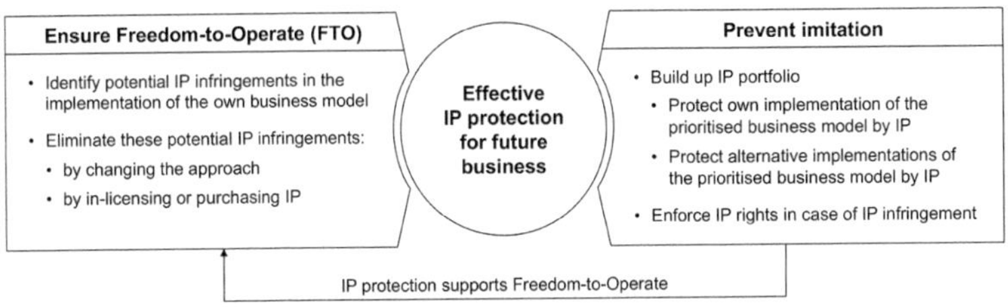

Figure 7.3 A value-driven IP strategy

In order to ensure your own FTO, you must check for all relevant countries whether the implementation of your future business model or one of its alternatives infringes any third-party rights (eg, patents, utility models, designs, trademarks or copyrights).

Overall, this is a costly but necessary undertaking. If your implementation is not free of third-party rights, remedial action must be taken at an early stage. Two basic responses to this are possible, as shown in Figure 7.3:

- Changing the approach: In this case, you try to avoid the IP violation by choosing a different approach. Let's return to our e-scooter start-up: if it recognizes that a design detail of its wheel hub motor is protected by a patent of a potential competitor, it can try to avoid this IP infringement by redesigning it. Similarly, it will have to choose a new company or product name if its intended name is already protected by a third-party trademark that also covers the application for e-scooters. The start-up will also have to respond in a similar way to an already assigned Internet domain name.
- In-licensing or purchasing IP rights: An alternative to changing your approach is to in-license or purchase IP rights from the owner of the IP rights that would be infringed through implementation of your business model. Often, a licence limited to your own field of use is sufficient. For example, if our e-scooter start-up discovers that the patent holder for the design detail of its wheel hub motor is only active in the business field of large engines for the construction industry, it

could try to obtain an exclusive licence for the patent which is limited to use in the micro-mobility market. In the case of technologies which are standardized worldwide, such as telecommunications technologies, the patent holders of these technologies are obliged to grant a licence on terms which are 'fair, reasonable and non-discriminatory (FRAND)'.

The nature of IP rights as prohibitive rights is what enables them to be used to prevent imitation. As Figure 7.3 shows, the goal is to build up a suitable IP portfolio for this purpose. This can be done either by generating your own IP rights or by in-licensing or purchasing third-party IP rights. In doing so, one must also consider what protection is needed in which countries. To ensure that the IP portfolio created in this way can also be legally enforced to prevent imitation, it must have the following characteristics:

- IP protection for own implementation: Your own planned implementation of the prioritized future business model and its alternatives will be protected by all kinds of IP rights, such as patents, utility models, designs, trademarks and copyrights. The aim is to prevent potential competitors from directly copying your customer offerings. Our e-scooter start-up must, within the scope of IP protection for its own implementation, protect not only the basic technology of the wheel hub motor, but also – by means of a design protection right – the coloured design elements that shimmer through the spokes and thus draw the customer's attention to the wheel hub motor and its customer value.
- IP protection for alternative implementations: In addition to preventing competitors from direct copying of your own customer offer, you will also wish to prevent them from circumventing it or finding alternatives to make the same or a confusingly similar customer offer. It is therefore necessary to think about what ideas competitors might come up with in this context and to protect these implementations yourself through IP rights of all kinds. The point here is not to implement these implementations in your own customer offer, but rather to prevent others from doing so. So our e-scooter start-up should, for example, come up with other motor and brake concepts that have a similar value to the wheel hub motor and patent them to keep potential future competitors away.

A value-driven IP strategy is a unique strategic competitive tool. It is similar to other value-driven functional strategies, in that it contributes to the creation of unique customer value; but it differs significantly from the other functional strategies in the following aspects:

- IP rights are prohibitive rights: The owner of an IP right can prohibit a third party from doing something. In this respect, IP differs significantly from all other functions in the company, which can only aim to create products or services which are better than those of competitors, but cannot directly influence competitors in any way.
- IP rights have an effect on the future: Depending on the country and the applicable law, the prohibitive effects of an IP right often extend well over ten years into the future. The activities of all other functions in the company have no such binding future effect, but depend on market and competitive conditions.
- IP rights are priority rights: Whether someone is granted an IP right depends not only on questions of content, but also on the date of application, as generally only the first applicant will be granted an IP right. Therefore, in IP activities, it is not only important to apply for an IP right, but also to be fast in doing so. This is particularly important in business crisis situations: IP filing activities that have been reduced for cost reasons cannot usually be compensated for by increased filing rates later on. In all other business functions, such as R&D, however, this is largely possible.

4. The value-driven IP strategy in practice

The subject of the discussion thus far has been the concept of a value-driven IP strategy. We have seen how a value-driven IP strategy interacts with the strategic activities of all other functions in the company; and how conceptually a value-driven IP strategy can be used to build up effective IP protection for future business, thus enabling the IP strategy to be used in a targeted manner as a unique strategic competitive instrument. Now we turn to business practice and look at how to conduct the discussion on the future business model in a structured manner and derive IP protection step by step.

4.1 Description of a business model with the 'business model canvas'

As a result of the prioritization of the future business model and its alternatives according to Figure 7.1, the employees in all functions should have the same vision of the company's future.

In practice, the methodology of the 'business model canvas' (Blank/Dorf 2012; Osterwalder/Pigneur 2019; Ries 2011) has proven to be very effective when it comes to conducting efficient and structured discussions about the future business model in companies. Originally, the business model canvas was used primarily in the start-up world, but it has now become very popular with established companies too.

We will look at the business model canvas using the example of our e-scooter start-up. Of the three possible business models previously outlined, the start-up team has decided not to pursue the 'e-scooter sharing' model for the time being, because the initial investment that would be required for sufficient distribution of the scooters in cities seems too big. The 'e-scooter wheel hub motor supply' business model is also being put on hold, because the margin potential in this business is perceived as too low. The 'e-scooter sales' model, on the other hand, appears to be interesting after initial talks with potential customers. For this reason, the e-scooter team has drawn up an initial draft of the business model canvas, which is shown in Figure 7.4.

The business model canvas describes a specific business model that is characterized by a certain unique customer value which it is intended to

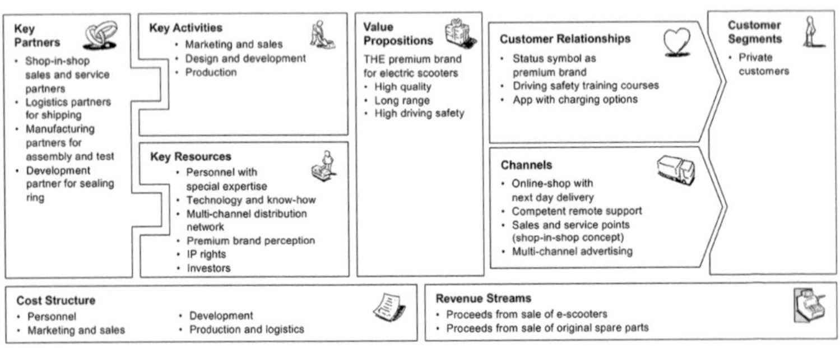

Figure 7.4 Draft 'business model canvas' for the e-scooter sales business model

be delivered ('customer perspective'), and by the way the organization wants to deliver that customer value ('operational perspective'). If you want to analyse different business models, you will need to create a separate business model canvas for each business model.

At the outset, we characterized a business model by answering the following questions:

- Customer perspective: Who pays for what; why; how much; and in what way?
- Operational perspective: How and at what cost does the organization generate this 'what'?

The business model canvas answers precisely these questions (see Figure 7.4). The customer perspective is represented on the right-hand side by the fields 'Customer segments' ('Who?'); 'Value propositions' ('What?' and 'Why?'); 'Revenue streams' ('How much?'); and 'Customer relationships' as well as 'Channels' (together, 'In what way?'). The operational perspective is found on the left-hand side, in the fields 'Key activities', 'Key resources' and 'Key partners' (together, 'How?'); and 'Cost structure' ('At what cost').

The term 'canvas' comes from the fact that in practice, this basic scheme is often hung on the wall as a large print-out and the contents of the business model are worked out in workshops and entered in the individual fields. The associated visualization of the business model contributes greatly to developing a common understanding among the discussion participants. For this reason, the business model canvas is also very well suited for prioritizing the future business model and its alternatives according to Figure 7.1 in cross-functional strategy workshops.

A value-driven IP strategy must protect all nine fields of the business model canvas. In addition, it must take into account aspects that are of an overarching nature. A deep understanding of these nine fields is therefore essential for the development of a value-driven IP strategy. The following short description can only serve as an introduction; for further details, please refer to the rich literature already cited.

4.1.1 Value propositions

As previously explained, the primary objective of a company is to offer its customers products or services that are of greater customer value to them than comparable offers from competitors. This is intended to trigger a purchase decision on the part of the customers, combined with a corresponding willingness to pay. For this reason, it is best to start working on the business model canvas by filling in the two fields of 'Value propositions' and 'Customer segments', which are strongly interdependent. Very different aspects can contribute to the special customer value – for example, special product performance; special possibilities for customer-specific adaptation of the product; a special design; or special possibilities for cost savings. With regard to the latter, for example, with software-as-a-service solutions, customers avoid buying, installing and operating software on their own computers and pay only a monthly user fee instead.

According to Figure 7.4, our e-scooter start-up has set itself the goal of becoming THE premium brand for electric scooters. From the customer's perspective, this will be apparent not only from the high quality of the materials and the workmanship of the e-scooters, but also from two aspects in particular: the long range of battery charge and the high level of driving safety thanks to the scooter's powerful braking system. The start-up's founders are convinced that the wheel hub motor they have invented will give them a big advantage over the competition in terms of range and braking power.

4.1.2 Customer segments

The 'Customer segments' that match the 'Value propositions' can also have very different characteristics. For example, the offering could be aimed at mass markets, niche markets or highly diversified markets. There are also business models that simultaneously address very different customer groups; these are known as 'multi-sided'. These include, for example, the business models of credit card companies. A credit card company needs a large number of credit card users; but at the same time, it also needs a large number of shops where the use of this credit card is possible. Many Internet platforms, such as Amazon and Airbnb, also work in this way.

According to Figure 7.4, the e-scooter start-up in our example is initially targeted at the customer segment of private customers who, as far as micro-mobility is concerned, want to cover short distances comfortably, quickly and safely, whether professionally or privately. The start-up could then relatively easily expand its business activities later on to include the sale of e-scooters to electric scooter rental companies.

4.1.3 *Channels*

The customer value must reach the customer segments in an appropriate manner. The field 'Channels' describes how a company makes customers aware of its own offer; how customers evaluate the offer in comparison to competing offers; how the purchase process and the delivery of the product or service work; and how customer care looks after the purchase process. All of these activities can be performed in many different ways – for example, indirectly via the Internet or directly through retail stores or sales representatives. You also need to decide whether these activities should be performed by your own organization or by partners, or a combination of both.

According to Figure 7.4, our e-scooter start-up uses various channels to reach private customers. There is an online shop where experienced customers can order an e-scooter and have it delivered to their home by parcel. In addition, competent remote support is available for any queries. Customers who would first like to obtain information in person or to test drive an e-scooter can be reached through sales and service points. In order to establish a high-quality brand image, a 'shop-in-shop' concept with a corresponding corporate design will be pursued, with excellent sales and service partners – for example, leading sports or two-wheeler shops. Advertising will be carried out through multi-channel advertising via social media, print media and event marketing.

4.1.4 *Customer relationships*

Every company wants satisfied and permanent customers. To achieve this, a company must clarify what relationships it wants to build with its customers and how these relationships can be maintained cost effectively. Different approaches are possible depending on the business model. Some business models depend heavily on personal advice from a sales or service employee. In others, customers prefer self-service via the Internet or at vending machines. In others still, companies use customer loyalty programmes to make customers feel that they belong to a group that enjoys special advantages. Obviously, the design of customer relationships is also closely related to the design of channels.

The e-scooter start-up wants to become THE premium brand for electric scooters. In order to achieve this goal, it must devote particular attention to customer relationships. This includes positioning the brand as a status symbol for modern people with high-quality requirements and high willingness to pay. Special customer events such as free driving safety training courses can strengthen customer loyalty. A smartphone app with an overview of public charging options for e-scooters, combined with exclusive conditions, could keep customers mobile easily at all times and strengthen customer loyalty.

4.1.5 Revenue streams

The design of revenue streams must also be geared towards customer value. Customers will only be prepared to pay for something that brings them a concrete value. The method and timing of payment will also influence the customer value. Conceivable options include the sale of a product; rental or leasing (eg, for real estate or cars); consumption-based user fees (eg, for hotel accommodation); and non-consumption-based access fees (eg, for memberships in sports clubs or flat-rate smartphone tariffs). There are also a variety of options for pricing and discounts. Many business models – such as inkjet printers – also use a combination of revenue streams, such as low initial costs with high subsequent consumption costs.

According to Figure 7.4, there are two main revenue streams in our e-scooter start-up. One comes from the sale of the e-scooters; the other from the proceeds from the sale of original spare parts to the sales and service partners.

4.1.6 Key resources

'Key resources' are what a company needs in order to achieve the intended customer value. Human resources are an important resource for most companies, especially those that require employees with special knowledge and experience. Physical resources – such as production facilities, retail stores, vehicles or computer equipment – can also be key resources; as can financial resources. For start-ups, the latter include financing through venture capital; and for established companies, access to other forms of capital markets such as credit lines with banks. An essential part of the key resources is the company's IP portfolio, which protects the business model.

According to Figure 7.4, the e-scooter start-up has identified as a key resource its personnel, who must have special expertise in mechatronics, software development, design and marketing. The technology of the wheel hub motor and the associated know-how are also critical to success; as are the IP rights, which should effectively protect the business model with its unique customer value. A carefully cultivated perception in the market as a premium brand is also an important resource for business success. In addition, investors that the start-up must still win over are among its key resources, because only the financial strength and support of the investors will allow the business to scale up quickly.

4.1.7 Key activities

The 'key activities' are core competencies of the company which, from an operational perspective, are necessary to deliver customer value. In the case of product businesses, these often include competencies in development, design, testing and manufacturing. In service businesses such as car repair or medical services, the key activities often lie in the ability to solve certain problems efficiently and to have an appropriate knowledge and quality management system in place. In business models based on Internet platforms, key activities often relate to the ability to analyse transactions on these platforms very efficiently using artificial intelligence tools and draw conclusions to optimize platform operation.

Our e-scooter start-up has the classic key activities of a company that offers an innovative product to private customers: marketing and sales, design and development, and production.

4.1.8 Key partners

Partnerships with other companies are an important component of a successful business. It does not make sense – and is not necessary – to carry out all activities and have all resources yourself. Non-critical parts or services for which there are several comparable suppliers can be easily purchased from a partner and will usually afford a cost advantage over in-house production, because the supplier has a significantly larger production volume. Key partners are those that are relevant to the functioning of your own business model and usually are not easily interchangeable. These include distribution partners or strategic manufacturing alliances with other companies. A partner from which a patent licence on acceptable conditions is absolutely necessary is also a key partner. For start-ups, partnerships with established companies can be extremely helpful if they are designed as win-win alliances (Freytag 2019). To avoid confusion: in the business model canvas, 'customers' and 'partners' are different actors; whereas in everyday business life, these terms are often used synonymously to emphasize close relationships with customers.

According to Figure 7.4, the shop-in-shop sales and service partners are decisive for the e-scooter start-up, because this is the only way it can establish a broad presence quickly and cost effectively. Assembly and testing are also largely outsourced and most components are also purchased externally. These include the wheel hub motor developed in-house. The motor is built by a contract manufacturer and uses, among other things, a highly innovative sealing ring that was developed together with a development partner. In deriving the IP strategy, we will see later that the sealing ring is critical to success, which is why the development partner for the sealing ring is a key partner for our e-scooter start-up; whereas ordinary sealing rings would certainly be non-critical purchased parts.

4.1.9 Cost structure

The operational side of the business model canvas leads to costs for running the business. In the 'Cost structure' field, the aim is to identify the main cost blocks and their driving factors. For example, one must understand exactly what the fixed and variable cost components in the business model are; and what cost degression is possible in relation to sales volume. This provides a basis for cost, liquidity and financial planning, and the associated optimization options. Together with sales and financial planning, cost planning flows into the financial part of the business plan.

In the case of our e-scooter start-up, in addition to personnel, marketing and sales, as well as development, represent large cost blocks with a strong fixed cost character. The costs of production and logistics, on the other hand, are largely variable due to outsourcing to partner companies and depend on the actual sales of e-scooters.

4.2 Systematically ensuring freedom to operate and preventing imitation

Following the joint preparation of the business model canvas for the prioritized future business model, the persons responsible for all functions of the company – and especially the IP experts – will have a clear common vision of the unique customer value of the future business and its implementation. The same applies to possible alternatives to this prioritized future business model. This concludes the first phase shown in Figure 7.1. Those responsible for the individual functions in the company can now proceed to develop their individual value-driven functional strategies in accordance with the second phase shown in Figure 7.1. Based on the common understanding of the company's future achieved in the first phase, these individual functional strategies will be well aligned.

We now turn to the activities of the IP function of the company and consider in detail how a value-driven IP strategy is developed and implemented in practice there.

IP expertise in start-ups is usually obtained by consulting an experienced external patent attorney, because newcomers cannot rely on in-house IP experts in the same way as established companies. In order for the external patent attorney of a start-up to provide targeted support for the development of a value-driven IP strategy, he must be well informed – like the in-house IP experts in established companies – about the discussions regarding the prioritization of the future business model and the unique customer value to be achieved. Ideally, the patent attorney should participate in these discussions. The aspects described below are also described (from the perspective of patent attorneys) as a supplement in Chapters 1 and 2. Chapter 1 provides a general overview of the individual legal aspects of IP rights in general; while Chapter 2 addresses this using the example of a medical technology start-up (see Chapter 2, section 5).

To develop a value-driven IP strategy as shown in Figure 7.1, the following tasks are now on the agenda based on the description of the prioritized future business model and its alternatives as shown in Figure 7.3:

- Ensure Freedom-to-Operate (FTO) by identifying potential violations in the implementation of the company's own business model and eliminating these problems by changing approach or in-licensing or purchasing IP; and
- Prevent imitation by building up an IP portfolio to protect the company's implementation of its business model and alternative implementations.

The following guidelines for the systematic development of a value-driven IP strategy have proven to be effective in practice. In particular, a company should:

- Go through the business model canvas field by field to ensure completeness, while also consciously looking for overarching aspects;
- In all considerations, always put the idea of unique customer value in the foreground, which is represented by the business model and to which the IP strategy should contribute. This helps in considering the fields of the business model canvas as an important orientation, but not losing sight of the basic goal. The IP strategy – and especially IP protection to prevent imitation – is by no means always just about a 'great ingenious idea'. Little things can be just as important if they lead to the desired result;
- Very consciously exploit all potential IP types – from patents, utility models, designs and trademarks to copyrights – as a means of protection in order to avoid unconsciously focusing excessively on patents. In order to effectively prevent imitation, one should also examine the extent to which IP rights could be combined to optimize their effect;
- Examine the extent to which it is better to license or purchase IP rights rather than registering them yourself;
- Ensure that all countries potentially relevant in the future are included in the analysis;
- Consider the IP strategy as a team task between internal and external IP experts and employees of other functions in the company, thinking not only of R&D, but also of marketing, production, purchasing and other departments. In established companies, these functions are usually represented by individual departments; while in start-ups, they are often performed by members of the founding team;

- Keep in mind all considerations – not only the company's own industry and the competitors that are currently active in it. Companies that are active in completely different industries may also be relevant: they could own IP rights to technologies that have a cross-sectoral effect; or they could suddenly appear as 'disruptive' competitors in the company's own sector in the future, possibly adopting a completely different approach to pursue the same customer value; and
- Take into account that a value-driven IP strategy must cover both the prioritized business model and its alternatives. If the alternatives differ only slightly from the prioritized business model, there will be strong synergies in ensuring FTO and preventing imitation. However, if the alternatives deviate significantly, the overlaps may be very small, so that the additional expense involved would be considerable; in many such cases, it will be necessary to concentrate on critical areas and avoid covering the alternatives completely.

The temporal aspect plays an essential role in several respects:

- Ensuring FTO involves testing for the infringement of third-party IP rights, but this is valid only at the time it is executed. This test must therefore be repeated at suitable intervals.
- IP rights are prohibitive rights and in general, the first application date is what counts. Therefore, one must be quick.
- The market, technology and competitive environment are continuously evolving and the IP strategy must therefore be adapted accordingly. Major changes may even have repercussions on the prioritized future business model. In any case, the validity of the prioritized future business model must be reviewed regularly, and at least once a year as part of the budget cycle.

An effective value-driven IP strategy and its implementation can only be realized by consulting an experienced IP expert, who will usually be based at an external patent law firm in the case of start-ups and in the in-house IP department in the case of established companies.

4.3 Examples and notes from practice

The previous recommendations for the development of a value-driven IP strategy are now supplemented by practical advice below. These notes do not claim to be exhaustive, but are intended to serve as suggestions –

especially for start-up entrepreneurs who are just getting to grips with the topic of IP. Our e-scooter start-up again serves as an example.

The founders are trying to ensure FTO in the e-scooter business as follows:

- Because they developed the wheel hub motor while they were still studying at university, they must clarify to what extent they have the rights to this invention. If necessary, they must negotiate with the university on the conditions under which they can acquire or license these rights. Details on this issue are set out in Chapter 3 (in particular, section 2.6) from the perspective of a patent attorney. In Chapter 4, this topic is supplemented by practical advice from a university chair holder.
- Because a constructive detail of the wheel hub motor is already protected by a patent of an electric motor manufacturer, the founders must either consider whether they can design this part differently or negotiate a licence. It may suffice if this licence is limited to the application of the constructive detail in motors in the field of micro-mobility and to certain countries.

The founders want to prevent the imitation of the e-scooter business through several different measures:

- First, they protect the company name and logo by filing a trademark application.
- They also apply for patents on the technology of the wheel hub motor, whose claims they generalize as far as possible. In their regional application strategy, they make sure to cover all future relevant countries. Because the founders want to present their e-scooter at a trade fair soon, and patent examination and grant take some time, they apply for a utility model in parallel. Utility models are weaker than patents; but they are granted more quickly and still allow the derivation of a prohibition claim against a competitor, if necessary.
- In order to ensure that the wheel hub motor and the added value associated with it are immediately recognizable, the founders attach an eye-catching design element to the wheel hub motor itself, which shimmers through the wheel spokes, and protect it by means of a design protection right. They also have a short, catchy melody composed that sounds as soon as the scooter is switched on. They protect this melody with a trademark as a sound mark.

- An essential design detail of the wheel hub motor is the seal that seals the axle against the motor housing and prevents water from running into the motor when the scooter is moving through deep puddles. The founders developed this seal together with a specialist seal manufacturer, taking care to secure the exclusive right to use the seals in the micro-mobility field. This allows them to prevent the manufacturer from supplying the same seals to potential competitors.
- Because weight plays a major role in the wheel hub motor, it is possible that in future, the motor could be built not as a casting, but by means of a 3D printing process in a light and extremely stable honeycomb construction. In order to prevent new competitors from entering the market and keep this path open, the founders are considering what this alternative could look like and are applying for patents on the design and the necessary manufacturing processes – even though they do not currently intend to build the motor in this way.

The role of software in the development of IP strategy is becoming increasingly important in light of the growing trend towards digitization. Just as widespread as fatal is the opinion that software-related inventions cannot be protected by IP and therefore need not be addressed. For details on IP rights and software, please see Schwarz/Kruspig 2017; only a few of the essential aspects will be mentioned here:

- Basically, the source code of software is protected by copyright without any further action. However, this protection only prohibits direct copying of the source code. The reprogramming of the basic idea behind the program code is not affected by this.
- In most countries, software as such is not patentable. However, if software is part of a process that solves a technical problem, it may very well be patentable, and this patent can then also have a prohibitive effect.
- Finally, the use of open source software (OSS) must also be carefully considered. On the one hand, OSS libraries are a significant help in making rapid progress in software development. On the other hand, 'open source' does not automatically mean 'freely available'. As soon as the user of OSS no longer uses it only for himself, but passes it on to third parties as part of a product, the underlying licence agreements – such as the GNU ('General Public Licence') – must be observed. In the simplest case, only the naming of the original author will then be necessary. However, the licence agreements to which one automatically agrees when using OSS can sometimes go so far that the software

in which the OSS is integrated automatically becomes OSS itself under the same licence conditions ('copyleft'). As a rule, a company will wish to avoid these circumstances, unless it is pursuing an explicit strategy of using OSS to indirectly promote its own business model. Further information on OSS can also be found in Chapter 1, especially sections 3.1 and 4.

In particular, these practical examples should illustrate how broad, important and often underestimated the field of IP strategy development is. Start-ups would be well advised to deal intensively with the subject of IP.

5. Organizational implementation of a value-driven IP strategy

The value-driven IP strategy described so far has proved itself in practice many times over, both in start-ups and in established companies.

Nevertheless, the traditional invention-driven IP strategy approach still prevails in many companies. In this approach, IP essentially serves to protect inventions made within the company. This approach has serious disadvantages, which will be discussed in more detail below. Understanding the differences between value-driven and invention-driven IP strategies is a prerequisite to establish a value-driven approach to IP strategy in an organization.

This issue is as relevant for start-ups as it is for established companies. Both should seek to ensure that all employees in the company have a value-driven rather than invention-driven understanding of IP strategy, which does not depend on the size of an organisation.

5.1 Differences between value-driven and invention-driven IP strategies

The main difference between a value-driven IP strategy and an invention-driven IP strategy is the starting point.

With a value-driven IP strategy, the cross-functional strategic prioritization of the future business model is the starting point. The functional strategies – and thus in particular, the IP strategy – are derived from this, as shown in Figure 7.1. This means that after the joint prioritization of the future business model, the persons responsible for all functions in the company will have the same vision of the future and will try to make this vision a reality through their functional strategies.

In the case of an invention-driven IP strategy, by contrast, the starting point is an invention that a developer makes in the company. The developer knows that he should contribute to the innovative power of the company and that inventions are therefore expected of him.

These different starting points lead directly to different goals of value-driven and invention-driven IP strategies.

- A value-driven IP strategy aims to secure effective protection for future business, whereby two tasks must be fulfilled: ensuring the company's own Freedom-to-Operate (FTO) for the implementation of the prioritized future business model; and preventing imitation of that business model by competitors.
- By contrast, in an invention-driven IP strategy, inventors aim to demonstrate their innovative strength and thus contribute to innovative products and services of the company. In addition, inventors want to protect their creations with IP so that only their own company can use them. The number of invention disclosures and patents granted per developer is often an important innovation indicator in the company and a component of variable salary.

The different goals of value-driven and invention-driven IP strategies logically result in different approaches.

- According to Figure 7.3, a value-driven IP strategy actively ensures the company's own FTO in implementing the prioritized business model by analysing whether third-party IP rights could potentially be infringed as a result and how such infringement could be avoided. In addition, IP is actively generated to prevent imitation. The previous section outlined how to proceed in this respect by using the business model canvas as an example. It was also explained that the protection-worthiness, and thus the quality, of the IP must be in the foreground. The point is to secure exactly those IP rights which are needed to achieve the best possible protection for future business. Among other things, as the examples above also show, all types of IP should be considered and systematically exploited; and in addition to the company's own applications, it should be examined whether in individual cases the in-licensing or purchase of IP rights might be a better choice.

- In contrast, an invention-driven IP strategy does not focus on clarifying FTO for future business. The IP department is usually commissioned by the development department with 'patent clearing' at the end of the development process. The same applies to orders from product management when design or trademark issues are involved. In an invention-driven IP strategy, IP filing by definition takes place at the initiative of the inventor, who believes he has invented something interesting which might be protectable. Thus, the focus here is on protectability, rather than on protection-worthiness. Whether an application for protection is filed and how it is structured will depend on the inventor's and patent attorney's knowledge of the company's current and future business model. In addition, as inventions generally emerge from the development department, the focus is more on patents than on other IP rights. As innovative strength is measured by the number of patent applications filed by a company, the in-licensing or purchase of IP rights plays a role at most in the clearing of IP rights, but is not an integral part of the IP strategy.

Therefore, a value-driven IP strategy generates effective IP protection for the company's prioritized future business in a targeted manner. By contrast, in the case of an invention-driven IP strategy, the protective effect for future business is unclear, as the above discussion has shown.

In this context, the stability of the business environment also plays a decisive role. The longer a company has been active in the market and the less the business environment changes, the less important the differences between value-driven and invention-driven IP strategies become. This is because it can then be assumed that the company already has a sufficient IP portfolio, and that all employees know the business model and its further development very well and know what is important. In these circumstances, the 'right' and 'sufficient' invention disclosures come from the development department; the product management and marketing departments give 'right' and 'sufficient' thought to design and trademark protection; and the IP department knows exactly how to structure applications and also keeps an eye on whether third-party IP rights may be infringed.

However, because nowadays one cannot assume a stable business or a stable environment, a value-driven IP strategy is crucial to success – especially for two types of companies:

- Start-ups: By definition, start-ups do not yet have a business that is stable, but are looking for a business model (see Figure 7.2). For this reason alone, a value-driven IP strategy for start-ups is an absolute necessity. This approach also fits perfectly with the business model canvas methodology, which is the standard strategy instrument in the start-up world.
- Established companies in times of digitization: Digitization and the transformation it entails present significant opportunities – but also risks. The previously rather stable environment in which established companies operated is becoming increasingly unstable. Strategically, the associated uncertainties about the future of the business are countered with scenario analyses and the prioritization of these scenarios. This is precisely the starting point of the value-driven business strategy, according to Figure 7.1. The more uncertain the future is, the more the prioritized future business model and the potential alternatives will differ; and the more the IP strategy must ensure that both the prioritized business model and its alternatives are sufficiently protected, to be as well prepared as possible for the future. In this way, the application of the value-driven IP strategy becomes a competitive advantage in the digital transformation.

These observations on the differences between value-driven and invention-driven IP strategies are deliberately kept in black and white to highlight the crux of these statements. However, reality certainly also has shades of grey.

At this point, you may wonder how to deal with a spontaneous ingenious idea of an inventor in the research department which does not seem to fit within the process of a value-driven IP strategy illustrated in Figure 7.1. Of course, the company will consider this idea; but the decisive question here too concerns which criteria to apply. If you first apply the criteria of the value-driven IP strategy and ask yourself how this ingenious idea fits into the effective protection of the future business model, you have already taken an important step forward. And if the idea does not fit at all, or has many other applications outside the future prioritized business model or its alternatives, you can examine whether you can lucratively sell or out-license the associated IP rights. A spontaneous ingenious idea is therefore also highly welcome and valuable in the course of a value-driven IP strategy. However, it is important to separate the two key questions:

- What does the ingenious idea contribute to the effective protection of the future business?
- What is its commercial value outside of this business?

Some established companies, such as Siemens (Siemens 2019), have their own organizational unit that deals with the commercialization of IP and technology beyond the focus of their own business. For example, companies that market medical products for human healthcare could attractively out-license the IP rights with which they protect those products to companies in the veterinary healthcare sector and limit the licences to application in veterinary healthcare. In this way, these companies can generate additional revenues without being restricted in any way in their main market of human healthcare.

5.2 Establishing a value-driven IP strategy

The differences between value-driven and invention-driven IP strategies illustrated in Figure 7.5 automatically also define the different roles that the IP function plays in both approaches in companies from an organizational point of view.

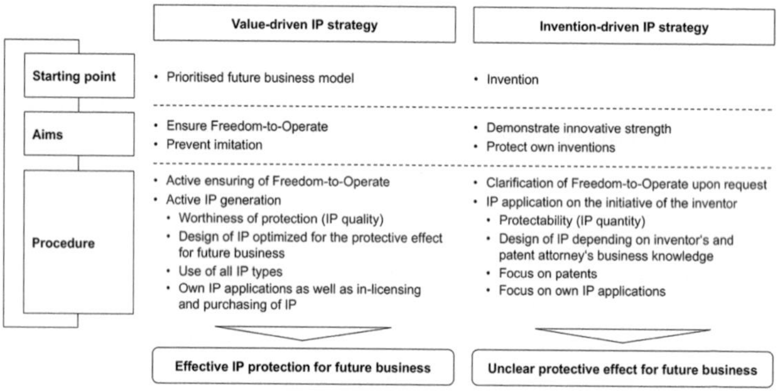

Figure 7.5 Differences between value-driven and invention-driven IP strategies

In the case of a value-driven IP strategy, the IP function is involved from the beginning of strategy development (see Figure 7.1) and contributes intensively to the prioritization of the future business model.

- In particular, this means that the IP experts also speak the language of the strategy, marketing, development and production departments; that they can handle strategic approaches such as the business model canvas; and that they are also familiar with the corporate strategy and the market, the technology and the competitive environment in terms of content. It is the IP experts themselves, and not their colleagues in the other functions, who must effect the transfer from the strategic level to the IP specialist level and thus, in particular, the translation into legal terminology.
- IP work is thus an integral part of the business. It interacts closely with all other organizational functions. In particular, the contribution of the IP function to the success of the business becomes directly apparent to all other colleagues in the company.

In an invention-driven IP strategy, on the other hand, the IP function is often included only towards the end of the product development.

- Often, the IP function essentially interacts with the development department with regard to patent applications and has difficulty motivating the developers to submit a sufficient number of invention disclosures. It is not uncommon for development departments to become particularly creative towards the end of the fiscal year and submit a large number of invention disclosures in order to meet their targets for the number of inventions.
- The other functions in the company consider the IP function to be largely decoupled from the business and regard it as a legal department without a great understanding of the market and with little relevance to the business. This impression is often reinforced by the fact that in the event of a conflict of IP rights, the supposedly strong IP portfolio proves to be unhelpful and legally difficult to enforce because it does not sufficiently cover the actual business model.

How should this be handled in practice?

- Companies should ensure that they pursue a value-driven IP strategy from the very beginning. This is particularly important for start-ups, especially in view of their limited resources and the need to convince investors of the quality of their IP portfolios.

- For established companies, a well-considered change management project is necessary to make the transition from a traditionally established invention-driven IP strategy to a value-driven IP strategy. This project must be supported by the management together with the heads of all organizational functions of the company.

Based on these explanations of the differences between a value-driven IP strategy and an invention-driven IP strategy, and the related roles of the IP function in the company, it is easy to determine where a specific company currently stands between these two poles and what the main starting points for change should be.

It has proved successful in established companies to first explain the benefits of a value-driven IP strategy to IP employees in workshops in theory and by means of concrete examples in practice. Cross-functional pilot projects can then be launched in the company according to the procedure shown in Figure 7.1. If the success of these pilot projects is then made known throughout the entire company, the application of the value-driven IP strategy can be successively extended across the company, thus establishing this approach on a permanent basis.

6. Summary

The task of a company is to create satisfied customers by offering a unique customer value which is better than those offered by its competitors. For this reason, customer value is the best target for a company's business strategy. This is called a 'value-driven business strategy' and the corresponding IP strategy is called a 'value-driven IP strategy'. A value-driven IP strategy can effectively protect future business.

The development and implementation of a value-driven IP strategy are integral to the development and implementation of a value-driven business strategy, and take place in two main phases (see Figure 7.1):

- In the first phase, a careful strategic analysis defines the vision for the company in the form of a prioritized future business model and possible potential alternatives. The persons responsible for all functions in the company – whether strategy, research, development, marketing, sales or the IP function – are involved in this activity.
- In the second phase, the persons responsible for all functions in the

company develop coordinated value-driven strategies for their functions based on this, in order to realize their vision of the prioritized future business model and prepare for the potential alternatives.

The effective protection of a future business and its potential alternatives through a value-driven IP strategy involves two crucial factors: ensuring Freedom-to-Operate (FTO) and preventing imitation (Figure 7.3). This ensures that the planned implementation of the prioritized future business model does not infringe third-party rights and that a portfolio of IP rights is developed which makes it as difficult as possible for other companies to enter the market as competitors with identical or similar offerings.

A value-driven IP strategy is of particular importance for start-ups:

- Start-ups must first find the right business model (Figure 7.2). To this end, they must make hypotheses about the market, competition and technology, test them out and gradually develop their future business model on this basis. Start-ups must also consider the issue of IP protection of their future business from the outset. They must ensure that they have FTO for their business and must prevent potential competitors from imitating their business idea. Investors will examine these points carefully when making their investment decisions.
- For start-ups, a value-driven IP strategy is therefore ideally suited to the parallel search for the right business model and its protection. In the start-up world, the business model canvas is often used as an instrument for business model development. Its nine fields map the relevant elements of a business model completely and clearly (see Figure 7.4, which concerns our example e-scooter company). To apply a value-driven IP strategy in practice, start-ups must consider, for each of these nine fields, how to ensure FTO and prevent imitation. Start-ups must consider all types of IP rights – from patents to utility models, designs, trademarks and copyrights; and must also consider a forward-looking regional filing strategy.

A value-driven IP strategy is also indispensable for established companies:

- As soon as established companies can no longer assume a stable business environment, they can only effectively protect future business through a value-driven IP strategy. An invention-driven IP strategy is not suitable for this purpose (see Figure 7.5).
- Such a situation of change is particularly prevalent today due to the

transformations that have resulted from digitization. New technologies such as 3D printing and the Internet of Things will change the existing business models of established companies and facilitate new ones. New competitors will put established companies under pressure in a disruptive way.

- The basic principles of a value-driven IP strategy and its implementation are the same for established companies as for start-ups. This means that start-ups which pursue a value-driven IP strategy will not have to change – especially if they grow over time into larger, established companies.

A value-driven IP strategy is thus a unique strategic competitive instrument for both start-ups and established companies to effectively protect future business.

8 IP management in the start-up lifecycle

Christina Lubinski and Christoph Viebig

1. Introduction

IP is an important asset for companies. However, companies – especially resource-constrained start-ups – often underestimate the strategic value and importance of IP. While managing IP is a core activity of most mature companies, start-up entrepreneurs frequently discount the issue until it becomes an obvious problem and can no longer be ignored. However, continuous and proactive IP management not only helps entrepreneurs to stay out of trouble, but can also provide the company with an important competitive advantage.

Although scholars have begun to study the importance of IP, the strategic value of proactively and continuously managing the legal dimensions of a business is still underappreciated, in both academic research and entrepreneurial practice (Bagley 2008, 2010; De Leon and Fernandez Donoso 2017). Undoubtedly, there are many opportunities to gain value from IP in early-stage start-ups. While other chapters in this book engage in detail with the different types of IP (see Chapter 1), this chapter takes a research-oriented perspective, providing a systematic overview of the current literature on IP management from strategic management and entrepreneurship research. In particular, we set out to highlight three research findings, which in our opinion are of great relevance for entrepreneurs and founding teams.

Our starting point is the assumption that IP management is a moving target, dynamically evolving over the course of a venture's lifecycle. We argue that entrepreneurs should avoid a static approach to their IP management and instead remain flexible and adaptive. Building on established venture lifecycle approaches, we show which IP-related problems entrepreneurs face at different stages of the venture's lifecycle and how best to address them.

Second, we show how IP management is inextricably intertwined with venture legitimacy. We posit that IP should be a crucial area of activity in early-stage start-ups because it addresses stakeholders' concerns about the future development of the venture. Because start-ups in the early days typically lack a strong record of accomplishments, the signalling effect of professional IP management is particularly important and valuable to them. Hence, signalling trust to external stakeholders through IP management addresses a prominent problem: the venture's 'liability of newness' (Stinchcombe 1965).

Finally, for many new ventures, the complexity of IP management derives from the need or desire to manage IP not just in their home country, but also across national borders. This step exposes them to different legal environments. We thus conclude by exploring some of the most common issues with cross-border IP management for start-ups.

As our chapter will show, entrepreneurs experience many IP challenges as trade-offs. We identify and discuss the most common of these IP-related trade-offs and highlight the stage in the lifecycle at which they most frequently emerge. Trade-offs are challenging for entrepreneurs because there is no optimal solution to them. Instead, entrepreneurs must base their response to them on an evaluation of the pros and cons and reflect on both short and long-term consequences. By discussing common trade-offs, we provide a roadmap for start-up entrepreneurs to manage their IP systematically and proactively.

2. Lifecycle models and venture legitimacy

IP management is a dynamic rather than a static field of activity in organizations. This is particularly true for start-ups, which in the early days often radically 'pivot' their business model, technology and team structure and therefore go through distinct stages of development. As new entrepreneurial ventures progress, the requirements and opportunities of IP management also change.

We present these challenges in the context of venture lifecycle models, which the academic literature has long discussed and debated. Lifecycle models typically present IP challenges chronologically, helping us to see when they emerge and how entrepreneurs can best address them. A word of warning: the ideal or typical venture lifecycle is an abstraction. Start-ups will undoubtedly experience the transitions between the stages in different ways and at different points in time. Nevertheless, understanding the transitions between the stages of a venture's lifecycle is important for entrepreneurs, as it helps them to look ahead, plan and prepare for upcoming IP-related challenges.

IP management always addresses two questions:

- What is the best way to manage a venture's IP (content)?
- How does the IP strategy affect the legitimacy of an early-stage venture (signal)?

Recent scholarship has looked closely at the legitimacy of start-ups and its findings are relevant for understanding the strategic value of IP management. In the following section, we will first briefly introduce the literature on lifecycle models and legitimacy, and then address the concrete IP challenges that emerge in an early-stage venture over time.

2.1 Venture lifecycle models

Business historian Alfred D Chandler (1962) was arguably one of the first to introduce and systematically explore the idea that companies go through predictable development stages. Since then, different lifecycle models have been developed and tested across various academic disciplines (Gaibraith 1982; Kazanjian 1988; Greiner 1997; Fisher et al 2016). By and large, the different models convey similar ideas and differences between them are frequently more semantic than content driven. In this chapter, we follow Fisher et al's (2016) model, for two primary reasons. First, this model was designed to describe early-stage ventures. While it was developed specifically for technology start-ups, it is equally suitable for non-technology ventures if they are interested in external financing rather than being self-funded or primarily socially driven ventures. It thus fits the purpose of our analysis. Second, and more importantly, the model is one of the few that incorporates both the transitions between the different stages of a venture's evolution and the particular legitimacy issues that arise with them (Figure 8.1).

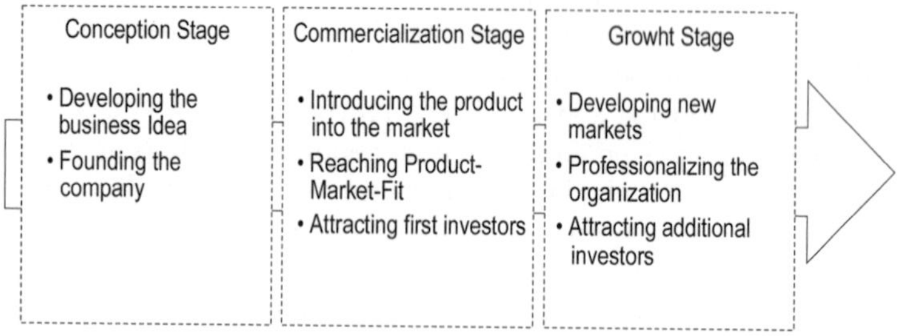

Figure 8.1 *The lifecycle of a start-up according to Fisher et al (2016)*

Fisher et al (2016) describe start-up development in three stages:

- the conception stage, when entrepreneurs first perceive of a business idea and the venture becomes established;
- the commercialization stage, when the founders achieve product/market fit and outside investors enter the business; and
- the growth stage, when larger infusions of capital become necessary to expand operations, build formal organizational structures and expand into new markets.

The three stages differ not only regarding the venture's activities, but also regarding the resources needed for further development. In each of the three stages, new stakeholders enter the scene (eg, business angels, venture capitalists (VCs) or strategic partners). It is often challenging for start-up entrepreneurs to manage these relationships because each of the stakeholders follows different conventions and has different expectations for its relationship with the founding team.

2.2 The conception stage

During the conception stage, entrepreneurs conceive of the business idea and form the start-up. Scholarship on this stage characterizes it by its resource constraints and an egalitarian decision-making structure within the early founding team. The corporate culture is informal and creative, with few or no formalized functions and standardized processes (Wasserman 2012). Even at this earliest stage in the lifecycle, entrepreneurs can encounter IP-related issues. Specifically, they may face potential claims that former employers may have on ideas of the founders or their early hires; with the question of when to start addressing IP challenges; and with collaborations with outside partners. In addition, entrepreneurs must reflect on the role that IP management in these very early days can play in establishing and communicating legitimacy and professionalism to relevant outside stakeholders.

2.3 The commercialization stage

The transition from the conception stage to the commercialization stage is marked by several 'inflection points', such as completing the development of the first product or service, establishing product/market fit and closing a round of external funding beyond 'family, friends and fools' – the infamous 'three Fs' that often act as first investors for start-ups. At this stage, angel investors and selected seed-stage VCs become attractive sources of venture financing (Fisher et al 2016), which raises the question of how IP management affects the relationship with them. During the commercialization stage, the attention gradually shifts from technology risks and product development to professional sales and marketing, as well as to more formal processes and less centralized consensus-driven decision making (Wasserman 2012). Tangible and demonstrable milestones become more important; and solid IP management and partnerships with respected IP lawyers can turn into competitive advantages for the entrepreneurs. Dominant IP challenges at this stage include the continuous trade-off relating to resource allocation (invest now versus later). Typically, it is also at this stage of greater visibility for the venture's products or services that competitor claims may become an issue for the start-up, which then raises a series of new IP issues, as well as questions about the start-up's general approach to IP management.

2.4 The growth stage

Finally, at the growth stage, companies seek a broader base of financial resource providers, including VCs and, if applicable, institutional investors – for example, in the context of an initial public offering. At this point, the organization will have a steady revenue stream from a standardized line of products or services. Structures and processes are formal, written and well understood by employees. Decision making tends to be more decentralized across functions and hierarchies. Top-level hires come primarily from a pool of experienced and seasoned executives (Wasserman 2012). These processes are reinforced by investors having a stronger voice on start-up boards. Prior research suggests that VCs on start-up boards usually come with an agenda to professionalize (Hellmann and Puri 2002). At this stage, most of the earlier discussed IP issues will likely have been resolved. However, at the growth and expansion stage, IP management across national borders often becomes more immediately relevant and, if it has not been addressed earlier, brings up a new set of IP challenges.

2.5 Venture legitimacy

Protecting IP is obviously important for a venture's competitiveness and business success. However, it also plays an important role in building a start-up's reputation. Start-ups do not have a long track record of achieving milestones and therefore, as noted in the introduction, are confronted with the 'liability of newness' (Stinchcombe 1965; see also Aldrich and Auster 1986). Ultimately, this liability increases the risk of failure; and it is an important part of the entrepreneurs' job to manage these risks and establish a trustful relationship with stakeholders. Dermont Berkery (2008: 1), a US-based VC, pointedly declares: 'New companies are guilty until proven innocent. Most of them fail. Investors know this. Entrepreneurs don't – or at least choose not to believe this.' It is thus crucially important for start-ups to address their legitimacy challenge.

One easy yet important way of acquiring legitimacy for a new venture is securing defendable IP. The reason for this link between legitimacy and IP is that research on the success factors of start-ups shows that IP is positively correlated with the financial success of start-ups (Mann and Sager 2007; Schwarzkopf 2016). Therefore, the relationship between start-up entrepreneurs and investors, and the bargaining position of the former, are heavily dependent on the ability both to manage IP rights and to successfully communicate their relevance and value to external stakeholders.

The field of legitimacy research is extensive (for an overview, see Suddaby et al 2017), and several scholars have applied its findings to the experience of start-up entrepreneurs (Fisher et al 2016; Islam et al 2018). Suchman (1995: 574) defines 'legitimacy' as 'a generalized perception or assumption that the actions of an entity are desirable, proper, or appropriate within some socially constructed system of norms, values, beliefs, and definitions'. IP management has a signalling effect towards relevant external stakeholders, with direct consequences for developing or destroying venture legitimacy.

Zimmerman and Zeitz (2002) find that there is a 'legitimacy threshold' in new ventures below which start-ups are unlikely to raise necessary resources. Before a start-up has reached the first legitimacy threshold, it is hard to attract investors and other important collaborators. However, the relationship between legitimacy and resource acquisition is not linear. While a minimum of legitimacy is necessary to be perceived as an interesting investment object, subsequent increases in legitimacy provide only decreasing returns (Pollock and Rindova 2003). From this, we can conclude that investing in legitimacy is most relevant during the transitions from one lifecycle stage to the next, when the entrepreneurs must convince a new group of stakeholders of the venture's potential. Start-up legitimacy is also not stable, but can be reduced or destroyed by activities that are not perceived as 'desirable, proper, or appropriate' (eg, see Elsbach 1994; Jonsson et al 2009). It must therefore be proactively managed, but also maintained and if necessary repaired (Garud et al 2014).

From this short overview of the literature on venture lifecycles and legitimacy, we can conclude that IP must be managed holistically. Entrepreneurs should consider both the management of IP rights and the signalling effect of a professional IP management towards external stakeholders, both of which are inextricably intertwined. One finding from previous lifecycle research is that entrepreneurs should pay special attention to the transitions between the different lifecycle stages because these are the moments when (new) IP-related problems emerge, which then have long-term consequences for the success and survival of the company.

3. IP challenges during conception stage

The conception stage is the stage during which entrepreneurs most easily forget or side-line IP management, due to the many seemingly more pressing issues in their day-to-day activities. Yet already at this stage, entrepreneurs may encounter a series of IP and legitimacy challenges, which can turn into severe short- and long-term problems. In addition, many entrepreneurs lack legal competences and access to experts in the early days of the venture, when resources are scarce and must be allocated with great care.

3.1 The information trade-off

When new ventures are formed, the previously existing employment relationships of core individuals (founders, early hires) often become an issue of concern (for details, see Chapter 4). Sometimes entrepreneurs will start a new business right out of school or while unemployed. However, often individuals decide to take the plunge while still employed by another company. In those instances, it is important to investigate whether employers may have claims to employees' ideas and could enforce agreements that prevent employees from using ideas, confidential information and client contacts for the benefit of another company. Previous employers can obtain an interim order inhibiting the founders from continuing with their business, using confidential information or contacting the employer's clients.

In this situation, an aspiring entrepreneur's information trade-off may revolve around the timing of revealing his intentions to the employer. Informing employers early may facilitate negotiations over IP rights (see below) and lead to early settlement of the issue. However, it can simultaneously alert employers to the employee's intention and to the idea. Having realized the potential value, the employer may decide to exploit it autonomously or prevent others from doing so for strategic reasons.

When employees develop an idea for a business, it is often difficult to tell where, when and how the idea first emerged. Did they develop the idea during working hours or during their free time? Did they come up with the idea based on their experiences during the job? Employers' rights to ideas and confidential information vary by country; and in larger countries, even regionally. Employment contract conditions are also idiosyncratic. Finally, the rights of the previous employer are also shaped by the employee's role within the company. Highly compensated top managers, for example, are subject to more stringent restrictions than lower-level employees.

When people leave previous employment relationships to start a business, time usually favours the previous employer. An employer can remain inactive until such time as the former employee's venture becomes successful enough to deserve its attention (whether for monetary or strategic reasons), and then decide to take action. The threat of an impending lawsuit will inhibit attempts to start a new business and, if the business is nonetheless started in the face of this threat, create barriers for future funding opportunities – an important factor for the venture's legitimacy with outside stakeholders such as early hires, banks, partners and family and friends who may consider an investment.

Therefore, it is in the new venture's best interests to negotiate a settlement as soon as possible – preferably before the individual in question leaves his employer. It is at this time, prior to the employee leaving, that the employer is most aware that the idea will never reach fruition without the employee's efforts, and therefore that the aspiring entrepreneur's bargaining power is greatest. Depending on how strong the employer's claims are, one possible outcome may be for the new venture to give up a piece of equity in return for a release from any claims to the invention. An early decision to actively manage IP rather than waiting for a problem to occur has the advantage of predictability and gives legitimacy for future negotiations to the start-up. This also applies to all hires of the new start-up, whose employment contract should clearly give all emerging IP rights to the company to avoid future conflicts. For all these questions, expert advice can help to mitigate the challenges.

3.2 The patent application trade-off

If a person develops a patentable idea while still employed (before starting a new venture), another trade-off to consider may concern the timing of patent filings. While an earlier filing date will generally be advantageous to the aspiring entrepreneur in terms of claiming priority over competing claims, the same early filing date will also make it easier for the previous employer to argue that the person finalized the invention during his tenure at the company, and hence that rights may belong to the former employer. Reaching agreement with the employer before that happens is therefore crucial to securing IP rights long term.

3.3 The resource trade-off

Where there is no issue with a previous employer, aspiring entrepreneurs may still need to guarantee the IP rights of a technology, copyright or trademark that is not legally theirs before launching a venture.

Resource-strapped start-ups experience another straightforward trade-off: early investment of time and resources in IP management takes away resources from all other early-stage activities, such as developing products, services or platforms; hiring staff; renting office space; and setting up a website. It can slow down the start-up process and require significant financial resources – especially if the services of a lawyer are needed. On the other hand, IP protection is often a crucial building block of the proof-of-concept process and a necessary requirement to attract early hires, partners and – not least – investors. Paradigmatic of this challenge is German start-up Curaluna, which developed a 'smart nappy' that sends an alarm to a mobile phone as soon as a baby requires a nappy change. The founding team successfully pitched their idea in an episode of German TV show *Die Höhle der Löwen* (similar to the UK show *Dragons' Den* and the US/Australian shows *Shark Tank*), and received an investment offer from Carsten Maschmeyer, one of the panel members. However, during the due diligence after the show, the experienced investor withdrew his offer when he realized that the start-up had failed to secure a crucial patent for its invention (Schäfer 2018).

3.4 The timing trade-off

While the availability of resources in early-stage start-ups is one aspect to consider, another is the timing of IP management activities. Over time, entrepreneurs will be able to acquire more knowledge about their products or services, come increasingly closer to product/market fit and understand better what their main value proposition will be. These details will help them to file for the most appropriate IP rights, but are often unclear in the first stage of the venture development. On the flipside, managing IP later in the development cycle comes at the risk of being unable to secure necessary rights or securing them only at higher costs.

Many entrepreneurs, and even authors who write guidebooks for entrepreneurs, underestimate the importance of this timing trade-off. For example, the lean start-up model (Ries 2011) – a famed methodology for start-up entrepreneurship – suggests that entrepreneurs should 'fail fast' and 'fail forward'; meaning that they should test and iterate products and services rather than developing them in-house behind closed doors and without feedback from the market. While this approach has great advantages for finding product/market fit (one of the main indicators signalling transition to the commercialization stage), it also comes at a cost. On the one hand, such an approach provides competitors with important information which they can leverage to develop and secure IP. On the other hand, it discloses the technology – or at least significant parts of it – to the public; something which makes it more difficult to file patents and secure other important IP rights.

3.5 Public institutions during the conception stage

Proactively engaging in IP management sends a strong and positive signal to stakeholders who are toying with the idea of investing time or money in a start-up. However, in the resource-constrained early days of the conception stage, entrepreneurs often find themselves struggling with the challenge of finding time and money for this process. Public agencies and initiatives can play an important role in dealing with these challenges (Islam et al 2018).

One special scenario regarding guaranteeing IP before taking the plunge is the case of university spin-offs (see Chapter 5 for more information on this issue). Research on university spin-offs and academic entrepreneurship is becoming increasingly prominent, and the questions of IP and the general commercialization of university research are core interests of this stream of research (Rothaermel et al 2007). As universities are increasingly challenged to go beyond their traditional research and educational mission, they are engaging in new venture creation (or partnerships to that end) and are exploiting academic research commercially (Shane 2004). Given that there is a growing need for universities to align IP incentives, many have founded technology transfer offices to organize the process of university spin-offs (see Chapter 4, section 2.2). Those offices provide both tangible and intangible support for start-ups' IP management, often at no or heavily reduced costs.

At the same time, technology transfer offices help to manage IP-related conflicts. A plethora of IP issues between firms and universities can emerge – in particular, as Hall et al (2001) show, when the research is expected to lead to less appropriable results and the duration of the research is relatively short. In such cases, it is quite helpful for inexperienced founders to collaborate with skilled technology transfer officers who can anticipate and manage IP-related issues.

Finally, in reaction to resource-related trade-offs, public institutions offer support for early-stage start-ups. The German government supports IP protection for start-ups with advice and financial resources. The Federal Ministry for Economic Affairs and Energy (*Bundesministerium für Wirtschaft und Energie Öffentlichkeitsarbeit*) invests in the *WIPANO – Wissens- und Technologietransfer durch Patente und Normen* programme, which assists companies with researching, detailing and filing for patents both in Germany and abroad, and helps with the costs of such activities. All companies that have not filed for patents in the preceding five years are eligible. In this way, even small and new companies can start to develop an IP management strategy and a portfolio of IP rights (*Bundesministerium für Wirtschaft und Energie Öffentlichkeitsarbeit* 2017; Erk 2018). By accelerating the professionalization process, the WIPANO programme can ultimately also help to manage the transition from the conception stage to the commercialization stage.

4. IP challenges during commercialization

Many of the earlier IP issues cast a long shadow when start-ups transition to the commercialization stage. Unaddressed issues can now turn into serious liabilities. Often these issues will impact the relationship with early stage outside investors. Given that start-ups often lack a track record of clear metrics, investors are challenged to evaluate them based on the perceived strength of the team and the potential of the business concept (Sahlmann 1997). As soft criteria matter most when evaluating relatively new ventures, signalling effects towards investors and other stakeholders matter a great deal.

4.1 The counselling trade-off

Investors perceive a venture as more legitimate if it is strategically positioned to protect and exploit its IP (Fisher et al 2016: 392). One element of a holistic IP management strategy is the choice of lawyer or law firm as sparring partner. This confronts entrepreneurs with yet another trade-off. Professional legal services that usually come at a high price may be difficult to afford for resource-constrained start-ups. However, choosing a more affordable service can create its own problems when it comes to highly complex issues around IP, including the lack of experience in flagging potential issues for the future.

In addition, selecting counsel has a signalling effect for outside partners and investors. Investors will avoid investing in a company faced with the possibility of lawsuits unless they are very certain about the outcome. For that reason, it pays to use a law firm that the start-up and investor community know and respect. Often, such firms will include law firms that the investors work with on a regular basis. For founders who face the dilemma of how to invest their scarce resources, any evaluation of the matter should consider not only the quality of the lawyer, but also the signalling effect. The quality and type of law firm selected communicate professionalism to potential investors, as well as to the founders' former employers who might be considering claiming rights.

Moreover, a stable partnership may generate what Orozco (2010: 694) calls 'legal knowledge' – that is, 'the outcome of learning among managers and attorneys working in a group', which in the long run may develop into an organizational routine and a competitive advantage. If companies find themselves engaging with IP on a regular basis, and if a lot of the company's value is tied up in IP, ventures may even consider hiring an in-house IP lawyer.

4.2 The patent registration trade-off

The process of registering a patent often takes several years. Therefore, it is crucial for entrepreneurs to think about patenting early in the commercialization stage. In Germany, patents can be registered through the German Patent and Trade Mark Office (DPMA) or with the European Patent Office (EPO). When choosing the registration process, entrepreneurs should not only consider practicalities, but also reflect on the strategic outcome of this decision.

Filing a patent at the DPMA is significantly faster and more cost effective compared to an application at the EPO. However, the resulting patent is valid only in Germany. Alternatively (or additionally), inventors have the option of filing a patent application centrally at the EPO. If the application is accepted, the EPO will file a national patent in all member states chosen by the applicant. Another option that inventors can choose, which has an even broader geographical scope, is to file under the Patent Cooperation Treaty (PCT). Inventors can file a PCT application at the DPMA or EPO, which allows them to 'reserve' their patent for up to 30 months in as many as 153 member states. Following this approach, entrepreneurs can buy time to decide on the 'crown jewel' countries – that is, those which are most important for future growth and expansion. The patents must be validated in these countries, which comes at some additional cost for the start-up. As the success of the product is as yet unknown, it is often difficult for entrepreneurs to decide on where to file a patent. However, it is imperative for the founders to critically reflect on the global potential of their inventions, even while building the start-up and improving their product or technology in one specific environment: act local, think global.

4.3 The scope trade-off

After deciding on the most important markets in which to secure a patent, the founders will also need to consider the types of patents they want to file. De Wilton (2011: 10) describes the strategic trade-off that start-ups face between filing narrow and broad patents. She argues that a narrow patent, which describes the core of the product, can be of high value if the described functionality 'solves a longstanding problem, relates to a standards-essential feature, or has wide user appeal relative to other known solutions'. Nevertheless, a narrow patent not only takes more time to file and often requires a highly paid technical or legal specialist; it is also prone to workarounds. As the core functionality is narrowly described in every detail, competitors can find an alternative solution that differs marginally from the original patent without violating it.

Broad patents require less curation in the application process. As they cover not only a specific functionality, but also a broader set of possibilities to solve a problem, it is more complex for competitors to develop a workaround without violating the patent. However, broad patents bear a higher risk of being voided in a legal confrontation. US-based SEO platform BrightEdge learned this lesson the hard way. The company filed a lawsuit on patent infringement against German competitor Searchmetrics, which had just entered the US market. In a four-year court battle, during which the US branch of Searchmetrics declared bankruptcy, the court eventually ruled that the patents were too broad and unspecific, and were therefore invalid. Eventually, this decision allowed Searchmetrics a new entry into the US market (Hüsing 2018).

A start-up's IP strategy also has a decisive impact on its business model. In analysing start-ups with different business models – such as 'pay per use', franchise or multi-sided platforms – Bonakdar et al (2017) find a strong relationship between business models and IP strategy. Hence, the choice of IP strategy is not an isolated or peripheral decision in the process of venture creation, but rather an imperative and substantial element of designing a viable business. Other scholars have shown that companies which perceive their IP as an asset independently of their products and engage in strategies to utilize their IP – for instance, through licensing – are more likely to internationalize and grow (Symeonidou et al 2017). In the commercialization stage, start-ups often adjust their business models or even pivot from one business model to another. In these processes, entrepreneurs must think carefully about how to align and, if necessary, realign their IP strategy with other aspects of their business strategy.

4.4 The enforcement trade-off

As the visibility of the new venture increases, competitors' claims over IP may create obstacles for the further development of the business. Start-ups differ in their approaches to IP confrontations with competitors. Some try to discourage competitors systematically from taking legal action, while others actively look for violators to sue them. If faced with a lawsuit, some firms opt for avoidance, even at the cost of losing a potentially valuable asset. Others invest in the process of IP conflict resolution, even if that means shouldering significant financial obligations and engaging in lengthy lawsuits that divert attention away from the day-to-day running of the start-up.

Once a start-up detects a violation of its IP, management must decide whether to enforce its IP rights. Suing a competitor over IP violations is costly, in terms of both financial resources and time. Egym, a tech start-up based in Munich, fought for more than three years against a competitor that claimed a violation of one of its patents (EP 0 853 961). In 2016, Munich Regional Court I decided in favour of Egym and ruled that this was not a case of patent violation. However, reflecting on the process, the founders stressed that the investment needed systematically puts larger companies with more resources at an advantage over start-up entrepreneurs (no author 2016). Involvement in an IP-related lawsuit can also cause uncertainty among important stakeholders, such as employees and investors, and can thus undermine the company's legitimacy. Investors will generally avoid investing in a company involved in an unresolved lawsuit; and key hires may hesitate because they cannot be entirely sure whether their job will be secure if the company loses the conflict.

The loss of legitimacy is not only tied to the companies involved in the lawsuit, but might even affect an entire product or market category. Radically innovative products are more prone to losing legitimacy than products based on incremental innovations in established markets. Therefore, start-ups in relatively new market segments may delay lawsuits against patent violators if they fear that the public attention may put the entire product or market category in question.

Another reason to delay a lawsuit is even more strategic. A competitor using another's party IP might have structured its entire business process around this IP. Therefore, the damage from losing this IP through an actual or threatened lawsuit can be quite substantial. In most cases, the damage increases the longer the patent has already been used. German company IDnow, which offers software for video identification over smartphones, engaged in a lawsuit against its direct competitor, WebID. IDnow won the initial lawsuit and WebID had to temporarily change the technology it used (Schlenk 2017). This was undoubtedly a major setback for the start-up, forcing the entrepreneurs to significantly change its business processes until WebID eventually won the case on appeal in 2020 (*IT Finanzmagazin* 2020).

4.5 Collaborations

Finally, collaboration can also be a reasonable approach towards IP management. Instead of perceiving potential competitors as threats, de Wilton (2011) suggests that start-ups should see them as potential partners and collaborators. Especially in markets that the start-up is as yet unable or unwilling to serve, licensing IP can be a rewarding and financially lucrative strategy. Occasionally, companies may even strategically decide to give up IP rights, with the goal of sustainably developing new markets. In 2014, Tesla CEO Elon Musk published a blog article explaining that the company would make its patents freely available (Musk 2014). Even though this decision seemed harmful to the development of the company at first, it had a clear strategic purpose. By allowing Tesla's competitors to use the patents and build electric cars, the market for them – still small at the time – developed at a faster pace (Chambers 2014). The car manufacturers – almost all of them international brands – would not have been willing to pay a licensing fee which ultimately would have strengthened their competitor, Tesla. As they were still heavily investing in R&D around internal combustion engines, the only way to speed up market development was to allow them to freely use the existing patents. While giving up patents requires a developed market position, it is an option for companies to swiftly transition to the growth stage.

5. IP challenges during growth stage

In the growth stage, start-ups regularly expand beyond their initial markets. In this expansion process, entrepreneurs must adapt their IP strategy to new markets and reflect on the different cultural and legal environments. Start-ups that reach the growth stage have successfully established their business models in their home market. Their track record may even make them interesting targets for mergers and acquisitions. At the same time, the transition is also a transformational and risky event, which may 'reset the organization's liabilities of newness clock and reexpose the organization to the risk of failure' (Fisher et al 2016: 392). A well-developed, carefully executed international IP strategy can help to mitigate this challenge, increase attractiveness for potential buyers or serve as the foundation to reach maturity independently.

5.1 The entrepreneur's blueprint

When start-ups enter a foreign market for the first time, they often make decisions 'as if' they were in a familiar context. Ignoring important contextual differences, they stick to their notion of 'how things work'. This phenomenon – sometimes referred to as the 'entrepreneur's blueprint' – is common in the case of many activities, such as hiring (Wasserman 2012) or splitting equity and allocating salaries (Baron and Hannan 2002), in which entrepreneurs make decisions based on previous unrelated experiences gained in a fundamentally different context.

In the context of IP management, start-up entrepreneurs entering an international market with an unfamiliar legal and cultural context are prone to the risk of taking their 'IP blueprint' as the basis for decision making. To avoid the 'blueprint' trap, entrepreneurs must first investigate the different context and be aware of their (potentially limited) mental map for decision making. In talking to other start-ups and local or international IP lawyers, entrepreneurs can develop a better understanding of the cultural and legal differences. In a second step, entrepreneurs must critically reflect on and eventually challenge their blueprints. It is crucial to continuously question their interpretations of the unfamiliar context and distinguish between knowledge that they acquired by investigation and ideas transferred from unrelated experiences.

In recent years, the German start-up scene has become increasingly internationalized, especially towards the US (GTAI 2019). Expanding to the US is not only attractive for German start-ups due to the large market; other common reasons to open a branch in the US or even to move headquarters across the Atlantic include the flourishing investors scene – especially VC – and the presence of exceptional talent. VCs often require the start-ups they invest in to be located in close proximity. This provides them with a higher level of control and affords start-up entrepreneurs better access to the VC's network and resources. However, to successfully operate in the US, entrepreneurs must be aware of and overcome their German or European 'blueprint' and build a comprehensive understanding of the US legal system, including IP. While a full discussion of the issue of IP for start-ups in the US legal system is beyond the scope of this chapter, the following sections provide a brief introduction to some important differences regarding IP (for more details, see Bagley and Dauchy 2018).

5.2 Common and civil law as context for IP management

The US legal system is a common law system, which is based on the idea that the court decision of a legal dispute sets a precedent for following conflicts of the same type. It is the dominant legal system in English-speaking countries and one of the two legal frameworks of the Western world. The other one is civil law. This principle, as applied in Germany, is based on generic or more abstract laws that cover many specific cases. Under the latter system, it is not the precedent that determines the resolution of a legal conflict, but a general law. For IP, these differences play a decisive role not only in how IP-related disputes are resolved, but also regarding the filing of patents and trademarks.

Patent registration in Germany is based on the 'first-to-file' principle. The party that is first to apply for a patent with the DPMA or the EPO will be granted the patent. In 2013, the US became one of the last countries in the world to switch to the first-to-file system. However, while the general principle of granting patents is now the same, there are striking differences in trademark registration. In Germany, the registration of a trademark also relies on the first-to-file principle: the company or individual that first registers a trademark owns the right to use it. In the US, by contrast, trademark registration is based on the 'first-to-use' principle: the first party to use a trademark has the right to register it. While entrepreneurs in the US can also register a trademark before they have used it, this is no guarantee – in contrast to the position in Germany – that another company has not used it already and still has the right to register it. This difference is important for German start-ups expanding to the US market and highlights the need to register trademarks early.

5.3 IP and staff

In a stage of international growth, IP challenges arise not only in a company's relationship towards competitors, but also internally. Employees have access to various trade secrets, such as costumer contacts, manufacturing techniques and business processes. To turn a business element into a trade secret, companies in the US must declare what they define as 'trade secrets' and develop a strategy to keep them 'secret'. Otherwise, the company will have a hard time enforcing the trade secrets in case of a legal conflict. Once key employees who had access to trade secrets leave the company, they are in an advantageous position to compete with it, either by working for a competitor or by founding their own venture. Acknowledging this advantage, some states – such as New York – allow for so called 'non-compete agreements'; while others – such as California – prohibit such agreements in order to benefit employees and protect their right to switch employers (Marx et al 2015). Such agreements forbid a former employee, for a certain period after leaving the company, from working for a competitor and from founding a new company in the same space and industry. Non-compete agreements must be reasonable in time and geographic scope in order to be enforceable.

This type of legal contract is exemplary for challenges in the growth and internationalization stage of a start-up. On the one hand, it shows that German entrepreneurs must overcome their home blueprint. When internationalizing, US start-ups have an advantage because they are trained to expect differences not only between countries, but also within a given country. On the other hand, in their growth and expansion stage, entrepreneurs must also rethink how they manage their own IP processes and their employees' relationship to the company's IP.

5.4 International IP management

It is not only the case that the legal situation around IP rights and conflict resolution differs between countries and states; but also that different cultures, languages and business attitudes require different IP strategies, especially regarding brand/product names, trademarks and designs. Sometimes names will already have been registered as trademarks in foreign markets. In this case, a company must think about whether it is viable and worthwhile to buy the trademark, or whether it is preferable to enter the market with a new trademark. Planning the market entry of its e-health platform, the founder of German start-up Junomedical discovered that the trademark had already been registered. He adjusted the firm's name to Qunomedical in order to avoid legal conflicts and have a single brand name internationally (Project A Services GmBH & Co KG 2017). Another reason to change a product or company name is an unintended meaning or connotation in a foreign language. In expanding beyond the European market, travel platform GoEuro changed its name to Omio (Fockenbrock 2019). Founder and CEO Naren Shaam commented on the name change: '[Over the last 15 years] GoEuro has served us well, supporting us in making travel easy for millions of people travelling to and within Europe. But our ambitions are much larger than Europe' (Omio 2019). When considering renaming a start-up, the founders must carefully weigh the options of adopting a unified company or product name for all markets or having different names in different markets. Having multiple product or company names in various markets is the less costly strategy, as the trademarks need only be registered on a per country basis. However, this strategy might dilute the brand or product value. Especially in the process of raising additional capital for growth or exiting the company, an ambiguous brand strategy might be harmful.

In case of exiting the company or acquiring new capital for growth, IP can play an important role. VCs and other institutional investors value secured IP and especially patents as a positive signal for venture success (Conti et al 2013). VCs not only pick start-ups with strong IP strategies, but also support them in further developing valuable IP (Baum and Silverman 2004). In collaborating directly with institutional investors and other firms from their network, start-ups might create shared IP. In developing IP together, start-ups can leverage their capabilities and develop valuable outcomes quicker and with little investment. However, shared IP can cause problems, especially if one of the companies is acquired. Start-ups must think ahead and plan for different scenarios. It is crucial not to fall into the trap of defining only one possible outcome, but rather also plan for alternatives. 'If ... then ... otherwise' clauses help entrepreneurs to define not just the consequences of reaching a milestone ('if ... then'), but also project how the company will react to not achieving said milestone ('otherwise ...'). It is a common mistake to plan only for the 'rosy' scenarios and fail to agree on how to deal with alternative outcomes (Wasserman 2012). Hence, planning for both positive and negative contingencies is key for the long-term success of a start-up.

6. Concluding remarks

IP management is and should be a core area of activity for start-ups at every stage of their lifecycle. A well-crafted IP strategy creates significant competitive advantages. It can erect barriers to entry or provide other obstacles to competitors; reduce overall costs; or be a source of revenue when utilized in licensing or franchise models. Indeed, business strategy and strategic IP management are closely intertwined and have a shaping influence on each other. At the same time, IP strategy is a field that helps start-ups to deal with the challenge of legitimacy. In the absence of a track record of business successes or clear metrics to evaluate them, start-ups are often perceived as risky investments. The more that they can manage risks and present convincing strategies for predictable obstacles, the more likely that stakeholders are to engage with them. As start-ups evolve through different stages – that is, conceptualization, commercialization and growth – they are continuously challenged to convince relevant stakeholders of their potential and their ability to manage technology and market risks. Their IP strategy is a core part of this task; and if left unaddressed, start-ups potentially forgo an important and effective way to increase their market value.

Importantly, IP management is not a static task. As start-ups evolve, so too do IP challenges and opportunities. It is noteworthy that, in particular, it is the transition phases from one stage to the next that require the attention of management, because they bring about new challenges for managing IP. In addition to the new content challenges in IP management, the transitions from one stage to the next act as 'legitimacy thresholds' and start-ups must actively work on acquiring legitimacy with a new set of stakeholders at each stage of their development. Importantly, gaining legitimacy requires continuous investment. Therefore, holistic management of both IP and its perception helps entrepreneurs to smoothly progress from one stage to the next.

IP management has an impact both outside (competitors, investors, institutions) and inside (employees, co-founders) the company. IP decisions often come in the form of trade-offs. For example, during the conception stage, aspiring entrepreneurs may need to decide how and when to inform a previous employer about their intention to start a new business (information trade-off). Informing employers early may facilitate a concrete dialogue over IP rights; but it also increases the risk of alerting employers to the potential value of the idea. Another trade-off pertains to the timing of patent filings (patent filing trade-off). While an earlier filing date generally allows an aspiring entrepreneur to claim that he is the inventor, it also makes it easier for a previous employer to argue that the person finalized the invention while still employed, which may give the employer some rights to the idea. At each stage of the lifecycle, entrepreneurs face the challenge of deciding how much resources to invest into IP management (resource trade-off) – a difficult decision in the context of generally resource-starved early-stage ventures. Too much of an investment may slow down the start-up process because it channels attention away from other tasks. However, too little investment may discourage early hires, partners and – not least – investors to collaborate with the start-up because it fails to secure necessary IP rights. Because this is such an obvious dilemma, public agencies exist that help start-ups to deal with it.

While early and proactive IP management may seem and often is generally preferable, entrepreneurs can be encouraged to delay IP activities due to lack of information (timing trade-off). In many start-ups, entrepreneurs only slowly realize product/market fit and understand what their main value proposition is. These details are the basis for filing for the most appropriate IP rights. On the flipside, filing late obviously comes at the risk of being unable to secure necessary rights or being able to secure them only at higher cost (Figure 8.2).

When it comes to patent filings, there are a few trade-offs that entrepreneurs must address. The first concerns the choice of legal service or law firm. While an experienced lawyer may tie up a significant

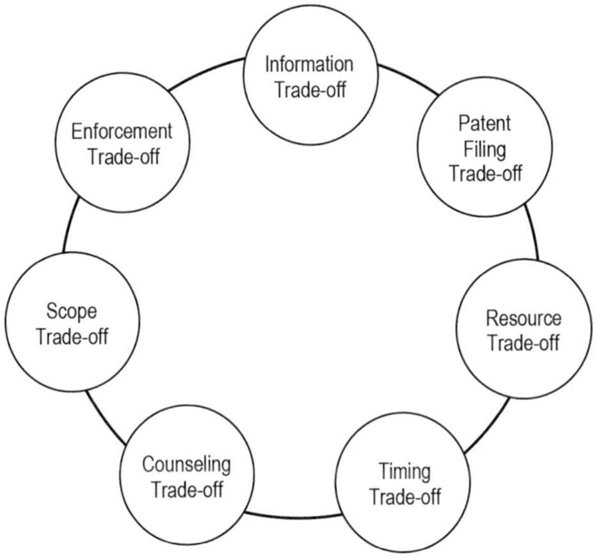

Figure 8.2 Overview of the most important trade-offs

number of financial resources, the decision may also send positive signals towards external stakeholders (counselling trade-off). In addition, there is a trade-off regarding the scope of the patent. Filing a narrow patent is more cumbersome to design and file, yet potentially prone to workarounds. A broad patent, in contrast, is harder to enforce in a legal conflict (scope trade-off). Finally, start-ups differ in how they approach legal conflicts. Not pursuing IP violators aggressively means potentially losing a valuable asset, but also not diverting attention from other business activities; while pursuing them means capitalizing on an asset, but also having to endure lengthy lawsuits and their costs (enforcement trade-off).

For many areas of IP management, start-ups will require expert advice. Indeed, Bagley (2008: 378) argues that the ability of management teams to have a productive dialogue with lawyers and to collaborate on solving complex problems is a managerial capability of great significance for innovation and competitiveness. We would add that this dialogue may not only help to predict and prepare for foreseeable IP problems, but can also address challenges relating to entrepreneurial blueprints – that is, taken-for-granted assumptions derived from prior, not necessarily identical experiences. This is particularly important when it comes to different legal environments, because seemingly small differences in facts can result in dramatically different outcomes. It is up to the entrepreneurial team to decide whether and how they want to engage with a sparring partner that can help to align law and strategy in IP management.

IP management in start-ups requires continuous investment; but if managed proactively, it can provide important competitive advantages for entrepreneurs. More than mature companies, start-ups are often forced to radically rethink their business model, strategy and team composition – they should remain flexible and go through a series of pivots. However, sophisticated IP management plays a crucial role in transitioning through different lifecycle stages, acquiring legitimacy with different groups of stakeholders and ultimately supporting the start-up's competitive positioning and success. Despite resource constraints, start-up entrepreneurs do well in acquiring legal astuteness and proactively addressing the challenge of IP management.

9 Aspects relevant to the valuation of start-ups, with a focus on intangible assets

Ashkan Kalantary

1. Introduction

The transformation from the industrial age to the service and information age has also changed the framework of the business valuation and transaction market. Digital business models usually have faster product, life and growth cycles. This is illustrated in particular by the speed at which companies now achieve so-called 'unicorn' status – the point at which a company's valuation exceeds the $1 billion mark.

While traditional software companies such as Avast Software took more than 20 years to achieve unicorn status, today's technology and data-driven companies are doing so in much shorter timeframes – for example, just 14 months in the case of Oculus Virtual Reality (Oculus VR) (see *Frankfurter Allgemeine Zeitung* 2014).

The basis of this rapid growth is the use of novel business models combined with modern technologies. Moreover, globalization and the opening up of international markets have significantly advanced this trend (see Kasperzak and Nestler 2010: 21; Stoi 2003: 175; Reimsbach 2011: 3).

In particular, intangible assets such as brand names, technologies and customer relationships increase companies' long-term competitiveness and thus cash-flow and growth expectations (see Kasperzak and Nestler 2010: 21; Stoi 2003: 175; Reimsbach 2011: 1). To this extent, innovations

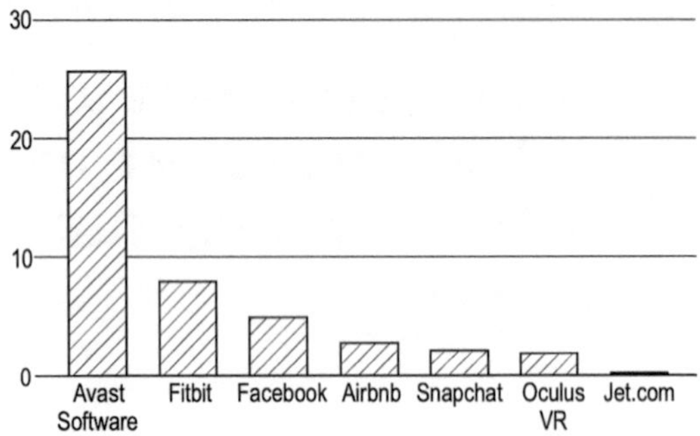

Source: Own presentation based on CB Insights 2019a; Unger 2016.

Figure 9.1 *Speed at which companies reach unicorn status in years*

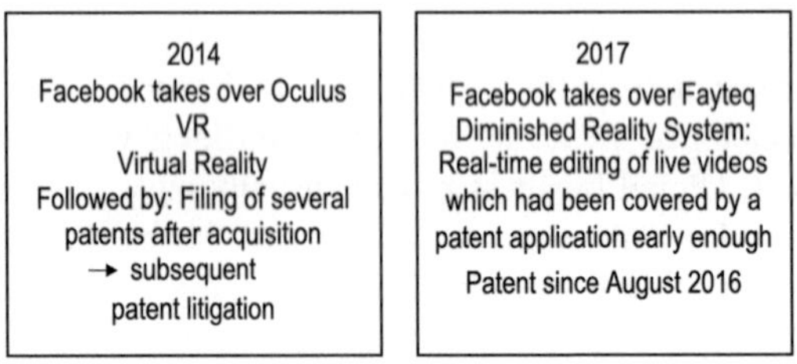

Source: Own presentation based on Facebook 2014; Kyriasoglou 2017

Figure 9.2 *Mergers between Facebook and innovative start-ups with intangible assets*

and new technologies have become increasingly important for company valuation (Figure 9.1).

The recoverability of intangible assets is important, for example, in case of internal restructuring or the sale of the company. For innovative start-ups in particular, they comprise a large part of the asset structure following a business combination. Studies show that across all industries, intangible assets account for more than 50 per cent of the purchase price (see Günther and Ott 2008: 920). Thus, the correct valuation of a company is dependent on the correct valuation of intangible assets. Current examples show that patented technologies in particular are of greatest relevance here (see Figure 9.2).

In 2014, Facebook acquired Oculus VR for approximately $2 billion (see *Süddeutsche Zeitung* 2014; Facebook 2014), whereupon Oculus VR filed a number of patents (CB Insights oJb). The subsequent patent lawsuits that were filed – which could potentially have been avoided by the early filing of patents (see section 4 below) – reveal the vulnerability of technology-driven companies (see Wolfe 2017; Heath 2017).

Three years later, Facebook purchased German start-up Fayteq, which had already patented its technology in 2016 ('Method and image processing system for removing a visual object from an image', US 9,412,188 B2) (CB Insights nd; TU Ilmenau nd; Kyriasoglou 2017). With the help of this technology, live videos can be modified in real time, allowing the removal and addition of new image content and thus enabling videos and films to be modified for specific target groups. This technology can be used, for example, across countries in the marketing industry.

The fast pace of innovation-driven start-ups has the advantage of rapid and high market penetration and accelerated market success, but also the danger of greater imitation. Therefore, innovation-driven start-ups in particular are dependent on the protection of their inventions. A distinction can be made between software and hardware-based business models. The protection of inventions in technology/hardware-heavy industries (eg, medical technology, VR, mobility) – the so-called non-digital area – is particularly relevant. According to studies, approximately 24% of German start-ups have a non-digital hardware focus (see Kollmann et al 2018: 26).

2. Proration of the subject of valuation

A company valuation is an assessment of the company's future success value. This is an uncertain value, due to its prognostic character. The value can be estimated mathematically from the expected returns (so-called 'cash flows') or based on the transaction price.

In the valuation theory of the market objectivity of transaction prices on the capital markets, preference is given to cash-flow forecasts based on an individual enterprise value. However, the market valuation of companies is mainly limited to listed companies, so cash-flow based company valuation is highly relevant in practice.

The cash-flow forecast in particular serves as the basis for this. The challenge in evaluating individual technologies lies in the ability to distinguish individual cash flows from overall corporate cash flow. While this can regularly be extrapolated for an established company from the analysis of historical figures, it is more difficult for start-ups with limited or no financial history.

The situation is similar with the value drivers of innovative start-ups. As in the examples above, these lie in particular in intangible assets.

Intangible assets are characterized by certain features that make their valuation difficult:

- Inventions, brand names and customer relations are unique. It is difficult to derive a comparative value from past transactions such as securities or machinery.
- It is not uncommon for their financial value contribution to unfold through interaction with other tangible assets, making it difficult to isolate their cash flows.
- The inability to isolate their cash flows leads to a lack of historical financial figures that can be used to extrapolate the cash flows.

Therefore, methods have been developed in literature and practice to derive the value contribution of intangible assets for companies. However, before these methods can be discussed, it is necessary to further delimit the valuation object.

3. IP rights as a reference framework for the valuation of intangible assets

While the boundaries between unprotected intangible assets are blurred, the advantage of the distinction between IP rights is that the intangible asset to be protected is more specific. This also facilitates trade and thus valuation. As has been shown in the previous chapters, the protection of IP plays a significant role, especially for start-ups. Having clarified in Chapter 3 the importance and applicability of inventor law for start-ups, the following section discusses the different types of IP rights. The focus here is on the different functional orientations of patents with which intangible assets can be protected.

Table 9.1 *IP rights and their term*

Type	Maximum duration (in years)
Patents	20
Utility models	10
Registered trademarks	Indefinitely renewable
Registered designs	25

Source: Own presentation based on DPMA 2019.

Different types of IP rights can be defined (see DPMA 2019; Kasperzak and Nestler 2010: 183). The different types of IP rights have different terms after which the protection of the intangible asset expires. This refers, on the one hand, to the loss of legal significance after the expiry of the term; and on the other hand, to the technological and economic obsolescence caused by the advancement of technologies. Table 9.1 sets out the different types of IP rights and their respective maximum term of protection.

For a detailed description of IP rights, see Chapter 1, section 2 on the categorization of IP.

The maximum term of the intangible asset is of particular relevance for cash-flow-related valuation, as it determines the term within which future surpluses can be generated. While intangible assets without IP rights regularly present challenges in determining the term, this can be clearly determined in the case of IP rights – with the exception of trademark rights, as these are indefinitely renewable.

In the following, the focus is on the patent as an instrument of IP protection for the technological inventions of start-ups. In order to derive cash flows, it is important as a first step to determine whether the technology to be evaluated comprises one patent only or is spread over several patents (see Kasperzak and Nestler 2010: 181ff). For further differentiation, it is therefore helpful to assess the different functional orientations of patents (see Kasperzak and Nestler 2010: 181ff).

These are as follows:

- protective function;
- blocking function;

- financing function;
- cooperation function;
- stockpile function; and
- reputation function.

The protective function has the highest functional relevance for start-ups. This is the basis for excluding third parties from using the invention. As a result, the monopoly income for the patent owner, which is limited at least to the patent term, unfolds (see Kasperzak and Nestler 2010: 181ff). This forms the basis for the sustainable and relevant development of the value of the start-up. As patenting is usually preceded by a long and complicated application process, start-ups should start the patenting process early on.

The blocking function, on the other hand, is usually more likely to become relevant in the later phases of the start-up, as it provides only indirect benefits compared to the protective function. Its purpose is to hinder the competitive environment by restricting the scope for action, which is associated with the market exclusion principle or the occupation of new research fields (see Kloyer 2004: 425).

Especially for start-ups, the procurement of capital is of existential importance. Through their financing function, IP rights can be used as an argument for securing external financing (see Kasperzak and Nestler 2010: 182). It is not uncommon for new applications for IP rights to be the reason for initiating a financing round and updating the assessment of the start-up (see *Süddeutsche Zeitung* 2014; Facebook 2014).

For cross-company patents, the cooperation function also plays a decisive role. Start-ups often operate across sectors. One example is Facebook, which, through its acquisition of Oculus VR, is now enabling VR applications for companies. Such patents, which previously had no relevance in the media sector, are becoming increasingly important.

When patents are applied for, but exploited only at a later stage, this is known as the stockpile function. It allows the company to occupy fields of technology on the one hand; and to be able to act flexibly in the future on the other (see Mazzoleni and Nelson 1998: 275 et seq; Hermans 1991: 87).

The publication of an invention can also serve as an indicator of success and thus fulfils a reputation function (see Knyphausen 1993: 784). This is particularly relevant for start-ups in the exit phase, as it can be used to generate positive momentum in an IPO.

4. Reasons for valuation and factors determining the value of patents

The valuation of intangible assets is carried out for a specific purpose. There are various occasions for patent valuation for start-ups:

- debt financing;
- accounting valuation; and
- dispute valuation.

As previously indicated, patent value can play a significant role in providing security for future financing rounds. Due to the lack of historical figures, the assessment of the start-up in financing rounds is often based on the subjective ideas of both the buyer and the seller. A valuation of the underlying patents can serve as the lower limit of the sales value, taking into account other assets. The company value should exceed the value of the sum of all assets in the case of a single sale.

As a result of growth and the increase in borrowed capital, the accounting-related valuation of patents plays an important role. The publication of accounting information keeps creditors and owners informed about the value of patents as key value drivers. At the latest when the company goes public, patents should be valued in accordance with International Financial Reporting Standards (IFRS). However, patent valuation also plays an important role in the so-called 'purchase price allocation' according to IFRS 3 when the start-up is sold.

Finally, the determination of IP value in the event of a legal dispute can also play a decisive role for start-ups. This is illustrated by prominent court cases such as those involving Oculus VR (see Heath 2017; Wingfield and Isaac 2017). US holding company ZeniMax Media accused Oculus VR of stealing important elements of the technology and thus of IP infringement. The complaint was based on the fact that a former ZeniMax employee had helped to develop the VR technology at the time and ZeniMax was never compensated for this. ZeniMax won the lawsuit and received $250 million in compensation for the infringement (Gilbert 2018).

In addition to the reason for valuation, there are several factors that determine the value of patents which must be taken into account. These include legal indicators, patent strategy and patent function, as well as the exploitation process (see Kasperzak and Nestler 2010: 185 et seq). These are independent of the maturity of the company and are therefore also relevant for start-ups.

4.1 Legal indicators

As indicated above, the age of the patent is highly relevant to its value. The shorter the remaining term of the patent, the shorter the economic life or the term of expected cash flows (see Kasperzak and Nestler 2010: 185 et seq). Unlike trademarks, patents generally do not increase in value over their term. Through marketing investments, the brand value can increase over time.

The scope of protection of a patent influences its value: the larger the secured monopoly, the higher the potential returns. Accordingly, there is a positive correlation between the number of patent claims, the regional scope and the value (see Kasperzak and Nestler 2010: 185). This is where start-ups often reach their limits. The patenting process is long and complex. Nevertheless, examples such as the Oculus lens show that a broad scope of protection is desirable.

Legal disputes must also be included in the assessment. Victory in a patent case can increase the value of a patent; whereas a pending or lost patent dispute can reduce its value. The influence of a patent dispute on value is referred to as the 'conflict value' of a patent (see Wurzer and Reinhardt 2006: 4, margin 60 et seq; Harhoff et al 2003: 1352).

4.2 Patent strategy and purpose

Not every patent is directly exploited. There are company-specific reasons for not exploiting a patent, which must be used to determine the value of the patent subjectively. This company-specific value contribution can be significant – for example, if the IP right owned by a competitor would have a higher value contribution than that of the inventor which uses the patent as a blocking patent to exclude competitors (see Kasperzak and Nestler 2010: 186 et seq). Due to their limited resources, start-ups must consider whether the benefit from the blocking or stockpiling function is greater than the investment that must be made in the patenting process.

4.3 Exploitation

To determine the value of a patent, the cash flows to be allocated are used. The exploitation of a product invention (new features or types of use) can lead to increased sales and, in the case of a process invention, to more efficient production processes. For this reason, the invention's economic chances of success are relevant. Accordingly, the influencing factors can result from higher sales or savings in manufacturing costs (see Kasperzak and Nestler 2010: 188 et seq).

5. Approaches to patent valuation

There are various approaches to the valuation of patents, which are explained in more detail below. The selection of the respective method is based on the underlying data and the function of the patent value. The following considerations are based on Castedello et al (2018: 587 et seq), Kasperzak and Nestler (2010: 189 et seq) and Moser (2011: 17 et seq).

5.1 Market-oriented approach

The market-oriented approach is based on two methods. The first assumes that the price of the intangible asset can be observed in the market. With the exception of tradable licences, this is rarely observed in practice (see Castedello et al 2018: 589). The second method – the analogy method – is based on market participants' estimates of past transactions of patents, using the transaction prices of patents that have already been issued. Here, an analogy of the patented technology is assumed, although this is not normally the case. The market-oriented approach is made more difficult by the fact that the basis for comparison is not sufficiently large for patents placed on the market under similar conditions and close to the valuation date (Hommel, Buhleier and Pauly 2007: 371 (372); Castedello et al 2018: 589). Innovative technologies in particular have many distinguishing features and are therefore not comparable.

5.2 Net present value-oriented approach

The net present value-oriented approach refers to the expected future cash flows. Since, as described above, these cannot be derived directly for individual patents, alternative methods are used in valuation practice to determine the cash flows. A distinction is made between the licence price analogy method (relief from royalty method); the incremental cash-flow method; and the multi-period excess earnings method (see Castedello et al 2018: 591 et seq).

The licence price analogy method is a common method of patent valuation due to the fact that patents are often strategically exploited to grant rights of use. This approach is based on the consideration that patent owners save the costs of obtaining the rights of use externally. The notional royalties incurred in licensing the intangible asset are determined. These notional royalties are then regarded as value-added and discounted to the valuation date (see Castedello et al 2018: 593 et seq).

The licence price analogy method combines both net present value-oriented, cost-oriented and market price-oriented valuation approaches, and is therefore referred to as the 'chameleon' of valuation methods (Beyer and Mackenstedt 2008: 338 (344); Castedello et al 2018: 593).

In order to calculate these notional payments, the company first determines customary market licence rates for benefit-equivalent patents. The meaningfulness of the result therefore depends on the quality of the database from which the licence rates are taken. For this reason, thorough analysis of the licence analogy must be conducted in advance of the calculation, such as by checking the comparability of the licence with the valuation object and examining various parameters. These include the scope of the licence; exclusivity; the reference value of the licence (patent-relevant sales); and the rights and obligations of the contractual partners. The numerical example in Figure 9.3 illustrates the practical application of this approach.

Under the incremental cash-flow method, the cash flows of an entity with the patent being measured are compared with the cash flows of an identical entity without this patent, and the resulting difference can be explained by patent-specific cash flows. This allows conclusions to be drawn about the additional profit resulting from the patent. A prerequisite is that the

Time (in years)	1	2	3	4	5
Patent relevant sales (in k EUR)	300	350	420	470	530
License income before taxes (in k EUR) at a license rate of 3 %	9,00	10,50	12,60	14,10	15,90
30 % taxes (in k EUR)	2,70	3,15	3,78	4,23	4,77
License income after taxes (in k EUR)	6,30	7,35	8,82	9,87	11,13
Present value of license income after taxes (in k EUR at a discount factor of 8 %)	5,83	6,30	7,00	7,25	7,57
Determined initial value of the patent: 33.95 k EUR					

Source: Own calculation and presentation

Figure 9.3 *Numerical example of patent valuation using the licence price analogy method*

notional cash flows for the business concept with and without the intangible asset must be realistically estimated. In practice, such cash flows are often difficult to estimate, since an identical business model without a patent is difficult to depict – especially for technology-intensive and thus patent-dependent products.

Another capital value-oriented approach to patent valuation is the multi-period excess earnings method, which is used when further assets are to be valued. In this method, the expected cash flows of the company are reduced by notional leasing rates for supporting assets, which result from the interest on the capital employed (return on asset) and the impairment in value due to the use of the supporting assets (return of asset) (Nestler 2008: 2002 et seq). The multi-period excess earnings method assumes that the cash flows of supporting assets are deducted from the turnover of the entire company. The remaining – residual – cash flow is then allocated to the patent.

Two different methods can be used to calculate patent-specific success (see Table 9.2):

- Gross lease method: Patent-relevant earnings before interest and taxes (EBIT) + depreciation and amortization – contributory asset charges

(payments for supporting assets) = patent-specific success.
- Return on asset method: Patent-relevant EBIT – return on assets (as notional royalties) = patent-specific success.

The multi-period excess earnings method is applicable only if the assets influence the future success of the company. Thus, the patent must represent the central asset. This method is not suitable for the valuation of supporting intangible assets.

Table 9.2 *Patent valuation using the multi-period excess earnings method*

Patent-relevant EBIT Patent-related sales - costs)	
Gross lease method	Return on asset method
+ Amortization and depreciation / Contributory asset changes	/ Return on asset
= Patent-specific success	

Source: Own presentation based on Kasperzak and Nestler 2010, p 193.

5.3 Cost-oriented approach

If the future value contribution of the patent cannot be determined at the valuation date, the value of the patent is estimated approximately using the cost-based approach (calculation of the investment amount). This involves including the costs of the IP right for the invention in the valuation. There are two ways of determining the current value of the patent using this approach (see Castedello et al 2018: 605 et seq).

The costs of a new valuation object are determined on the basis of the replacement cost approach or the reproduction method, using cost information that refers to current market conditions (IDW S 5, para. 49).

The current value of the patent is determined by weighting the historical costs with an inflation price index (see Smith and Parr 2000: 194). However, this often does not take economic effects into account, which is why patents are often undervalued. This can be remedied by using current market prices as a guide.

First, the costs are measured according to one of the abovementioned variants. Subsequently, value-diminishing aspects and the remaining useful life must be taken into account, since the valuation date does not coincide with the date of invention and filing of the patent. Finally, the tax savings from the deduction of the costs incurred are deducted. Figure 9.4 illustrates this calculation using a numerical example. However, this approach has been criticized because higher costs cannot be equated with higher benefits (see Dreßler 2006: 35).

Cost type	Costs (in €)
Research and development costs	
Personnel costs	500.000
Material costs	18.000
External consulting costs	10.000
	528.000
Property right costs	
Patent application	550
Ongoing patent costs (cumulative)	3.000
	3.550
Total	531.550
Depreciation (60 %)*	-265.775
Tax savings (35 %)**	-159.465
Patent value	106.310

* in the 10th year (assuming a maximum term of 20 years)
** notional taxation

Source: Own calculation and presentation.

Figure 9.4 *Numerical example for the calculation of the patent value using the replacement cost approach*

6. Accounting for intangible property rights

Intangible assets are one of the largest value drivers for many start-ups, as in the example described of Facebook's takeover of Oculus VR. However, these intangible assets are still too rarely taken into account in the annual financial statements because many national valuation guidelines prohibit the recognition of internally generated intangible assets. Although International Accounting Standard (IAS) 38 requires the recognition of these value-enhancing assets under certain conditions, this value-enhancing potential is still too rarely exploited (see Kasperzak and Nestler 2010: 41).

6.1 Capitalization of intangible assets according to national and international standards

This section discusses the differences in the capitalization of intangible assets under national standards on the one hand and international standards on the other. The discussion compares the German national law – the Commercial Code (HGB) – and international regulations (IFRS). A company domiciled in Germany can prepare IFRS financial statements in addition to the individual financial statements in accordance with the HGB. The exceptions to this are capital market-oriented companies, for which consolidated accounting is mandatory under IFRS; although the HGB remains the most important accounting standard for the annual financial statements of German companies and for the consolidated financial statements of medium-sized groups of companies without capital market orientation (Startup Guide Ionos 2018).

As a matter of principle, internally generated intangible assets are accounted for in accordance with IFRS using the same criteria as those acquired. Since 2010, however, it has been possible to capitalize development costs (Hans Böckler Stiftung 2011). Since then, accounting companies have had the option under the HGB to capitalize internally generated intangible assets such as patents and other IP rights on the balance sheet. This is important for start-ups, as they were particularly affected by the prohibition on capitalizing self-created IP rights at that time.

As a result, the scope for action under tax law was very limited; but above all, essential IP rights based on the developments of the founding team were not reported as fixed assets. As a result, the assets of start-ups were not sufficiently recognized and thus made financing rounds more difficult (Engel 2010).

The option to include self-created intangible assets as assets on the balance sheet is based on Section 248(2), sentence 1 of the HGB. However, this is restricted in the course of that section, to the effect that self-created intangible assets are subject to an accounting ban if the following items are involved (Bundesanzeiger Verlag 2019):

- self-created brands;
- print titles (special designations under which printed matter, such as newspapers, appears);
- publishing rights (copyrights, such as authors' rights granted to the publisher, and the rights to reproduce and distribute literary and musical works);
- customer lists; and
- comparable rights of fixed assets (eg, registered designs and utility models).

As it is not possible to clearly differentiate between the production costs of the intangible assets just listed and the expenses for general corporate development, they may not be capitalized (IAS 38.63). Another reason why such items may not be included in the balance sheet is their uniqueness, which means that there is no active market (IAS 38.78). Overall, it is therefore not possible to separate these production costs from goodwill beyond reasonable doubt (Bundesanzeiger Verlag 2019).

As already described, in contrast to the HGB, there is no capitalization option for internally generated intangible assets in IFRS accounting, but rather an obligation to capitalize them. However, the same accounting prohibitions exist as under the HGB (Hans Böckler Stiftung 2011).

If the option, which is enshrined in German law and is mandatory in IFRS, is exercised, there is an increase in profit because the costs of preparing the intangible assets do not directly impact the result, but are distributed over the assumed useful life. In return, the results of subsequent periods are reduced by the respective amortization charges (Hans Böckler Stiftung 2011).

6.2 Accounting differences between research costs and development costs of intangible assets

Intangible assets are of particular importance for start-ups which have developed or purchased patents or design rights. These can be capitalized as fixed assets and can thus contribute to an increase in the value of the company.

If the general conditions are met – that is, if the IP right can be independently exploited and valued – the start-up can make use of the option to capitalize the costs (Engel 2010).

The fact that IAS 38 requires that manufacturing costs be separated into research and development costs creates a problem of delimitation. According to IAS 38.54, research costs may not be capitalized, but must always be expensed in the period in which they are incurred.

It must be possible to clearly separate the research period from the development period, so that costs can be capitalized. Production costs may be shown on the balance sheet only if it can be demonstrated that a future economic benefit will be generated. This is not the case for research activities, as the aim is to gain new knowledge in order to develop new materials, products or processes and identify their areas of application (Hans Böckler Stiftung 2011).

If it is not possible to distinguish between research and development, companies must allocate the costs of the entire production process to the research phase (IAS 38.53) (Pellens et al 2017: 398).

However, as soon as the recoverability of intangible assets can be demonstrated on the basis of various criteria, these are development costs that must be recognized as intangible assets, which must be recognized on the balance sheet (IAS 38.57) and amortized. If the following conditions are cumulatively met, the attributable expenses must always be capitalized as development costs in accordance with IAS 38 (Hans Böckler Stiftung 2011; Pellens et al 2017: 398 et seq):

- the given technical feasibility of completing the intangible asset (IAS 38.57a);
- the intention of completion and subsequent use or sale (IAS 38.57b);
- the ability to use or sell the intangible asset (IAS 38.57c);
- proof of a future economic benefit of the intangible asset (IAS 38.57d);
- the availability of resources to ensure completion, use or sale (IAS 38.57e); and
- the valuation of expenditure in connection with the development of the intangible asset (IAS 38.57f).

If costs are not capitalized, they must be disclosed as expenses for the current period and may not be capitalized at a later date, even if the previously listed capitalization criteria are met (IAS 38.68; IAS 38.71; Pellens et al 2017: 339).

By adjusting amortization periods, the actual value of the IP right can be adjusted to the indicated item in the balance sheet after the effective recognition of the intangible asset (Engel 2010). In general, amortization increases the costs in a period and affects the profit for the period. Companies may adjust the costs to their economic situation or to the accounting objectives, which impairs the information function and the transparency of the profit for that period for investors (Kirsch 2008).

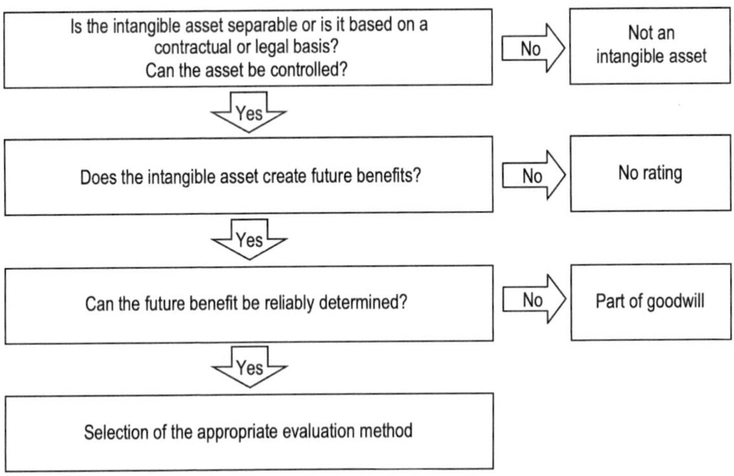

Source: Own presentation based on Siegrist and Stucker 2007.

Figure 9.5 Requirements for the capitalization of intangible assets

Figure 9.5 presents a heuristic according to which start-ups can decide whether the requirements for capitalization of intangible assets are met.

6.3 Subsequent measurement of intangible assets

In the context of subsequent measurement, a distinction must first be made as to whether the asset has a definable useful life. For this purpose, it must be determined at the time of acquisition whether the useful life is definite or indefinite (Kalantary 2012) for the respective item, whereby an indefinite useful life need not be indefinite in accordance with IAS 38.91. If there are no indications that the intangible asset will no longer generate positive cash flow for the company from a certain point in time, then a useful life is indefinite. However, planned future expenditure that is intended to increase the asset is not a reason for an indefinite useful life (Pellens et al 2017: 401).

In the event that an intangible asset has an indefinite useful life, no scheduled amortization is to be carried out; instead, the asset is to be subjected to an impairment test at least once a year and checked for impairment (Kalantary 2012).

If the useful life is limited, its duration must be determined (Kalantary 2012). For example, patents have a maximum useful life of 20 years and are generally amortized over this period. If the useful life is determined, the International Accounting Standards Board provides two models for subsequent measurement.

There is an option for the subsequent valuation of intangible assets according to either the cost method or the revaluation method. Under the cost method, the company capitalizes the intangible asset at cost at the time of acquisition and reduces this value by all accumulated amortization and impairment losses (IAS 38.74; Hans Böckler Stiftung 2011; Kalantary 2012). Consequently, a useful life and method of amortization must be defined (Pellens et al 2017: 401).

According to IAS 38.97, amortization must begin when the intangible asset is put into operation. Internal and external factors are decisive for the length of the useful life. If the intangible asset is based on IP rights, their useful life must not extend beyond the validity of the rights. An exception is made if the legal rights are renewable or renewal is virtually certain and a comparison with the future benefits expected from the asset is not associated with significant costs (IAS 38.94). The depreciation method must follow the purpose and fulfilment of the benefit. Examples of depreciation methods that may be applied are the defined benefit method, the straight-line method and the declining balance method (IAS 38.98). If the course of the realization of the benefit cannot be reliably determined, the asset must be depreciated using the straight-line method. If it becomes apparent in the course of the useful life that the depreciation period or method has been forecast significantly incorrectly, current and future depreciation must be adjusted to the real situation (Pellens et al 2017: 404).

The revaluation method is based on the fair value at the time of revaluation. The revalued amount must be adjusted for accumulated depreciation and impairment losses (IAS 38.75). The revaluation model may be applied to intangible assets only if an active market exists for these assets (IAS 38.75 and IAS 38.81). As this is usually not the case for intangible assets, this method is of little significance in practice (Hans Böckler Stiftung 2011; Kalantary 2012).

7. Summary

In the previous chapter, it was shown that intangible assets are becoming increasingly important in the age of digitization. Especially for start-ups with a software and digital focus, the recoverability of patented technologies is of great importance. IP protection not only serves to protect and promote intellectual creation, but is also a decisive factor in the development towards innovation and investment protection for start-ups.

Accordingly, IP rights can provide decisive competitive advantages. To ensure that these assets classified as intangible assets are also visible to investors, it is important that they are also reflected in the balance sheet. However, not only debt financing, but also accounting-related valuations and the determination of the value in dispute are reasons for the valuation of patents. The value drivers here are primarily the strategy, function and exploitation of IP rights.

In practice, various valuation methods have been established for the valuation of intangible assets, the choice of which will depend on the existence of corresponding data. If there is an active market in which patents already traded can be compared with the valuation object, the market-oriented approach is preferable. However, since active markets rarely exist in which objects of comparison exist, the net present value-oriented approach is used in most cases, in which a valuation is made on the basis of expected income. If estimating the future value of the patents involves a high degree of uncertainty, the cost-based approach is the remaining alternative.

Annual financial statements can be prepared in accordance with national or international standards (IFRS), whereby the national legal requirements have mostly been adapted to the accounting rules of IFRS. For example, intangible assets can be capitalized not only if they were purchased, but also, under certain circumstances, if they were created in-house. In general, only development costs and not research costs may be shown on the balance sheet for internally generated intangible assets. There is a choice between two different methods for subsequent measurement. The cost method takes the asset into account at the time of acquisition, whereby this is reduced by scheduled depreciation and unscheduled impairment losses. In contrast, the revaluation method involves regular revaluation less scheduled depreciation. Since an active market must exist for this method, which is rarely the case for intangible assets, the cost model is considered to be the most significant in practice.

10 From IP to IPO – IP rights from the investor's perspective

Daniel Brüggemann

1. Introduction

'Venture capital' (VC) describes a sub-segment of the equity capital market. VC – which is primarily used to finance young, fast-growing, innovation-oriented companies – is also known in German as 'opportunity capital'.

Although the process by which potential investors meet start-ups can vary considerably depending on the founders, the technologies on which they are working and the development phase of the company, the strength of a company's IP position is an increasingly important factor for investors (Hadzima, Bockmann and Butler 2010). This is particularly true in the technology and life sciences sectors.

The market for VC, one of the main sources of financing for start-ups, is highly competitive. Many young companies must compete for the attentions of only a few VC providers. A company's IP situation can make an important difference in attracting financing in this fundraising landscape, where investors encounter numerous founders seeking support for new, unproven technologies.

Research has shown that there is a strong correlation between the success of a company that goes public or is successfully sold in a trade sale and its ownership of IP. This correlation is even greater when companies have good or strong IP relations (Hadzima, Bockmann and Butler 2010). Start-ups should have a good patent strategy, freedom to operate and good prospects of patentability if they hope to obtain financing for the development of their technologies.

This chapter therefore aims to give founders insight into the relevance of IP rights from the perspective of VCs. The views and experiences of VCs with respect to patent requirements will be discussed.

The chapter will explain how investors assess and value IP of start-ups when considering a stake in a start-up. In view of the growing interest of German founders in establishing a presence in international markets and the associated search for foreign networks and growth capital, the protection of IP abroad will also be discussed, using China as an example.

By discussing these topics, the aim is to encourage start-ups to consider the strength of their IP position and their IP strategies when preparing for discussions with potential investors.

2. How start-ups are financed

Start-ups can be financed by equity capital, debt capital or a combination of both.

The possibilities of internal financing without equity in the early phases of companies through the unpaid work of the founders – so-called 'sweat equity', as well as 'bootstrapping' – are limited. To secure the continued existence of the company, financing by external capital providers is of immense importance (Eilenberger and Haghani 2008: 10).

In addition to business angels and incubators, typical sources of self-financing include risk capital, which is discussed in this chapter (see Figure 10.1).

Many of the financing sources used by larger companies – such as bank loans, bond issues and initial public offerings (IPOs) – are difficult or impossible to access, especially for young start-ups. Start-ups often lack tangible assets that can serve as collateral for a loan. Negative cash flows are another reason why banks and other credit institutions, as well as the public stock markets, have historically been unwilling to provide capital to finance the business plans of start-ups.

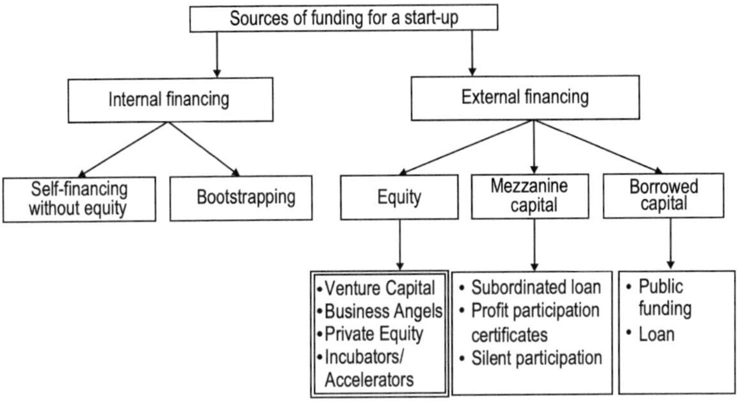

Source: Own representation, based on Hahn (ed) 2014: 34.

Figure 10.1 *Differentiation of financing sources for a start-up*

Due to the ever-increasing number of start-ups, a financing ecosystem has emerged in recent decades that is specifically tailored to the needs of these emerging companies and that balances the risk appetite of investors with the financing needs of start-ups.

Private equity funds provide the working capital that enables young private companies to grow and develop successfully. This is a long-term investment process that requires careful consideration and active monitoring. In this chapter, we will look at the category of private equity most relevant to start-up companies: VC.

VCs finance high-risk, illiquid ideas, which have not yet proven their worth by purchasing shares while the companies are still in private ownership. VCs provide financial support for start-ups with products and services that have not yet proven themselves on the market. However, they bear the risk and lack of liquidity only if they can get an adequate return on their efforts and therefore expect high return targets to justify the risks they bear.

2.1 What is 'venture capital'?

VCs invest primarily in young companies that promise rapid growth due to the development of innovative products for large markets. VCs are a kind of financial intermediary that performs three main functions:

- analysing potential investments and selecting companies to invest in;
- monitoring these companies and providing value-added services to them; and
- exiting from investments in these companies through an IPO or a sale to a strategic investor, such as a large corporation.

Start-up teams need investment capital to implement their business plans. VC is the provision of equity capital to these start-up companies which, due to the early stage of their development, do not yet have a sufficient track record to obtain investment capital from traditional sources (eg, public markets or credit institutions).

Although less than 0.25 per cent of companies receive VC funding, Kaplan and Lerner (2010) estimate that about half of all genuine IPOs are co-financed by VC. Gornall and Strebulaev (2015) estimate that listed companies that have previously received VC support account for one-fifth of the market capitalization and 44 per cent of the R&D spending of US listed companies. In line with this performance at the company level, Harris, Jenkinson and Kaplan (2014, 2016) find that VC funds have historically outperformed public markets on average after fees.

As shown in Figure 10.2, VCs act as financial intermediaries, collecting money from investors and then investing this capital in start-up companies. Indeed, Kaplan and Strömberg (2001) and Gompers and Lerner (2001) argue that VCs are particularly successful in solving an important problem in the market economy: connecting entrepreneurs that have good ideas but no money with investors that have money but not enough ideas.

The success of VC-supported companies is linked to the fact that VCs close a financing gap and take measures that contribute to value creation. VCs are therefore by no means passive investors. Once they invest in a company, they take an active role in an advisory capacity or as a member of the company's supervisory board. They monitor the progress of the company; develop incentive plans for the entrepreneurs

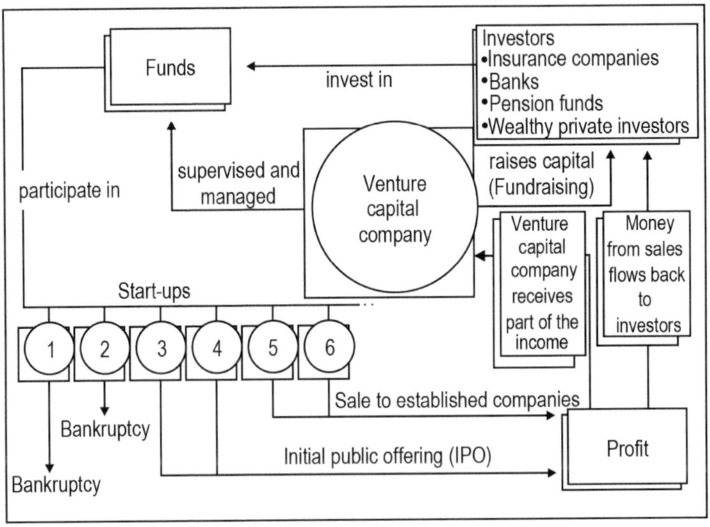

Source: Papendick and Schmalholz 2002: 128.

Figure 10.2 The architecture of the venture capital business

and the management; and set financial and product-related targets for the company. VCs often also help their portfolio companies to find talent by providing recruitment and hiring support through their networks. Some VCs even help their companies to develop and retain employees. Many larger VCs provide ongoing training, coaching and proactive solutions to help start-up executives meet the challenges of scaling. They also provide access to consultants, accountants, lawyers, investment bankers and often other companies which are potential customers for the start-up's products, or which can help in sales. VCs are an important part of the start-up ecosystem.

> Venture capital is much more than a financing instrument or an asset class. It is the central fuel for entrepreneurship, innovative future technologies, and strong growth – an elementary factor in the international competition among technology locations. (BVK 2018)

Thanks to the success of these initiatives, the operating model established by the early VCs has proven its worth to date (Horowitz 2010). Under this model, VC firms take partial ownership of the company to which they provide capital (Zider 1998). VC financing thus traditionally closes the crucial gap between the early financing of seed capital through '3F' financing by 'friends, family and fools', as it is called in the jargon, and later investment rounds. (This term describes, with slight irony, the origin of capital through family and friendly relationships, and through 'fools' who invest in a start-up at an early stage despite the above-average risk.)

Without the flow of information and the liquidity of the public markets, VC investments offer significant opportunities for investors with a specific risk profile – both for enormous profits and for huge losses. The importance of the willingness of VCs to invest in risky companies should not be underestimated. This willingness is of considerable help to founders whose companies, due to their limited assets, usually do not have early access to low-cost capital. 'Uncertainty is inherent in start-up companies, as their innovative products and business plans are not yet tested at this stage' (Cable 2011).

Given the difficulty for new start-ups to achieve early success in their chosen markets, many promising start-ups are liquidated without VC after initial progress proves unsatisfactory (Tian and Wang 2014).

This risk tolerance not only prevents the premature exit of a risk capital provider; research has also shown that those VCs which are more tolerant of failure tend to select more innovative start-ups to invest in. Start-ups supported by such VCs have more successful IPOs and produce a larger number of patents, which tend to be patents that have a greater impact on their respective markets (Tian and Wang 2014).

2.2 Snapshot of US VC

The modern VC industry effectively started in 1946 and grew slowly in its first 35 years. New sources of capital from pension funds led to rapid growth from the early 1980s onwards. This period of rapid growth came to an end in the mid-1980s, but returned in the mid-1990s. It culminated in a boom and a crash at the turn of the century, when the dotcom bubble burst in 2000.

Since then, the market has grown to record figures. In 2018, the US raised 66 per cent of the world's VC and 51 per cent of the world's VC was invested in US companies. In the US, IT and healthcare are the dominant sectors for VC investment; and Silicon Valley and the Boston, Massachusetts area account for about half of all US VC (NVCA 2019).

2.3 The European VC market compared to the US and Asia

After many years of underfunding, the European VC landscape is now developing well. Nevertheless, studies show clear deficits due to obstacles to VC in Europe. According to a study by the German Private Equity and Venture Capital Association eV (BVK 2018), Germany has a clear need to catch up on VC investments.

In 2017, VC in the amount of around €1.1 billion was invested in Germany. In the US, by contrast, this figure stood at around €63.8 billion. This means that VC investments in Germany account for just 0.035 per cent of gross domestic product (GDP). In the US, this figure stands at approximately 0.371 per cent of GDP.

Also in comparison to Asia, the German and European figures increasingly diverge. While Europe and Asia were equal in terms of annual VC investments in 2012, the difference between them is now huge. With VC investments totalling €62.8 billion in 2017, Asia is now almost on a par with the US and has overtaken Europe. China in particular is increasingly investing state funds in the form of VC.

Start-ups in Europe therefore find a much smaller local market for VC than their counterparts in the US and Asia.

This becomes particularly problematic in the important later investment phases when companies must finance their market access and growth. In these important phases, European companies lack financing opportunities compared to their Asian and US competitors. In the US, more than half of all VC investments – over €34 billion – fall into the late phase. In Europe, at €5.9 billion, this figure is just 38 per cent. On average, €24.4 million per company flows in at the late stage in the US; in Europe, this figure is almost 38 per cent lower, at €15.1 million (median values Q1 2018; BVK 2018) (see Figure 10.3).

Too little VC leads to a vicious circle. The reasons for this are, on the one hand, too many bureaucratic and tax obstacles; and on the other hand, the fact that European institutional investors (eg, insurance companies

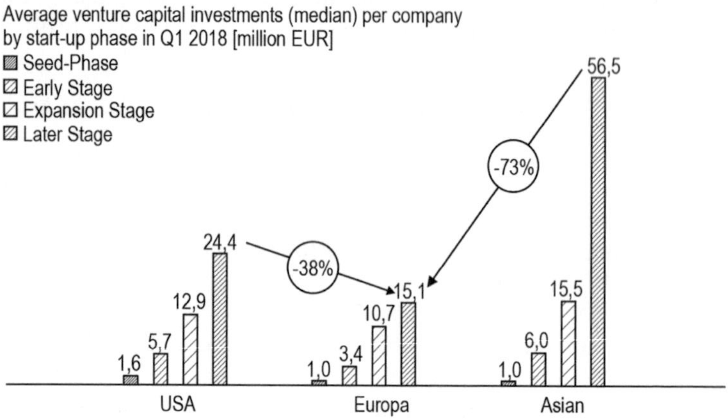

Source: BVK 2018.

Figure 10.3 *Venture capital investments per company by start-up phase in Q1 2018*

and pension funds) rarely participate in VC funds. As a result, there is a lack of large VC funds that can service the capital-intensive investments of late-stage financing. The consequence is a lack of success stories of start-ups that have enabled their investors to achieve extraordinary returns and that would enable entrepreneurs to reinvest capital in the system.

All these points lead to a lack of capital formation and limited scaling of local companies, which in turn inhibits VC investment.

The BVK, representing over 200 private equity companies, proposes the following measures to break the vicious circle and promote VC:

- Later-stage investments by VC funds should be encouraged by the state with a leverage mechanism between private and public money.
- A public VC fund of funds should be established, in which large private institutional investors also participate.
- Examples of successful (German) start-ups should be actively disseminated by the state to increase the general attractiveness of VC investments.
- The legal framework for VC should be improved. This concerns the following points:

  - abolition of value added tax on remuneration for the management of VC funds (management fee);
  - introduction of legal tax transparency for VC funds;
  - extension of depreciation possibilities for VC investments; and
  - extension of the German 'INVEST' grant to investments in VC funds.
- Modernization of the pension system (promotion of funded pension provision) should be accompanied by the promotion of citizens' participation in the VC market – and thus in the returns from the digital economy.
- Universities and research institutes should be supported through an Excellence Initiative to enable them to bring their research results to market and commercialize them through the creation of innovative start-ups.

2.4 Financing phases of companies

Figure 10.4 shows that start-ups negotiate with different investors to finance their business plans depending on their stage of development due to their different risk profile and capital requirements.

In early-stage financing, additional capital is provided to companies. In later phases, such as the takeover of a company by its management (management buy-out), capital flows exclusively at shareholder level. Table 10.1 shows the different financing phases of companies.

In practice, it is not always possible to distinguish clearly between the different phases of the lifecycle, and the length of these phases can also vary depending on the sector in which the start-up is active. For example, companies in the biotechnology sector have considerably longer research phases than the relatively short planning of, for example, e-commerce start-ups.

Table 10.1 *Different financing phases of companies*

Seed financing	Financing of the development and implementation of an idea into usable results up to prototype, on the basis of which a business concept is created for the foundation of a company.
Start-up financing	The company in question is in the process of being set up or has recently started business, and has not yet sold its products or has not sold them on a large scale.
Expansion financing	The company has reached the break-even point or is already generating profits. The funds are used to finance additional production capacity, product diversification or market expansion and/or further working capital.
Bridge financing	Financial resources made available to a company in preparation for an IPO, primarily with the aim of improving the equity ratio.
Management buy-out	The takeover of a company by the existing management. Management holds over 10 per cent of the company's shares.
Management buy-in	The takeover of a company by an external management. The management holds over 10 per cent of the company shares.
Leveraged buy-out	A majority takeover of the company by equity investors. The management holds less than 10 per cent of the company shares.
Turnaround financing	The financing of a company that is expected to recover after overcoming difficulties (eg, sales problems).
Replacement capital	The purchase of shares in a company from another investor or shareholder.

Source: Own representation, based on BVK 1997: 8.

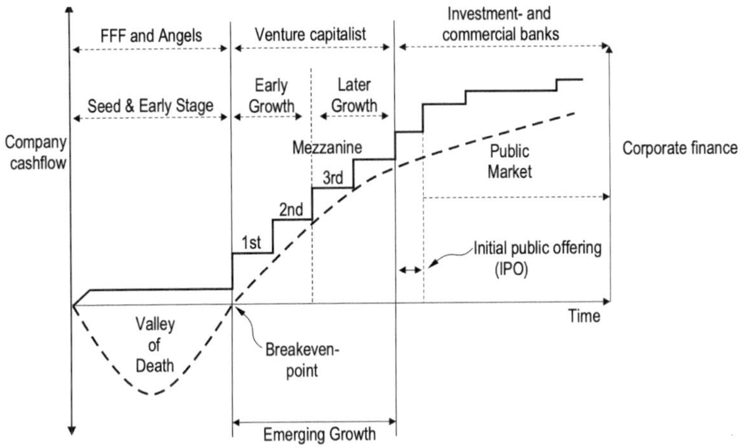

Source: Own representation, based on Hahn 2014: 34.

Figure 10.4 Financing the start-up lifecycle

2.5 Patents as a financing instrument?

Both economists and legal scholars have looked at how patents are used by new companies to promote innovation. Some academics have tried to answer this question with empirical methods. Their perspectives help to shed light on the interdependence of new technologies, patents, start-ups, and their financing.

For example, in a review of the academic literature, Bronwyn H Hall (2019) examines the reasons why the possession of knowledge assets could be useful for raising funds. She analyses the empirical evidence on patent ownership and its impact on the ability of firms to obtain further funding at different stages of their development. It is stated that in most technology-intensive sectors, patent applications (granted or pending) are associated with several positive outcomes: they help to attract VCs, increase the amount of funds received and correlate positively with future growth and the survival of the company.

Haeussler et al (2014), whose study focuses on UK and German biotechnology start-ups, also find that filing for a European patent increases the probability of obtaining VC financing. In a similar vein, Engel and Keilbach (2007) examine the early-stage financing of start-ups and find that filing for a patent with the German Patent and Trademark Office prior to the establishment of the company strongly predicts that VCs will later participate in the start-up.

Patents therefore not only contribute to innovation by motivating inventors; they can also be used as a financing instrument (Lemley 2000). In a broader sense, patents can serve as a signalling device for an innovative firm and help to eliminate information asymmetries between innovative firms and investors (Long 2002; see also Chapter 8, section 2.5).

Investors – especially at an early stage – are often faced with the challenge of identifying how innovative a target company is. In this scenario, a patent portfolio can close information gaps and enable the investors to identify the company's potential more easily.

The following section looks at how investors evaluate IP strategies and aims to provide food for thought on how to prepare the founders of start-ups for IP-related discussions with investors.

3. IP strategy from an investor's perspective

IP is an essential part of the value creation in a technology-based company and as such is a crucial element in raising VC for start-ups.

As described in section 2.1, VCs invest in young, high-growth companies to finance their expansion and usually accompany them up to the trade sale (ie, the sale of the start-up to an established company) or IPO, so that VCs and other investors such as business angels can monetize their investments.

However, as VC is characterized by high default risks and asymmetric information, IP assets can signal the prospect of future profits through market entry barriers and first-mover advantages when evaluating start-ups (Harhoff 2009; Brassell and King 2013).

IP is therefore important in convincing investors or lenders of the market opportunities available to the company to commercialize the product or service in question. Occasionally, a single powerful patent can open up a range of financing opportunities. Finally, IP rights on the creative results or innovations of the products or services that a company wants to market promise a certain degree of exclusivity and thus a higher market share if those products or services prove successful with consumers.

Different investors attach different importance to IP rights and may value IP in different ways. In practice, however, there is a clear trend towards increasing reliance on IP rights as a source of competitive advantage for companies. As a result, investors and lenders are increasingly focusing on companies with a well-managed IP portfolio.

The founders of a start-up must therefore understand the commercial value of their start-up's IP assets; ensure their correct valuation, by professionals where appropriate; and possibly pay attention to the requirements to include self-created intangible fixed assets as an asset on the balance sheet (see also Chapter 9). In any case, the founders should include the IP assets and IP strategy in their business plan when presenting it to potential investors.

When drawing up a business plan and preparing for the investor pitch, start-up entrepreneurs should pay particular attention to their IP management to ensure that their IP assets are aligned with the overall business strategy and objectives of the company. Start-ups should be clear about how IP will contribute to the overall business success and be able to communicate this clearly.

When start-up entrepreneurs are talking to potential investors, IP assets can help to strengthen their arguments for obtaining corporate financing. In discussions with potential investors, the start-up can prove from the outset that the future business is well protected by IP rights. When applying for equity financing or a loan, the investor or lender – be it a business angel, VC or financial institution – will check whether the new or innovative product or service offered by the start-up is protected by a patent, utility model, trademark or related rights. Investors that evaluate an investment in a company at an early stage usually want to learn more about the company in two ways: through the business plan and through the pitch. These will be discussed in the following sections.

3.1 Integration of the IP strategy into the business plan

A comprehensive discussion of business plans is beyond the scope of this chapter. Below are a few basic IP-related aspects that founders should consider when drawing up their plans. Companies trying to raise VC usually own IP. And indeed, the quality both of this IP and of the management team are often the two most important aspects of a VC's investment decision, alongside the target market and the business model.

The business plan that the founders prepare contains all relevant details about their business and IP-related aspects. More than just a document to attract investors, it provides the founders with the opportunity to carefully consider every aspect of their business and growth strategy.

Business planning is a process, a discipline; not a bound document. The scope of the thinking process depends on the phase of the product/business, the size and complexity of the market, and the financing requirements.

Simply put, a business plan is a living set of documents created from desk research, field research, discussions and deliberations of the founders and industry. The plan outlines how the company intends to finance and run its business.

The methodology of the 'business model canvas' (Blank and Dorf 2012; Osterwalder and Pigneur 2019; Ries 2011) has proven very useful in practice for the presentation of the business model (see Chapter 7). While the business model canvas focuses on the architecture of value creation and the profit model, the business plan mainly specifies the details. How should the company be organized? What is the market and competitors? What financing is required? The business plan is much more focused on external stakeholders (especially investors).

However, not every start-up needs a comprehensive business plan from the beginning. Especially with small early projects, the planning process itself is more important; so the focus should be on the business model. A business model (with the information from the business model canvas) and a simple financial plan are sufficient in the very early stages to quickly test assumptions about the market. Lean start-up pioneer Steve Blank is often quoted as saying: 'No business plan survives the first contact to customer.'

However, to successfully commercialize their products and services, the founders must have a realistic assessment of customer needs and benefits; an analysis of the market and competitors; a good sales strategy; and a plan for the right financing. Finally, in a dynamic environment, the original plan must of course be constantly adapted to reality.

As far as IP is concerned, the business plan should not discuss the confidential aspects, but clearly present the benefits and applications of IP.

It is also important not only to demonstrate the quality of the IP and the existence of a large market for its applications, but also to ensure that the founding team can successfully seize the opportunity. For example, the plan should detail the company's achievements to date, including information on previous rounds of financing and the development of products, partnerships and other important milestones.

If a very young start-up does not have much to show for itself, the plan should point to successes of the management team in previous projects or companies. These can give an indication of the team's ability to successfully overcome the many challenges of start-up life.

Potential investors should know where their money will go after reviewing the business plan. A detailed and realistic business plan, including a value-oriented IP strategy, provides investors with a roadmap that gives them an idea of how the company will operate in the future once financing has been secured.

Note

Non-disclosure Agreements from a VC Perspective

Start-up entrepreneurs may be concerned that a VC might share their idea for a new company or product with competitors or other founders. However, VCs do not usually sign non-disclosure agreements (NDAs) during the initial discussions on a potential investment.

Why do VCs rarely sign NDAs?

VCs talk to many start-ups and are likely to consider similar ideas in the same industry sectors. If the information that the VC firm would have to protect under an NDA is general in nature, this could effectively prevent the VC from investing in a particular industry.

Smaller VC firms in particular do not have the internal resources to adequately monitor compliance with NDAs. The cost of implementing such resources would be very high.

The process of reviewing NDAs, negotiating their terms and seeking advice from lawyers is very time consuming. VCs cannot implement them adequately for every potential investment right at the beginning of the talks. This would take up valuable time, which VCs would prefer to use in advising the founders in their portfolios.

So, what is the best way to proceed?

Founders need not reveal confidential information immediately to present their business ideas effectively. You can leave sensitive data or business secrets out of your presentations and keep them for later meetings. Founders must weigh the risk of disclosing information against the increasing likelihood of a potential investment during meetings. Start-ups should rely on trustworthy sources of recommendation before approaching angels or VCs. NDAs may then be appropriate during late due diligence. Nevertheless, NDAs should be closely tailored to the specific VC investment and not be a comprehensive confidentiality agreement. If an NDA is really needed, confidential information should be narrowly defined.

The best entrepreneur-investor relationships are based on mutual respect and trust. Start-up founders can demonstrate their judgement by requesting NDAs with the right timing.

3.2 *Caveat emptor* – IP in investor discussions

The term 'pitch' (originally a competition between advertising agencies for a company's budget) is now common in many industries where there is a battle for contracts. In the start-up scene, the pitch gives the founders the opportunity to present their business ideas to investors in an initial meeting within a short period of time and to convince them of their merits. If this is successful, there is a good chance of winning investment for the company and holding more detailed discussions.

3.2.1 *IP rights and investment conditions*

When an investor is interested in an IP-driven company, it will conduct a series of interviews to analyse, among other things, the IP assets that are valuable to the company and the related IP rights that protect those assets. Investors will pay particular attention to the risks associated with the use and monetization of IP. The outcome of this analysis has a significant impact on the negotiation of the investment terms and the preparation of a potential term sheet (ie, a written letter of intent recording the fundamental interest in carrying out the transaction). This is where assurances and warranties, indemnities, limitations of liability and the structure of the financial investment – such as financial terms linked to benchmarks, return on investment and other performance indicators – become relevant.

3.2.2 *Commercialization of IP rights*

During the discussion, the founders have the opportunity to show the VC where their invention or innovation fits into the market in relation to existing and potential competitors. The potential investor will also want to know whether the invention or innovation offers a dramatic and lasting advantage; and whether there are any 'compelling reasons' for building a company based on the innovation (Cardullo 2004). During the discussion, the investor will try to assess both the strength of the innovation and the ability of the founding team to successfully commercialize the innovative products or services. In order to help the founders prepare for IP-relevant investor talks, the next section contains possible questions to which investors will seek answers in their analysis.

3.2.3 *Questions on IP strategies from an investor's perspective*

Early-stage investors often say that there are three important things about start-ups: team, team, team. Investors at every stage of a company's development will want to be sure that the founders and their team know how to manage and use their IP.

But, much more than learning about the IP that is currently available, an investor will see IP discussions as an indicator of the management competence of the founders and the future success of the company. Especially in the very early stages, when experience shows that many companies can completely change their business plans, the founders have the opportunity to demonstrate their general understanding of the specifics of their industry and its different players, as well as their foresight, by discussing their IP strategy.

In the case of a relatively young company, it is likely that a large proportion of its IP rights will not yet have been created. In a dynamic, fast-growing environment, it is therefore particularly important to demonstrate to investors in a discussion that the management team knows how to strategically manage existing and future IP.

An investor will ask the following questions, among others.

3.2.3.1 IP ownership

- Does the start-up own the IP? Can the team guarantee that all the IP it claims is available to implement this option within the company? In order to obtain VC funding, it is important that a start-up actually owns the IP for its technology.
- Have the founders documented IP-relevant information right from the start? Does the start-up have strict guidelines for keeping records such as invention disclosures?
- Are there any obligations towards former employers, possible co-inventors or other third parties?

3.2.3.2 IP strategy

- Does the management team have a well-thought-out, value-oriented IP strategy that enables the start-up to take advantage of opportunities with confidence, manage risks effectively and plan for future cash flows?
- Is the IP strategy aligned with the business objectives of the founders and does it show a forward-looking plan to capture valuable IP in the respective industry?
- How does the IP fit into the founders' overall business strategy and how will the start-up benefit financially?

- Can the founders describe the future development of their IP? Can they credibly demonstrate that they understand the necessary success drivers for the growth of their start-up?
- Can the founders and their team prioritize the right development efforts? Can they separate the valuable ideas from the worthless ones while keeping the cash burn rate under control?
- How do the founders plan to minimize the risk of infringement of their IP rights by third parties?
- Will the founders be able to develop a market for their product and achieve a high market penetration?
- If an invention is relevant for foreign markets, have the founders thought ahead about international rights?
- Are the founders planning to establish strategic partnerships and license their IP to other companies?

3.2.3.3 *Products and competitors*

- What are the tangible benefits of IP and how is it integrated into products and services?
- Do the benefits of IP correspond to a major customer need, and will customers be willing to pay for it appropriately?
- Do the founders know their competitors? How does the IP of the start-up fit into the market compared to that of existing and potential competitors?
- Have the founders thought about whether their product is really superior to the competition and will be profitable on the market?
- Can IP assets reduce or discourage competition in the industry regardless of the start-up's business processes?
- Do potential new competitors risk infringing the start-up's IP rights by entering the market?

3.2.3.4 *Enforceability of IP rights*

- Is IP protection enforceable? Especially when IP is particularly critical to the success of a start-up, VCs want to be sure that IP rights really do provide the company with meaningful protection.
- Could the claims be too broad or too narrow, making it easy for competitors to circumvent the patent?
- How successful were the registrations? Investors may be wary of

companies where patent applications have been rejected too often. This could indicate that the start-up's IP rights may not be truly enforceable.

3.2.4 Other

Investors will want to know that the founders, among many other things, have thought through all potential IP-relevant issues and how they intend to use their IP in a competitive environment.

Patent portfolios are often closely examined together with independent consultants to avoid obvious problems with the applications filed by the founders. Start-up founders can offer investors additional security here by engaging competent and reputable IP advisers to support them in implementing their strategy. Investors know (unfortunately, often from experience) that only competently prepared patent applications can withstand litigation or proceedings regarding the validity of the IP rights.

The questions outlined above apply mainly to early funding rounds. In later and larger financing rounds, the focus will be different and independent IP audits – especially in the pharmaceutical, biotech and medical technology sectors – can be quite detailed.

In general, of course, every investor is different and every investment opportunity is different. A founding team will most likely meet investors who have different questions and priorities from those described here. The founders would be well advised to find out more about the potential investor. Has the potential investor already had positive or negative experiences with IP and IP rights? More about this in the next section ...

3.3 Evaluation – impact of IP

The evaluation of IP is difficult, due to its interdisciplinary nature. It is not without reason that there is a multitude of different valuation methods. There are many aspects of evaluating a start-up that go beyond the scope of this chapter; a few general and IP-relevant aspects follow.

In general, when evaluating a company, founders and initial investors, such as family members and business angels, will be confronted with the fact that a company and its IP may indeed have different values for different investors or buyers. Start-up valuation is more of an art than a science. For a detailed description of approaches that make this art more scientific, please refer to Chapter 9.

Determining the valuation for an established start-up in the growth phase can be relatively simple. Although there are certainly differences of opinion, there are at least cash flow, growth rates and other financial ratios that can help in deciding on the value.

But what if a young technology company generates little or no turnover, and perhaps does not even have a prototype? The complexity of the valuation also increases in proportion to the amount of intangible assets that exist. It is therefore extremely difficult to determine the exact value of a start-up while it is still in its infancy, as its potential success or failure is uncertain regardless of the quality of its IP. This is where investors and start-ups naturally often have different ideas about company valuation.

The previous experience of the investor also plays an important role in the assessment of IP. The founders will encounter a variety of perspectives here. Especially in the very early stages, potential investors may sometimes have very different opinions on IP and its contribution to company valuation.

For example, if a former portfolio company has generated a high return for investors by licensing or selling IP assets, in future those investors will be more interested in IP and in companies with strong IP portfolios.

The IP value is context sensitive, as it depends largely on the IP owners and the uses they find for the IP assets. Financial investors (eg, VCs) or strategic investors (eg, a group with a relevant market position) may have other associations with the asset. This is also due to the fact that they will have different ways of using the IP assets in conjunction with other assets they hold.

In the event of negative IP experiences, such as costly legal disputes with portfolio companies, investors will in future pay particular attention to the IP rights of third parties that a start-up might infringe with its product or process.

Investors that have had positive experiences in the past with IP in the form of trade secrets, such as proprietary manufacturing techniques and design specifications for products under development, will evaluate them differently.

Investors that received a significantly higher valuation due to IP when selling a previous portfolio company will in future place greater emphasis on the strategic development of IP and will be more positive about investments for IP protection.

If, on the other hand, the investor merely sees the costs of IP protection which, in its experience, cannot be enforced, it will prefer that the start-up's scarce funds be invested in further development and a quick product/market fit.

What types of IP are most important to the company? When should protection take place and what financial resources are available for it? Will the IP contribute to a higher company valuation in future capital increases? Founders and their investors should discuss these issues.

In a dynamic environment, reasonable people can easily disagree about issues where no data is available. The important thing is not to waste a lot of time on this, but to use the interactions wisely to learn from each other and agree on an IP strategy that everyone will continue to support in the future.

> A start-up becomes a company and eventually, that company gets valued on real value metrics. Someday it will have customers, and revenue, and profits. And investors will think, 'How many years of profits will I be willing to pay for that company?' A price-to-earnings ratio will be applied and it will be valued on the business fundamentals and not what can or could be.

Venture capitalists and seed funds and angel investors make or lose money on the journey from hypothetical value to real value. (Wilson 2019).

One final note: company valuation should always be just one aspect among many when choosing the right investor. Other important aspects – such as partly favourable/unfavourable provisions in the investment contract, industry know-how and market contacts – are often much more important than a few percentage points of the shares that are sold in a financing round with VC.

4. IP strategy: examples of winners and losers

Many IP-savvy founders and VCs know from experience that the valuation is highly dependent on the company's IP in the form of, for example, patents, trademarks, copyrights or trade secrets. When done correctly, investment in IP protection and the right actions can increase the value of a start-up and thus reward a corporate culture of active IP management. If done wrong, resources are potentially wasted, opportunities are missed, assets are lost and the start-up has greater vulnerability to competitors.

Below are some positive and negative examples of IP management of start-ups.

4.1 Positive examples

4.1.1 Nest

Thermostat start-up Nest had the foresight to apply early for patents for its intelligent thermostat. Due to the quality of its patents, Nest was able to successfully defend itself against Honeywell, a Fortune 100 manufacturer of household appliances, in a patent infringement lawsuit. Nest has also licensed patents from others to build on its patent portfolio.

Takeaway: Patents can help to protect against patent lawsuits from competitors.

(https://techcrunch.com/2013/12/11/tony-fadell-says-nest-has-100-patents - granted-200-filed-and-20O-more-ready-to-file/)

4.1.2 OneTrust

Very few tech companies reach a value of over $1 billion in an early financing round. OneTrust achieved unicorn status after raising $200 million in a Series A financing round at a company valuation of $1.3 billion. OneTrust holds 50 patents and 50 more are pending.

Takeaway: Patents can help a company to prevail against new and established competitors and have a strong positive impact on the company's valuation.

(www.forbes.com/sites/kenrickcai/2019/07/11/privacy-startup-onetrust-reaches-13-billion-valuation-from-series-a-funding-round/#3bffb0eb5fdO)

4.2 Negative examples

4.2.1 Ordrx, formerly Ordr.in

This start-up (supported by Google Ventures) was a restaurant e-commerce platform that enabled restaurants to upload their menus and take online orders. It had to close because it ran out of money due to a trademark infringement lawsuit (the name of the website).

Takeaway: The start-up's failure to control the trademark situation and to carry out the necessary research contributed to its failure, as it was unable to fend off a patent troll (according to the founder).

(https://domainnamewire.com/wp-content/ordrin.pdf; www.cbinsights.com/research/on-demand-startup-failures/)

4.2.2 Phytelligence

Agritech start-up Phytelligence had to shut down its operations just a few months before product launch after it failed in a dispute over the technology for producing an innovative apple variety called 'Cosmic Crisp'. Washington State University sued its own spin-off in a dispute over the distribution of what was hailed as the 'apple of the future'.

Takeaway: This is a sad story about the potential for conflict in contract negotiations between a public research institution and a start-up that was spun off from the university.

(www.geekwire.com/2019/agriculture-tech-startup-phytelligence-shuts-losing-dispute-cosmic-crisp-apple-variety/)

5. VC-financed market entry abroad - IP protection in china

As a comprehensive discussion of IP-relevant challenges for European and US-based start-ups abroad would go beyond the scope of this chapter, the following is an overview of IP-relevant aspects abroad using the example of China.

When China joined the World Trade Organization in December 2001, it signed up to the Agreement on Trade-Related Aspects of Intellectual Property Rights in order to align its IP regime with minimum international standards. Since then, China has strengthened its legal framework and amended its laws and regulations on IP protection to harmonize them with international practice. However, despite these improvements, companies in China still experience problems with IP protection.

In the past decade, the Chinese government has sought to move from a low-cost manufacturing economy to an innovation-based economy. This profound change in the economy and society has been driven by the increased number and quality of scientific publications and patents.

China's patent office received the highest ever number of patent applications in 2018 – 1.54 million, which represents 46.4 per cent of the total number of applications filed worldwide. This was as many patents as were filed in the offices ranked second to eleventh put together (WIPO 2019).

Asia has thus become the centre of global patent applications. In 2018, Asian patent offices received two-thirds (66.8 per cent) of all applications filed worldwide – a significant increase from 50.8 per cent in 2008 – mainly due to growth in China.

China aims to become a leader in science and intelligent technology, and knows that the creation of high-quality legal protection for IP is essential to this mission.

However, the protection of trademarks, copyrights and patents in China still presents numerous problems. The system in its modern form was only introduced relatively recently; and as a result, awareness of IP rights is still underdeveloped among many market participants compared to their counterparts in industrialized countries.

Due to the size of the market and ongoing difficulties in implementing a robust system of IP protection and enforcement, China presents unique challenges for foreign start-ups looking to do business there. However, Chinese authorities and courts are committed to tackling the problem. Progress has been made, particularly in China's so-called Tier 1 cities (Beijing, Shanghai, Shenzhen and Guangzhou).

The approach of Asian companies to IP management has also evolved in recent years. Many companies already rely on global best practices in the protection of IP. Licensing and litigation are increasing across the region, as companies realize that a high-quality IP portfolio is key to remaining globally competitive (Taylor 2018).

Companies wishing to do business in China should understand that there are significant differences between the IP laws in Europe and the US and those in China. The registration of rights in Europe and the US does not automatically lead to rights in China. It is important to understand the differences between the two systems, and to develop and implement a comprehensive strategy to protect IP in China.

The US-China Business Council has issued a best practices document (US-China Business Council 2015) recommending several strategies through which companies should try to identify and protect their IP in China. The aim is to prevent problems with IP from arising and to combat IP infringements once they have been identified. To protect their IP in China, companies should take the following steps:

- Develop and implement a corporate IP strategy in China.
- Conduct an initial audit of the company's activities in China to identify IP assets and IP risks. An appropriate level of protection should then be assigned to the risks to which it is exposed. It is recommended to make IP protection a core responsibility of the entire Chinese management team, and not just a function of the legal team.
- Understand the legal IP environment in China.
- Familiarize themselves with China's core laws and regulations for the protection of IP, such as those on patents, trademarks, copyrights and unfair competition.
- Take preventive measures to protect IP.
- Register their marks. If a company does not register its patents, trademarks and copyrights in China, its IP has no formal protection there. Early registration is an important preventive step to mitigate possible

future economic and legal difficulties.

- Address identified IP right infringements.
- Use official enforcement channels to pursue violations. Companies have access to three main enforcement channels in China – administrative, civil and criminal – with their respective advantages and disadvantages.

For a country that wishes to develop economically, it is essential to implement an effective and robust IP system tailored to local needs and conditions. In China, the protection of IP is an essential component of a complex innovation system that serves as a catalyst for economic development. Although there are still issues in China, the country has reached a transition point in its economic transformation where it is in its own interests to ensure stronger protection of IP, and it has therefore implemented major improvements in recent years. Similar transformations took place in Japan in the 1970s and in the Hong Kong Special Administrative Region, Singapore, South Korea and Taiwan in the 1980s; and also in Germany and the US (Assafa 1996: 120; Kingston 2005: 70, 658).

To succeed in China, start-ups should develop an integrated IP protection strategy that reflects the nature and scale of the IP problems and is based on a realistic assessment of internal goals and resources.

6. Summary and concluding remarks

IP is a crucial economic factor and proper IP management is a basic requirement for any emerging business.

For a start-up, IP protection can serve as a powerful tool to protect future growth and secure VC. IP protection is related to increased financing and a higher probability of business success. Although obtaining and protecting IP involves costs that may deter start-ups, this investment generally has a positive return when viewed in terms of future fundraising and the longevity of the business. A solid IP portfolio can also help to facilitate the future sale of the start-up.

Investing in start-ups – even those with strong IP rights – is very risky and can lead to capital losses. When evaluating companies to invest in, their

IP and how the founders protect and manage it will certainly be on the checklist of any potential investor.

Patents and other IP rights are not a prerequisite for obtaining financing or for the future sale of a start-up. A business model with unique customer benefits must always remain the main focus for the founders. However, a good IP strategy is an advantageous instrument to signal the value and potential of a start-up and the strategic thinking of the founders at an early stage and helps to effectively protect the company in the medium and long term.

Bibliography

Aldrich, H and Auster, ER (1986) Even dwarfs started small: Liabilities of age and size and their strategic implications. In: *Research in Organizational Behavior* 8, 165–98.

Bagley, CE (2008) Winning legally: The value of legal astuteness. In: *The Academy of Management Review* 33, 2, 378–90.

Bagley, CE (2010) What's law got to do with it? Integrating law and strategy. In: *American Business Law Journal* 47, 4, 587–639.

Bagley, CE and Dauchy, CE (2018) *The Entrepreneur's Guide to Business Law*. Fifth edition. Boston: Cengage Learning.

Baron, JN and Hannan, MT (2002) Organizational blueprints for success in high-tech start-ups: Lessons from the Stanford project on emerging companies. In: *California Management Review* 44, 3, 31.

Baum, JAC and Silverman, BS (2004) Picking winners or building them? Alliance, intellectual, and human capital as selection criteria in venture financing and performance of biotechnology startups. In: *Journal of Business Venturing* 19, 3, 411–36.

Beck'sche Online-Formulare Vertrag, 50. Edition 2019, Benedikt Pfisterer, 20.3 Share Deal.

Beisel, D and Andreas, F (2017) *Beck'sches Mandatshandbuch Due Diligence*. 3rd edition. Munich: Beck.

Berkery, D (2008) *Raising Venture Capital for the Serious Entrepreneur*. New York: McGraw-Hill.

Beyer, S (2008) *Grundsätze zur Bewertung immaterieller Vermögenswerte* (IDW 5). In: *Die Wirtschaftsprüfung* (*WPg*) 61(8).

Blank, S and Dorf, B (2012) *The Startup Owner's Manual: The Step-By-Step Guide for Building a Great Company*. Pescadero: K & S Ranch.

Bloomberg (2017) Silicon Valley's $400 Juicer May Be Feeling the Squeeze. www.bloomberg.com/news/features/2017-04-19/silicon-valley-s-400-juicer-may-be-feeling-the-squeeze. Accessed 16 December 2019.

Bonakdar, A et al (2017) Capturing value from business models: The role of formal and informal protection strategies. In: *International Journal for Technology Management* 73, 4.

Brassell, M and King, K (2013) Banking on IP? The Role of Intellectual Property and Intangible Assets in Facilitating Business Finance. The Intellectual Property Office of the United Kingdom. https://assets.publishing.service.gov.uk/government/uploads/system/uploads/attachment_data/file/312008/ipresearch-bankingip.pdf. Accessed 13 December 2019.

Bundesanzeiger Verlag (2019) *Immaterielle Wirtschaftsgüter zutreffend erfassen und abschreiben*. www.bundesanzeiger-verlag.de/xaver/bilanzplus/start.xav?start=%2F%2F*%5B%40attr_id%3D%27bilanzplus_15003304075%27%5D#_

_bilanzplus__%2F%2F*%5B%40attr_id%3D%27bilanzplus_15003304075%27 %5D__1568983715362. Accessed 20 September 2019.

Bundesministerium für Wirtschaft und Energie Öffentlichkeitsarbeit (2017) WIPANO – *Wissens- und Technologietransfer durch Patente und Normen. Ostbevern*: MKL Druck GmbH & Co KG, Programminformation.

BVK VC Studie (2018) *Treibstoff Venture Capital – Wie wir Innovation und Wachstum befeuern, Bundesverband Deutscher Kapitalbeteiligungsgesellschaften eV.* www.bvkap.de/sites/default/files/news/vc_studie_von_ief_bvk_roland _berger_treibstoff_venture_capital.pdf. Accessed 13 December 2019.

Cable, AJB (2011) Fending for themselves: why securities regulations should encourage angel groups. In: *University of Pennsylvania Journal of Business Law* 13, 107.

Cardullo, MW (1999) *Technological Entrepreneurism: Enterprise Formation, Financing and Growth*. Baldock: Research Studies Press Ltd.

Castedello, M et al (2018) *Bewertung und Transaktionsberatung: Betriebswirtschaftliche Bewertung,* Due Diligence, Fairness Opinions ua Dusseldorf: IDW Verlag.

CB Insights (2019a) The Global Unicorn Club. Current Private Companies Valued At $1B+ (including whisper valuations). www.cbinsights.com/ research-unicorn-companies. https://www.cbinsights.com/research-unicorn -companiesAccessed 9 September 2019.

CB Insights (2019b) The Top 20 Reasons Startups Fail. www.cbinsights.com/ research/startup-failure-reasons-top/. Accessed 16 December 2019.

CB Insights (nd) Fayteq. Patents. www.cbinsights.com/company/fayteq-patents. Accessed 22 August 2019.

CB Insights (nd) Oculus VR. Patents. www.cbinsights.com/company/oculus-vr -patents. Accessed 23 August 2019.

Chambers, C (2014) Tesla Giving Away its Patents Makes Sense. www.forbes.com/ sites/investor/2014/06/13/tesla-giving-away-its-patents-makes-sense/ Accessed 9 May 2019.

Chandler, AD (1962) *Strategy and Structure: Chapters in the History of the Industrial Enterprise*. Cambridge: MIT Press.

Christensen, CM and Raynor, ME (2003) The Innovator's Solution: Creating and Sustaining Successful Growth. Boston: Harvard Business School Press.

Coding VC (2016) How to De-Risk a Startup. www.codingvc.com/how-to-de-risk -a-startup. Accessed 16 December 2019.

Conti, A, Thursby, M and Rothaermel, FT (2013) Show me the right stuff: Signals for high-tech startups. In: *Journal of Economics & Management Strategy* 22(2), 341–64.

De Leon, I and Fernandez Donoso, J (2017) *Innovation, Startups and Intellectual Property Management*. Cham: Springer International Publishing.

De Wilton, A (2011) Patent value: A business perspective for technology startups. In: *Technology Innovation Management Review* 1(3), 1–11.

Diabetes Atlas (2019) www.diabetesatlas.org. Accessed 16 December 2019.

Dodgson, M, Gann, DM and Phillips, N (2014) *The Oxford Handbook of Innovation Management*. Oxford: Oxford University Press.

DPMA (2019a) *Markenschutz im Ausland*. www.dpma.de/marken/markenschutz _ausland/index.html. Accessed 12 December 2019.

DPMA (2019b) *Designschutz im Ausland.* www.dpma.de/designs/designschutz_ausland/index.html. Accessed 12 December 2019.

Dreßler, A (2006) *Patente in technologieorientierten Mergers & Acquisitions. Nutzen, Prozessmodell, Entwicklung und Interpretation semantischer Patentlandkarten.* Wiesbaden: Deutscher Universitätsverlag.

Eilenberger, G and Haghani, S (eds) (2008) *Unternehmensfinanzierung zwischen Strategie und Rendite.* Heidelberg: Springer.

Elsbach, KD (1994) Managing organizational legitimacy in the California cattle industry: The construction and effectiveness of verbal accounts. In: *Administrative Science Quarterly* 39(1), 57–88.

Engel, C (2010) *Aktivierung (bilanzielle) von Schutzrechten.* https://patentschutzengel.de/die-kanzlei/schutzrecht-wiki/aktivierung-bilanzielle-von-schutzrechten/. Accessed 20 September 2019.

Engel, D and Keilbach M (2007) Firm-level implications of early stage venture capital investment – an empirical investigation. In: *Journal of Empirical Finance*, 14(2), 150–67.

Erk, P (2018) *Patente Strategien: Ein Patent ist für ein Startup viel wert!* www.deutsche-startups.de. Accessed 20 May 2019.

Facebook (2014) Facebook to Acquire Oculus. https://newsroom.fb.com/news/2014/03/facebook-to-acquire-oculus/. Accessed 23 August 2019.

Fisher, G, Kotha, and Lahiri, A (2016) Changing with the times: An integrated view of identity, legitimacy, and new venture life cycles. In: *Academy of Management Review* 41(3) 383–409.

Frankfurter Allgemeine Zeitung (2014) *Facebook Kauft Oculus. Milliarden für Visionen.* www.faz.net/aktuell/wirtschaft/netzwirtschaft/milliarden-deal-facebook-kauft-oculus-12865286.html. Accessed 16 December 2019.

Freytag, R (2019) Strategic negotiations: three essentials for successful partnerships with startups. In: *Strategy & Leadership* 47(1), 19–25. https://doi.org/10.1108/SL-11-2018-0115. Accessed 1 November 2019.

Freytag, R and Weibel, B (2019) Why digitalization needs value-driven intellectual property strategies. In: *Les Nouvelles* December 2019, 268–273.

Gabler Wirtschaftslexikon (2017) *Start-up-Unternehmen.* https://wirtschaftslexikon.gabler.de/definition/start-unternehmen-42136/version-189893. Accessed 16 December 2019.

Gaibraith, J (1982) The stages of growth. In: *Journal of Business Strategy* 3(1), 70–79.

Galloway (2019) Yogababbel. www.profgalloway.com/yogababble. Accessed 16 December 2019.

Garud, R, Schildt, HA and Lant, TK (2014) Entrepreneurial storytelling, future expectations and the paradox of legitimacy. In: *Organization Science* 25(5), 1479–92.

Gassmann, O and Bader, MA (2011) *Patentmanagement – Innovationen erfolgreich nutzen und schützen.* Heidelberg/Dordrecht/London/New York: Springer.

Gilbert, B (2018) Facebook Just Settled a $500 Million Lawsuit over Virtual Reality after a Years-Long Battle – Here's What's Going on. www.businessinsider.de/facebook-zenimax-oculus-vr-lawsuit-explained-2017-2?r=US&IR=T. Accessed 26 August 2019.

Gompers, P and Lerner, J (2001) The venture capital revolution. In: *Journal of Economic Perspectives*, 15(2), 145–68.

Gornall, W and Strebulaev, IA (2015) The Economic Impact of Venture Capital: Evidence from Public Companies. Stanford University Working Paper.

Greiner, LE (1997) Evolution and revolution as organizations grow: A company's past has clues for management that are critical to future success. In: *Family Business Review* 10(4), 397–409.

GTAI (2019) *Start-Ups in den USA*. www.gtai.de/GTAI/Navigation/DE/Trade/Maerkte/Trends/Update-StartUps/Land-USA/trend-land-usa.html#2188952. Accessed 15 May 2019.

Günther, T and Ott, C (2008) *Behandlung immaterieller Ressourcen bei Purchase Price Allocations*. In: *WPg*, 11, H 1, 71–93.

Hadzima, J, Bockmann, B and Butler, A (2010) IP in early stage commercial and investment success, *Intellectual Asset Management* March–April 2010, 49.

Haeussler, C, Harhoff, D and Mueller, E (2014) How patenting informs VC investors – the case of biotechnology. In: *Research Policy*, 43, 1236–98.

Hahn, C (2014) *Finanzierung und Besteuerung von Start-up-Unternehmen*. Wiesbaden: Springer Gabler.

Hall, BH (2019) Is there a role for patents in the financing of new innovative firms? In: *Industrial and Corporate Change*, 28(3), 657–80.

Hall, BH, Link, AN and Scott, JT (2001) Barriers inhibiting industry from partnering with universities: Evidence from the advanced technology program. In: *The Journal of Technology Transfer* 26(1/2), 87–98.

Hans Böckler Stiftung (2011) *Rechnungslegung nach den* International Financial Reporting Standards (IFRS). www.boeckler.de/pdf/mbf_ifrs_kapitel2.pdf. Accessed 20 September 2019.

Harhoff, D and Wagner, S (2009) The duration of patent examination at the EPO. In: *Management Science* 55(12), 1969–84.

Harhoff, D, Scherer, FM and Vopel, K (2003) Citations, family size, opposition and the value of patent rights. In: *Research Policy*, 32, 1343–63.

Harris, R, Jenkinson, T and Kaplan, S (2014) Private equity performance: What do we know? In: *Journal of Finance*, 69(5), 1851–82.

Harris, R, Jenkinson, T and Kaplan, S (2016) How do private equity investments perform compared to public equity? In: *Journal of Investment Management* 14, 1–24.

Heath, A (2017) Mark Zuckerberg Reveals that Facebook Paid More than We Thought for Oculus VR. www.businessinsider.de/facebook-actually-paid-3-billion-for-oculus-vr-2017-1?r=US&IR=T. Accessed 23 August 2019.

Hellmann, T and Puri, M (2002) Venture capital and the professionalization of start-up firms: Empirical evidence. In: *The Journal of Finance* 57(1) 169–97.

Henn, G and Pahlow, L (2017) *Patentvertragsrecht*. 6th edition. Heidelberg.

Hermans, JP (1991) Strategies for Protection of Innovations, the Case of a Research-Intensive Multinational Corporation. In: Träger, U and Witzleben, von A (eds) *Patinnova '90 – Strategies for the Protection of Innovation*. Brussels: Kluwer Academic Publishers, 83–88.

Hommel, M, Buhleier, C and Pauly, D (2007) *Bilanzrecht und Betriebswirtschaft – Bewertung von Marken in der Rechnungslegung – eine kritische Analyse des IDW ES 5*. In: *Betriebs-Berater* (BB) 62(7), 371.

Horowitz, B (2010) How angel investing is different than venture capital. In *Business Insider*, March 2010. www.businessinsider.com/how-angel-investing-is-different- than-venture-capital-2010-3. Accessed 13 December 2019.

Hüsing, A (2018) *Searchmetrics entwickelt sich gut! Heftiger US-Patentstreit führt aber zu 14,4 Millionen Verlust*. www.deutsche-startups.de/2018/08/14/searchmetrics-patentstreit/. Accessed 10 May 2019.

IDW (2015) *IDW S5 Grundsätze zur Bewertung immaterieller Vermögenswerte*. In: *WPg* Supplement 3/2011: 98 et seq, FN-IDW 7/2011: 467 et seq, *WPg* Supplement 3/2015: 16f, FN-IDW 8/2015: 447 et seq.

IGE (2019) ip-search. www.ige.ch/de/ip-search.html. Accessed 12 December 2019.

Ilmenau University of Technology (nd) Diminished Reality. www.tu-ilmenau.de/vwds/forschung/diminished-reality/. Accessed 23 August 2019.

Islam, M, Fremeth, A and Marcus, A (2018) Signaling by early stage startups: US government research grants and venture capital funding. In: *Journal of Business Venturing* 33(1), 35–51.

IT Finanzmagazin (2020) *VideoIdent: Langer Rechtsstreit zwischen IDnow und WebID beendet*. In: *IT Finanzmagazin*. www.it-finanzmagazin.de/videoident-recht-idnow-webid-104505/. Accessed 19 May 2021.

Jonsson, S, Greve, HR and Fujiwara-Greve, T (2009) Undeserved loss: The spread of legitimacy loss to innocent organizations in response to reported corporate deviance. In: *Administrative Science Quarterly* 54(2), 195–228.

Kalantary, A (2012) *Fair Value-Bewertung immaterieller Vermögenswerte nach IFRS*. Frankfurt am Main: Lang.

Kaplan, SN and Lerner, J (2010) It ain't broke: the past, present, and future of venture capital. In: *Journal of Applied Corporate Finance*, 22(2), 36–47.

Kaplan, SN and Stromberg, P (2001) Venture capitals as principals: contracting, screening, and monitoring. In: *American Economic Review*, 91(2), 426–30.

Kasperzak, R and Nestler, A (2010) *Bewertung von immateriellem Vermögen. Anlässe, Methoden und Gestaltungsmöglichkeiten*. Weinheim: Wiley-VCH.

Kazanjian, RK (1988) Relation to dominant problems to stages of growth in technology-based new ventures. In: *Academy of Management Journal* 31(2), 257–79.

KfW-Gründungsmonitor (2019). *KfW Gründungsmonitor* 2019: www.kfw.de/PDF/Download-Center/Konzernthemen/Research/PDF-Dokumente-Gr%C3%BCndungsmonitor/KfW-Gruendungsmonitor-2019.pdf. Accessed 9 December 2019.

Kingston, W (2005) An agenda for radical intellectual property reform. In: Maskus, KE and Reichman, JH (eds) *International Public Goods and Transfer of Technology Under a Globalized Intellectual Property Regime*. Cambridge: Cambridge University Press, 70, 658.

Kirsch, H-J (2008) *Einführung in die internationale Rechnungslegung nach IFRS*. Herne: NWB.

Kloyer, M (2004) *Methoden der Patentbewertung*. In: Horváth, P and Möller, K (eds) *Intangibles in der Unternehmenssteuerung. Strategien und Instrumente zur Wertsteigerung des immateriellen Kapitals*. Munich: Vahlen. 419–31.

Knyphausen, DZ (1993) Why are firms different? *Der Ressourcenorientierte Ansatz im Mittelpunkt einer aktuellen Kontroverse im Strategischen Management*. In: *Der Betrieb*, 53, H 6, 771–92.

Kollmann, T, Henesellek, S, Jung, PB and Kleine-Stegemann, L (2018) *Deutscher* Startup Monitor 2018. *Neue Signale, klare Ziele*. Berlin: KPMG.

Kyriasoglou, C (2017) *Facebook kauft das Erfurter Startup Fayteq*. www.gruenderszene.de/allgemein/facebook-ubernahme-fayteq. Accessed 23 August 2019.

Lemley, MA (2000) Reconceiving patents in the age of venture capital. In: *Journal of Small and Emerging Business Law* 4, 137.

Long, C (2002) Patent signals. In: *University of Chicago Law Review*, 69(2).

Mann, RJ and Sager, TW (2007) Patents, venture capital, and software start-ups. In: *Research Policy* 36(2), 193–208.

Marx, M, Singh, J and Fleming, L (2015) Regional disadvantage? Employee non-compete agreements and brain drain. In: *Research Policy* 44(2), 394–404.

Mazzoleni, R and Nelson, RR (1998) The benefits and costs of strong patent protection. A contribution to the current debate. In: *Research Policy* 27, H 3, 273–84.

Morris, M, Schindehutte, M and Allen, J (2012) The entrepreneur's business model: toward a unified perspective. In: *Journal of Business Research* 58(6) 726–35.

Moser, U (2011) *Bewertung immaterieller Vermögenswerte. Grundlagen, Anwendung, Bilanzierung und Goodwill*. Stuttgart: Schäffer-Poeschel.

Musk, E (2014) All Our Patent Are Belong to You [sic]. www.tesla.com/de_DE/blog/all-our-patent-are-belong-you. Accessed 9 May 2019.

Narayanan, VK, Yang, Y and Zahra, SA (2009) Corporate venturing and value creation: a review and proposed framework. In: *Research Policy* 38(1), 58–76. https://doi.org/10.1016/j.respol.2008.08.015. Accessed 1 November 2019.

Nestler, A (2008) *Ermittlung von Lizenzentgelten*. In: *Betriebs Berater*, 63, H 37, 2002–2006.

no author (2016) *Wie gewinnt man einen mehrjährigen Patentstreit*? In: StartUPdate 01/2016, 7.

Omio (2019) GoEuro Will Become Omio. www.omio.com/press-releases?_ga=2.183454755.448615423.1557477125-327963341.1557477125. Accessed 3 December 2019.

Orozco, D (2010) Legal knowledge as an intellectual property management resource. In: *American Business Law Journal*, 47(4), 687–726.

Osterwalder, A and Pigneur, Y (2019) *Business Model Generation*. Hoboken: Wiley.

Papendick, U and Schmalholz, CG (2002) *Viel gewagt – und viel verloren*. In: *Manager Magazin*, 6(32), 26–32.

Pellens, B et al (2017) *Internationale Rechnungslegung*. Stuttgart: Schäffer-Poeschel.

Pollock, TG and Rindova, VP (2003) Media legitimation effects in the market for initial public offerings. In: *Academy of Management Journal*, 46(5), 631–42.

Project A Services GmbH & Co KG (2017) *Qunomedical Sammelt Mit Neuem Namen Weitere Millionen Ein und Baut Seine Präsenz auf dem Deutschen Markt aus*. www.project-a.com/de/media/pressemitteilungen-news/qunomedical-raises-2-million-dollars-and-changes-its-name-to-strengthen-brand. Accessed 3 December 2019.

Reimsbach, D (2011) *Immaterielles Vermögen in der Unternehmensanalyse. Bewertungsmethodik und Entscheidungsrelevanz*. Wiesbaden: Gabler.

Richtlinie (EU) 2016/943 des Europäischen Parlaments und des Rates vom 8. Juni 2016 über den Schutz vertraulichen Know-hows und vertraulicher Geschäftsinformationen (Geschäftsgeheimnisse) vor rechtswidrigem Erwerb sowie rechtswidriger Nutzung und Offenlegung (ABl. L 157 vom 15. 06. 2016), S. 1.

Ries, E (2011) *The Lean Startup: How Today's Entrepreneurs Use Continuous Innovation to Create Radically Successful Businesses.* New York: Crown Publishing Group.

Rothaermel, FT, Agung, SD and Jiang, L (2007) University entrepreneurship: A taxonomy of the literature. In: *Industrial and Corporate Change* 16(4), 691–791.

Sahlmann, WA (1997) How to write a great business plan. In: *Harvard Business Review*, July/August 1997, 98–108.

Schilling, K (2014) *Forschen-Patentieren-Verwerten: Ein Praxisbuch für Naturwissenschaftler mit Schwerpunkt Life Sciences.* Berlin/Heidelberg: Springer.

Schlenk, CT (2017) *IDnow Gewinnt vor Gericht Gegen Wettbewerber WebID.* www.gruenderszene.de/allgemein/idnow-webid. Accessed 16 June 2019.

Schwarz, S and Kruspig, S (2017) *Computerimplementierte Erfindungen – Patentschutz von Software?* Cologne: Carl Heymanns.

Schwarzkopf, C (2016) *Fostering Innovation and Entrepreneurship: Entrepreneurial Ecosystem and Entrepreneurial Fundamentals in the USA and Germany.* Wiesbaden: Springer Gabler.

Shane, S (2004) *Academic Entrepreneurship: University Spinoffs and Wealth Creation.* Cheltenham/Northampton: Edward Elgar Publishing.

Siegrist, L and Stucker, J (2007) *Die Bewertung von immateriellen Vermögenswerten in der Praxis–ein Erfahrungsbericht.* In: *Zeitschrift für internationale Rechnungslegung* H, 4, 243–49.

Siemens (2019) Siemens Technology Accelerator. www.siemens.com/sta. Accessed 1 November 2019.

Smith, G and Parr, R (2000) *Valuation of Intellectual Property and Intangible Assets.* 3rd edition. New York: Wiley.

Startup Guide Ionos (2018) *Rechnungslegungsstandards: Nationale und internationale Vorgaben.* www.ionos.de/startupguide/unternehmensfuehrung/rechnungslegungsstandards-nach-hgb-und-ifrs/. Accessed 21 September 2019.

Stinchcombe, AL (1965) Social structures and organizations. In: March, JG (ed) *Handbook of Organizations*. Chicago: Rand McNally, 142–93.

Stoi, R (2003) *Controlling von Intangibles – Identifikation und Steuerung der immateriellen Werttreiber.* In: *Controlling*, 15, H 3/4, 175–182.

Suchman, MC (1995) Managing legitimacy: Strategic and institutional approaches. In: *The Academy of Management Review* 20(3), 571.

Suddaby, R, Bitektine, A and Haack, P (2017) Legitimacy. In: *Academy of Management Annals* 11(1), 451–78.

Süddeutsche Zeitung (2011) *Wer hat's erfunden?* www.sueddeutsche.de/wirtschaft/krieg-um-patente-fuer-smartphones-wer-hat-s-erfunden-1.1134483. Accessed 16 December 2019.

Süddeutsche Zeitung (2014) *Facebook kauft Experten für virtuelle Realität*. www.sueddeutsche.de/digital/milliarden-uebernahme-von-oculus-vr-facebook-kauft-experten-fuer-virtuelle-realitaet-1.1921728. Accessed 23 August 2019.

Symeonidou, N, Bruneel, J and Autio, E (2017) Commercialization strategy and internationalization outcomes in technology-based new ventures. In: *Journal of Business Venturing* 32(3), 302–17.

Taylor, DO (2018) Patent Reform, Then and Now. SMU Dedman School of Law Legal Studies Research Paper 400; 2019. In: *Michigan State Law Review* 431.

Technology Readiness Level (2021), *oder Reifegrad einer Technologie*. https://de.wikipedia.org/wiki/Technology_Readiness_Level: Accessed 3 December 2019.

Tian, X and Wang, TY (2014) Tolerance for Failure and Corporate Innovation. In: *The Review of Financial Studies*, 27(1), 211.

Unger, A (2016) *So Lange Brauchen Einhörner bis zur Ersten Milliarde*. www.impulse.de/gruendung/gruender-news/start-up-wachstum/3160677.html. Accessed 9 September 2019.

University of Heidelberg (nd) *Umgang von Universitäten mit Privaten Drittmittelgebern*. www.uni-heidelberg.de/de/forschung/forschungsservice/industrie-und-sonstige-foerdermittelgeber. Accessed 3 December 2019.

US-China Business Council (2015) Best-Practices: Intellectual Property Protection in China. www.uschina.org/reports/best-practices-intellectual-property-protection-china. Accessed 13 December 2019.

USPTO (nd) USPTO's Prioritized Patent Examination Program. www.uspto.gov/patent/initiatives/usptos-prioritized-patent-examination-program. Accessed 12 December 2019.

Wasserman, N (2012) *The Founder's Dilemmas: Anticipating and Avoiding the Pitfalls that Can Sink a Startup*. Princeton: Princeton University Press.

Weibel, B (2013) *Strategisches IP Management – Aufgaben und Integration in die Wertschöpfungskette*. In: *Schweizer IP Handbuch*. Basel: Helbing Lichtenhahn, 153–77.

Weitnauer, W (2016) *Handbuch Venture Capital* 5. Munich: Auflage.

Wingfield, N and Isaac, M (2017) Mark Zuckerberg. Suit, Testifies in Oculus Intellectual Property Trial. www.nytimes.com/2017/01/17/technology/mark-zuckerberg-oculus-trial-virtual-reality-facebook.html. Accessed 24 August 2019.

WIPO (2019a) Patent Cooperation Treaty. www.wipo.int/pct/en/texts/articles/atoc.html. Accessed 12 December 2019.

WIPO (2019b) PCT-Patent Prosecution Highway Pilot (PCT-PPH and Global PPH). www.wipo.int/pct/en/filing/pct_pph.html. Accessed 12 December 2019.

WIPO (2019c) International Applications and National Security Considerations. www.wipo.int/pct/en/texts/nat_sec.html. Accessed 12 December 2019.

WIPO (2019d) Facts and Figures. www.wipo.int/edocs/infogdocs/en/ipfactsandfigures2018/. Accessed 12 December 2019.

WIPO (2019e) Paris Convention for the Protection of Industrial Property. www.wipo.int/treaties/en/ip/paris/. Accessed 12 December 2019.

WIPO (2019f) World Intellectual Property Indicators: Filings for Patents, Trademarks, Industrial Designs Reach Record Heights in 2018. www.wipo.int/pressroom/en/articles/2019/article_0012.html. Accessed 13 December 2019.

Wolfe, J (2017) Facebook virtual reality unit Oculus faces lawsuit over imaging patent. www.reuters.com/article/us-facebook-lawsuit/facebook-virtual-reality-unit-oculus-faces-lawsuit-over-imaging-patent-idUSKBN1792OT. Accessed 23 August 2019.

Wurzer, A and Reinhardt, D (2006) *Bewertung technischer Schutzrechte. Praxis der Patentbewertung*. Cologne: Heymanns.

Wurzer, AJ, Grünewald, T and Berres, W (2016) *Die 360° IP-Strategie*. Munich: Vahlen.

Zider, B (1998) How venture capital works. In: *Harvard Business Review*. November–December 1998, 131, 132.

Zimmerman, MA and Zeitz, GJ (2002) Beyond survival: Achieving new venture growth by building legitimacy. In: *The Academy of Management Review* 27(3), 414.

Index